EGYPT
AFTER
NASSER

EGYPT

——— AFTER ———

NASSER

Sadat, Peace and the Mirage
of Prosperity

THOMAS W. LIPPMAN

PARAGON HOUSE

NEW YORK

HOUSTON PUBLIC LIBRARY

R0159281695
SSC

First edition, 1989

Published in the United States by

Paragon House Publishers
90 Fifth Avenue
New York, NY 10011

Copyright © 1989 by Thomas W. Lippman

All rights reserved. No part of this book may be reproduced, in any form,
without written permission from the publishers, unless by a reviewer who wishes
to quote brief passages.

Library of Congress Cataloging-in-Publication Data

Lippman, Thomas W.
Egypt after Nasser : Sadat, peace, and the mirage of prosperity /
Thomas W. Lippman.—1st ed.
p.   cm.
Bibliography: p.
Includes index.
ISBN 1-55778-041-2
1. Egypt—Politics and government—1970–1981.   2. Sadat, Anwar,
1918–1981.   I. Title.
DT107.85.L56   1989   88-12155
962'.054-dc19   CIP

Manufactured in the United States of America

For my parents.
And for Sidney, my wife, who was there.

CONTENTS

CHRONOLOGY

Throughout this book, readers will find references to several events that have defined Egyptian history since the revolution of 1952 and have become part of Egypt's political vocabulary. The following chronology may be helpful to those unfamiliar with the details of these events.

1952, July 23–26: "The Revolution," a military coup organized by Gamal Abdel Nasser and a group of "Free Officers" in the armed forces. King Farouk, the last monarch, sails into exile in Europe.

1953, January 16: Political parties abolished by government decree.

1956, July 26: Nasser announces nationalization of the Suez Canal to finance construction of the Aswan High Dam.

October 29–November 5: The "Tripartite Aggression." Israel, Britain and France attack Egypt; United Nations arranges cease-fire.

1961, July 20: Government nationalizes all banks, insurance companies and financial institutions.

1967, June 4–9: Israel routs Arab armies in the "Six-Day War," occupies all of Egypt's Sinai peninsula east of the Suez Canal, the Gaza Strip, Syria's Golan Heights, East Jerusalem and the West Bank of the Jordan. Egypt breaks diplomatic relations with United States.

1970, September 28: Nasser dies. Anwar Sadat, his vice president and fellow "Free Officer," becomes president.

1971, May 1–13: The "Corrective Revolution." Sadat prevails in power struggle with former colleagues of Nasser, imprisons them, begins "correction" of Nasser's policies.

1972, July 18: Sadat announces expulsion from Egypt of thousands of Soviet military advisers and combat personnel.

1973, October 6–22: The October War, known in Israel as the Yom Kippur War. Egyptian troops cross Suez Canal, attack Israeli forces in Sinai. First successful confrontation of Israel by an Arab army ends in standoff, but Egyptians claim psychological victory.

1974, February 28: Egypt resumes diplomatic relations with United States after visit by President Nixon.

April 18: Sadat proclaims *infitah*, the opening of Egyptian economy to private investment and foreign capital.

1976, November 11: Sadat announces that multiple political parties will be legalized.

1977, January 18–19: Widespread rioting in Cairo and other cities over sudden increases in prices of staples. Army restores order. Government rescinds price increases.

November 19–21: Sadat's "peace mission" to Jerusalem. First visit by an Arab leader to the Jewish state.

1978, September 5–14: Sadat and Israeli Prime Minister Menachem Begin, after meeting in seclusion with President Carter at Camp David outside Washington, agree on framework for peace settlement. Other Arabs denounce accord as a separate peace and a sellout by Egypt.

1979, March 26: Peace treaty between Egypt and Israel signed at the White House.

1981, September 3–5: Sadat orders mass arrests of political opponents. More than 1,500 people, including prominent journalists, politicians and religious leaders, are locked up.

October 6: Sadat assassinated. Hosni Mubarak, vice president since 1975, becomes president.

1986, February 25–27: Security police conscripts riot, burn down tourist hotels; 36 people are killed. Army again restores order. More than 1,300 policemen are arrested.

1987, October 12: Mubarak begins second term as president.

CHAPTER

1

The Search for a Better Deal

The Egyptians are among the most demonstrative and least inscrutable people on Earth. Whether talking politics, selling tomatoes, welcoming a stranger, bidding at a camel auction, berating a child, mourning a death, or shrieking at a horror movie, they let themselves go. It is hard to misread their emotions.

So it was on October 1, 1970, when millions of Egyptian citizens poured into the streets of Cairo to vent their grief and shock at the funeral of Gamal Abdel Nasser. Nasser was the one great hero of independent Egypt, the brave officer who overthrew the monarchy, nationalized the Suez Canal, built the Aswan Dam, defied the imperialists. At his death the nation he personified was defeated and destitute and the Arab world he sought to lead was in turmoil, but he stood for Egypt, he was the hope of the common man, and the future without him loomed darker than the present.

And so it was again just seven years later, on the night of November 21, 1977, when Egyptians in uncountable masses gathered once more to shriek and salute in a collective outpouring of unmistakable feelings. But how different was the occasion, how much their world had changed in those seven years. They had come this time to pass judgment on an amazing event, President Anwar Sadat's journey to Israel, and hours before his plane touched down on the homeward flight it was clear what their verdict would be: stormy, passionate approval. At Nasser's funeral, the Egyptians mourned not only for him but also for themselves, bereft of hope. Now hope was restored—hope for peace and a better life. Sadat was

bringing it with him from Jerusalem, and the people turned out to
say yes: yes to peace with Israel, yes to ending the long fruitless
struggle that had exhausted their country and killed their sons.

Brown-skinned farmers from the provinces, cafe waiters and
messengers from Cairo and Alexandria, portly clerks in leisure suits,
students in comical T-shirts and flared jeans, black-eyed, black-
gowned women with gold on their wrists and children on their
shoulders, all were jubilant over the sudden imminence of peace.

As Sadat rode triumphantly through the mobs in his open car,
all Egypt was caught up in euphoric expectations of peace and
prosperity. Few seemed to regret that Sadat was now doing in
international affairs what he had already done in domestic matters—repudiating Nasser and his legacy. In the excitement, no one
could have imagined that Sadat would die unmourned only four
years later, slain while reviewing his own troops. On that night
Sadat was the hero of a resurgent Egypt. In his speech to Israel's
parliament, he had laid down stiff terms for ending the state of war
that had inflamed the Middle East for three decades, but the crowds
that greeted him upon his return were not chanting about the
occupied territories or the fate of the Palestinians. They were for
peace.

Two nights before Sadat's jubilant homecoming, I was at a
lonely helicopter pad on a parking lot behind the soccer stadium in
Ismailia, beside the Suez Canal, to watch him begin the journey
that transfixed the world, the first visit by an Arab leader to Israel.
Only a few of the president's intimate friends and a handful of
journalists were present. For security reasons, the hour and place of
his embarkation had been withheld from the public.

That was because nobody knew how the Egyptians would
respond to what Sadat was about to do. It was possible that the
spectacle of an Arab leader consorting with the Israelis—the hated
Zionists, the usurpers, the occupiers of Jerusalem—would bring
crazed mobs into the streets to demand the president's downfall; it
had happened once already that year, in riots over food-price
increases that challenged Sadat's regime.

But Egypt was as calm as a Pharaonic tomb while Sadat was in
Israel. The people went to their television sets, not into the streets,
and hardly a word of protest was heard. The explosion of emotion
on Sadat's return was one of joy and hope, not outrage. Con-
founding the predictions of the propagandists in other Arab coun-

tries, the Egyptians were ready for peace. They had borne the burden of the Arab struggle with Israel for nearly 30 years, and that was enough.

"Welcome, Sadat," they shouted. "Welcome, hero of peace. We are with you, Sadat, hero of war, hero of peace." The president, smiling and confident as if he expected no less, had read their mood correctly. Night was falling by the time he left Cairo International Airport and set out for his official residence, 10 miles away across the Nile. He could have been the target of a thousand invisible assassins on the roofs and balconies of the crowded city if the people were mutinous, but they were not. It made little difference to them whether the Iraqis or the Saudis approved of Sadat's bold breakthrough—the people were for peace.

It was not esteem for Israel that underlay this sentiment. It was need. Egypt could no longer afford war. The Egyptians had nothing to look forward to if the struggle continued except more privation and suffering, and to what end? To please the Saudis and Kuwaitis, who were awash in wealth they were not sharing with Egypt? To support the Palestinians, who were killing other Arabs in Lebanon? To curry favor with the lunatic Qaddafi in Libya? No, it was the Egyptians who had done the fighting, who had driven the Israelis back from the Suez Canal, whose cities were in ruins, and they had had enough.

Peace fever swept the country. With peace would come prosperity. The popular mood was captured concisely by a policeman who watched one of Cairo's rattletrap buses lurching along with the usual crowd of riders clinging precariously to the outside and said, "After peace comes, no more of that." Teachers, artisans, shopkeepers, laborers and Egypt's armies of petty bureaucrats shared that hopeful vision.

In those electrifying days, when Sadat and Egypt set the agenda for the world, reality was forgotten along with Nasser. Sadat was bringing peace, the Americans were back in Cairo and the Russians were gone. The future glowed with promise. But in the Middle East, where life is always volatile and politics always turbulent, a decade is a long time, and so it has proved in Egypt. Ten years after Sadat signed the peace treaty with Israel that resulted from his trip to Jerusalem, nothing remains of the euphoria of the moment or the acclaim for him. Egypt is a restless and disappointed nation, uncertain of its role in the region or the world.

The peace agreement turned out to be exactly the separate peace with Israel that its critics said it would be; the other Arabs did not follow where Egypt led, as Sadat had promised they would. Prosperity has not been achieved and probably is not achievable. The expansion of political freedom that followed Nasser's death has been restrained by rising religious tension. And Sadat's grand alliance with the United States, while it brought economic aid on which Egypt is now dependent, has also brought episodes of national outrage and humiliation.

Egypt seems to be waiting for something dramatic to happen. For two generations, the country lived in the spotlight of spectacular, riveting events that made it possible to overlook the rot in the shadows. One after another the dramas unfolded: war with Israel in 1948, the revolution that ended the monarchy in 1952, war with Israel, Britain and France in 1956, the Aswan Dam and the alliance with the Soviet Union, union with Syria in 1958, four years of war in Yemen in the 1960s, shattering defeat in the six-day war of 1967, the death of Nasser in 1970, the October war of 1973, peace with Israel in 1979, the assassination of Sadat in 1981.

What nation has lived at such a pace? Egyptians became accustomed to a theatrical environment and theatrical leaders. But Sadat's successor, Hosni Mubarak, is not given to impulsive gestures or grand strategies. He preaches patience, discipline, planning—fix the pipes, build the roads, set reasonable goals and work hard to reach them. This style of governance is appropriate for present-day Egypt, where Sadat left unsolved the very real crises of food, housing, health and public services that he inherited from Nasser. But Egyptians are uncomfortable with it. The lure of a prosperous future that won popular assent to the soul-wrenching agreement with Israel was ephemeral; Egypt has neither prosperity nor its cherished position of Arab leadership. Outside the international spotlight, Egypt is just another struggling Third-World country, nostalgic for the time—so few years ago!—when it commanded the attention of the world.

Sadat was able to make peace because Egypt's national pride, shattered in the six-day rout of 1967, was restored by the successful attack across the Suez Canal in the war of October 1973. Before the 1973 war, peace would have meant surrender; once Egypt and Israel could be seen as equals on the battlefield and the United States, in the person of Henry A. Kissinger, had nursed them through cease-fire negotiations, peace with honor became possible. The Egyptians wanted peace because they wanted what they were sure would come with it: economic opportunity and political freedom. A decade later they have approached the latter, at least by comparison with Nasser's repressive one-party police state, but they were deceived about economic progress.

Egypt has assets and strengths that are the envy of other developing countries. The Egyptians are a proud, homogeneous people, politically and culturally sophisticated, deeply conscious of a continuous existence as a nation that dates to earliest history. They had factories and railroads and universities when other communities of Africa and Arabia were tribal backwaters. Their land, while largely barren, is not without resources.

But the country's liabilities have overwhelmed its assets. Housing conditions are appalling, illiteracy is still widespread, disease is endemic. Mismanaged factories equipped with obsolete machinery produce inferior goods. Organizations are cumbersome, work habits are slovenly, and the state is committed to welfare and subsidy systems that exceed its resources. Every gain is outstripped by the unchecked growth of the population. Egypt has to keep running faster and faster just to stay in the same place.

A nation with such profound limitations as those of Egypt makes an uneasy ally for the United States, a weak link in the short chain of America's friends in the Middle East. The revolution in Iran, the vulnerability of Saudi Arabia and the menace of Libya helped Sadat extract ever greater commitments from Washington, commitments that have continued under Mubarak. These American commitments began as rewards for Sadat's anti-Soviet policies and his willingness to make peace with Israel. They have grown into a strategic investment magnified by the scarcity of alternatives.

Sadat turned Egypt's back to the Arab world, literally and metaphorically. He looked westward, and especially to the United States, for aid, allies and cultural input. He reached out to Americans through their television sets. In *Autumn of Fury,* a relentlessly critical account of Sadat's presidency and the assassination that ended it, Mohamed Heikal, Egypt's most eminent journalist, said that Sadat was

> the first Egyptian Pharaoh to come before his people armed with a camera; he was also the first Egyptian Pharaoh to be

killed by his own people. He was a hero of the electronic
revolution, but also its victim. When his face was no longer to
be seen on the television screen, it was as if the eleven years of
his rule had vanished with a switch of the control knob.

It is true that Egyptians do not wish that Sadat were still their
president; his vainglorious posturing, his grandiose proclamations,
his tolerance for corruption and intolerance of dissent reduced him
from national hero to national embarrassment in four years. But
Heikal's assessment of Sadat is that of a powerful acolyte of Nasser
who fell from favor under Nasser's successor; his judgment is
unfair. Sadat's achievements were geniune.

At Nasser's death, Egypt was a socialist-dominated, single-
party police state, politically paralyzed by a pervasive and abusive
security apparatus that was encouraged by Nasser's suspicious
nature. Censorship was in force. Travel was restricted. Economic
activity was calcified by restraints on currency, restrictions on international trade, fear of war and the government's record of nationalizing private assets. Sadat peeled this structure away layer by
layer. In 11 years as president, from 1970 to 1981, Sadat lifted
from Egypt the fear of war and death that had hung over every
family for a generation. He ended the economic and spiritual
paralysis brought on by defeat, repression and a misguided addic-
tion to socialism. And he became the only Arab leader to regain so
much as an inch of the territory captured by Israel in 1967—a
distinction he retains.

What Sadat could not do was deliver on the promise of material improvements in the daily lives of the people. Sadat was lazy,
and notoriously indifferent to the details of running the government. But even if he had been an energetic, hands-on leader like his
chosen successor, Mubarak, the differences would have been marginal. Egypt's aspirations simply exceed its resources.

By most statistical measurements, life for the Egyptian masses
has improved enormously since the revolution that ousted the
monarchy in 1952. Life expectancy is longer, primary school enrollment is higher, more homes are electrified, more people have access
to safe drinking water. These are not trifling achievements in a poor
country that was at war for 30 years.

But statistics are not the same thing as living conditions.
Illiterate peasant farmers are still destined to live exhausting lives of

perpetual labor in the fields; underpaid workers in gloomy factories
are still destined to live six or eight to a room in squalid buildings
along reeking alleys; restless white collar workers are still destined
to frustrating careers at make-work jobs in filthy offices, their wages
falling ever farther behind the cost of living.

To live in Egypt is like being an actor in several different plays
at once. Some are comedies, some are melodramas; whatever scene
is being acted at the moment contains a measure of truth: charm
and pride and achievement in one, laziness and ineptitude and filth
in another. The beauty of the Nile and the comfort of tradition give
way to noise and confusion. Consistency and order are hard to
achieve in a community where bus drivers sometimes improvise
their routes and stop for tea.

Amid the crowds, the scenes flash by with little time for
reflection. A 10-minute walk in Cairo or Alexandria brings a full
journey across the social spectrum, from malnourished children
defecating in the gutters and beggars maimed by surgery to make
them more pathetic, to portly polylingual businessmen with brief-
cases full of cash alighting from air-conditioned cars at foreign
banks.

In such a society, the establishment of an equitable and co-
hesive program of political and social action seems just as formida-
ble a task now as it did when the monarchy fell, nearly 40 years ago.
Sadat preached the establishment of a "state of institutions"—a
society in which law and legitimate institutions would ensure the
rights of the people, supplanting the repression and arbitrary rule
to which Egypt had become accustomed. He did not achieve it, and
in the end made a mockery of his own goal with mass arrests of
opponents, real and imagined, that he ordered just before his death.

But it was only in a nation at peace that it even made sense to
talk about the "state of institutions" and the transition to democracy, and Sadat pursued the goal of peace almost from the day he
took office. The objective remained a constant, even if his tactics
were breathtakingly unorthodox; he improvised as he went along,
the ultimate improvisation being the trip to Jerusalem.

He went to Israel because conventional diplomacy held out no
prospect of resolving a conflict that had left Egypt's territory occupied and its economy prostrate. Even unconventional diplomacy,
as practiced by Secretary of State Kissinger after the 1973 war, had
only altered the conditions of the stalemate, not broken it. The high

hopes aroused by the early Middle East policy declarations of President Jimmy Carter had dissolved in haggling over the conditions in which peace negotiations might be conducted.

In the mid-1970s, as Sadat looked for a way to rescue Egypt from war, the situation that confronted him was this: All the Arab nations had refused to recognize the existence of Israel as a sovereign state. Israel wanted acceptance as a nation and security for its people. In the six-day war of 1967, Israel had captured territory previously held by three Arab nations: Egypt's Sinai peninsula, the Golan Heights of Syria, and East Jerusalem and the surrounding territory on the west bank of the Jordan River, which had been part of Jordan. In the 1973 war, Egyptian troops crossed the Suez Canal and retook a slice of the Sinai. That was the first time any Arab army had engaged the Israelis successfully. It restored Egypt's morale and gave Sadat the aura of a hero, but it left Israel in control of most of the Sinai peninsula and of all the other lands it had captured in 1967.

The assumption that underlay all diplomatic efforts to resolve the Arab-Israeli dispute was that Israel was prepared to trade territory for peace. United Nations resolutions adopted after the 1967 and 1973 wars embraced the "territory for peace" principle, and the combatants accepted it. Kissinger's "shuttle diplomacy" achieved standstill cease-fire agreements. But the Arabs were unable to move beyond these to negotiations for a durable peace because they refused to negotiate directly with Israel; to do so would be tantamount to recognizing the Zionist state without any guaranteed return. The Israelis naturally insisted on face-to-face negotiations.

The Arab nations had pledged themselves to act collectively in negotiations and to accept no peace agreement that did not create a state for their stateless brethren, the Palestinians. They also had agreed that only the Palestine Liberation Organization could represent the Palestinians in international forums. Israel, however, refused to deal with the PLO in any way. The PLO was a sworn enemy of Israel's very existence and the Israelis would do nothing to accept it as a legitimate interlocutor.

Egypt, whose population exceeded that of all other Arab countries combined, was indispensable to the Arab cause. But the Arabs, despite their pledge of solidarity, were at odds among themselves; some Arab states, including Egypt, were willing to accept the existence of Israel on the basis of the territory-for-peace principle and self-determination for the Palestinians. Others were committed to the destruction of the Jewish state and would have no peace with the Zionists on any terms. Syria, which rejected peace, was closely allied with the Soviet Union. Egypt, which under Nasser had been a virtual client state of the Soviets, was turning toward the United States. Jordan felt itself threatened as much by the prospect of a revanchist Palestinian state on what had been Jordanian territory as it was by Israel. Syria suspected that Egypt might strike out and make peace on its own, but it had insurance against such an eventuality: Saudi Arabia was committed to the Palestinian cause, and Sadat, whose country was destitute, had been forced to go to the Saudis in 1976 to beg for cash.

Ismail Fahmy, the acerbic, cigar-smoking foreign minister who resigned rather than go to Jerusalem with Sadat, still insists that various parties to the conflict were on the verge of agreeing to meet at Geneva and hammer out an overall settlement when Sadat undermined that process by bolting off on his own. But if he really believes that, he is perhaps the only one who does. No formula was in sight for getting Egypt, Jordan, Syria, Israel and the PLO to the bargaining table, let alone achieving a settlement. Syria wanted a single Arab delegation, to limit Egypt's freedom of action, and insisted that Palestinians from the PLO be included on the Arab side.

Even if all these obstacles had been surmounted, Sadat understood that a conference at Geneva was not an end in itself. He knew it was possible that "the process would take 10 years and Egypt would get nothing," as William B. Quandt, a senior American participant in this diplomatic quagmire, said in his detailed account of it. Sadat could not wait 10 years.

Egypt in 1977 needed peace even more certainly than it had needed war in 1973. Sadat could not afford more interminable rounds of rhetoric, posturing, threats and negotiating over how to negotiate. He was convinced that some dramatic new approach was needed. He would have preferred that the United States devise a peace formula and impose it on Israel, but this was not a possibility, especially with the strong-willed Menachem Begin at the head of the Israeli government.

Fahmy said that the decision to go to Jerusalem was "not taken because Egypt was in a desperate position." Militarily, it was not, but economically it was. Sadat could not envision any way in which conventional diplomacy would free Egypt from the state of conflict that was destroying it, squandering its future. Sadat wanted to seize the moment. He was not crippled by the domestic weaknesses that hindered other Arab leaders—Egypt was not a precarious artificial state with an imposed monarchy, like Jordan, nor a pit of unrest run by a despised minority, like Syria—and he had reestablished Egypt's freedom of action by breaking with the Soviet Union and attacking Israel in 1973.

Sadat went to war in 1973 partly because overtures he had made to the United States had not produced the desired result— that is, the United States did not use its presumed power over Israel to force the Israelis to evacuate the occupied territories. According to Kissinger, Sadat was misled by William Rogers, Kissinger's predecessor as secretary of state under Richard Nixon. Rogers had assured Sadat that Washington would make an "all out effort" to achieve a settlement in 1971 when in fact that was a commitment "for which there was no White House support at all."

By the spring of 1971, in office only six months, Sadat had already said he would accept a peace agreement that would include recognition of Israel and respect for its independence (but not full diplomatic or trade relations); the price was Israeli withdrawal from the occupied territories. This was understandably insufficient for the Israelis, and they spurned the offer. And the United States was not going to force Israel's hand, because, as Kissinger later wrote, "as long as Egypt was in effect a Soviet military base we could have no incentive to turn on an ally on behalf of a Soviet client."

Sadat had told Nixon that "we are not within the Soviet sphere of influence," but the evidence indicated otherwise and the Americans were not convinced of Sadat's credibility. In fact, as Kissinger has admitted, they were not even paying attention, preoccupied as they were with the war in Vietnam, with detente and with Nixon's opening to China. One of Sadat's objectives in the 1973 war was to force the United States to take him seriously.

Egypt regained a sliver of the Sinai in that war, but territory was not the principal objective. There is still argument about which side won the war in military terms, both Egypt and Israel having been rescued from defeat by superpower intervention, but in Egypt there is no doubt that the war was a near-total success in terms of Sadat's nonmilitary objectives. It restored the shattered pride of the Egyptian people and their army; it traumatized the Israelis; it gave

Sadat the strength to negotiate peace with Israel over the protests of other Arabs because it was he, not they, who had engaged the enemy successfully; and it secured the involvement of the United States in the negotiations, not as a representative of Israeli interests but as a mediator.

After the war, Sadat looked to Washington to extend the temporary disengagement agreements negotiated by Kissinger into a permanent settlement. He told every interviewer, in a phrase that became a Cairo joke, that "the United States holds 99 percent of the cards" in the Middle East. He waited for the United States to play its hand, but a new stalemate set in—inevitably, given Kissinger's promise to Israel that the United States would never negotiate with the PLO and Arab insistence that no other group could speak for the Palestinians.

Jimmy Carter, who became president in January 1977, made encouraging remarks about Palestinian self-determination, but by the autumn of that year other pressures were driving Sadat to move faster than anyone else was prepared to go. He was facing serious domestic unrest: There had been food-price riots in January and an attempted uprising by religious extremists. Arab unity was in ruins; Egypt and Libya even went briefly to war that summer. Egypt's military equipment was obsolescent. And Sadat apparently believed that the United States and the Soviet Union were dragging their feet.

Sadat's trip to Jerusalem was essentially a public relations gesture—one of the most audacious ever undertaken. He could have made the same speech he delivered in the Knesset in his own parliament or at the United Nations, but it would not have had a fraction of the same impact on Israeli or American public opinion. He wanted popular sentiment in the United States to support American pressure on, and guarantees to, Israel, which he knew would be needed if Israel were to be persuaded to withdraw from Arab territory. Sadat had to sell the Americans, as well as the Israelis, on the genuineness of his peaceful intentions and on his sincere intention to override the collective veto other Arabs wanted to impose on his actions. That is why he allowed prominent American television journalists to travel with him on his plane from Cairo to Tel Aviv. The journalists were props for his magic show.

As much as Sadat wanted the Americans involved, he wanted the Soviet Union excluded. A return to Geneva and a renewal of the peace conference that had met there briefly after the war—which was the ostensible aim of all Middle East diplomacy even after the Jerusalem trip—would have reinjected the Soviet Union into a diplomatic arena from which it had been all but excluded. The Soviet Union, as co-chair of the Geneva Conference and principal arms supplier to Syria and Iraq, would have torpedoed the negotiations by insisting on maximalist positions on every issue. The Egyptians believed such Soviet participation would doom the negotiations to failure.

It is clear now that while Sadat's strategic aims in this period were consistent—peace and an alliance with the United States—he was making up his tactics as he went along, zigzagging on a course without maps, outside normal diplomatic channels. Egyptian officials met late into the night with American journalists such as myself to explain what Sadat was up to. We would go to the Foreign Ministry as late as 10 PM for background briefings and informal conversations about Egyptian policy. It was apparent during those meetings that the Egyptian diplomats themselves had often been surprised by Sadat's latest statements or actions and were providing the rationalization after the fact.

From accounts written later by participants in these events—Kissinger and Quandt on the American side, Ismail Fahmy and his successor Mohammed Ibrahim Kamel on the Egyptian—we know that Sadat's penchant for the grand gesture sometimes led him to give way on crucial issues without receiving any adequate return. Kissinger, for example, was amazed that Sadat expelled his Soviet military advisers without telling the Americans he was going to do it or extracting any reward for it. But for Sadat, instinct was policy. In the case of the Soviet Union his instinctive distrust and his desire to curtail Soviet influence in Egypt, and in the entire Middle East, were apparent from the early days of his presidency.

The Soviet Union had consistently supported the Arabs in their conflict with Israel. During the 1973 war, they backed their commitment with airlifts of arms and equipment. But for Egypt that partnership of convenience during the war was only a momentary reversal of a rapid deterioration in relations with Moscow.

Sadat's rupture with the Soviet Union was more a matter of expediency than ideology. Sadat detested communists, but that was not the reason he broke with Moscow. He would have continued to work with the Soviet Union if he thought it would advance the cause of Egypt, but he did not. He thought the Soviet leaders had lied to him. They could not or would not deliver the weapons he thought he needed to defeat Israel in battle, and they lacked any leverage over Israel that would have benefited Egypt in negotiations. Egypt under Nasser may have been a "client" of Moscow, as Kissinger said, but Egypt was not Cuba; Egypt is no one's surrogate. If Egypt went to war against Israel, it was because Egypt saw an advantage in doing so, not because Egypt put the interests of the Palestinians above its own or took orders from Moscow. If Egypt turned away from Moscow and toward the United States, it was because Sadat thought he could get a better deal.

Sadat wanted American support in peace negotiations; he knew the Soviets had no leverage over Israel. He wanted American money and technology for development. He wanted to extricate Egypt from international entanglements—such as the disastrous intervention in the Yemeni civil war of the 1960s and Nasser's abortive union with Syria—that had brought defeat and frustration on so many fronts, and he wanted to rebuild the country. To do that, he had to effect a change of near-revolutionary proportions in Egypt's political and economic life. Before he could begin development of a new system, he had to break down the old one. One wrenching step was the replacement of the Soviet Union by the United States as the principal source of aid and external political influence.

There was wonderful irony in this. Nasser had embraced the Soviets out of frustration with the Americans; now the circle was full. The Russians had built the High Dam at Aswan and the steel mills at Helwan, and had backed Egypt in every international arena. But Sadat showed them the door because the alliance had not led to military success or to economic progress, and he saw Egypt's main chance elsewhere.

I knew Russians who, years later, were still baffled at the collapse of their relationship with Egypt. They could not understand how their showcase Third-World partnership had broken up. The answer lay partly in Sadat's recognition that Egypt had not profited from its partnership with Moscow and partly in his frustration and disillusionment over what he regarded as duplicity in the Kremlin. Mohamed Heikal, who observed the deterioration of Egypt's ties to Moscow from the center of events, recalls that the Soviets irritated Sadat not only on large issues, such as their refusal

to deliver weapons on demand, but on trivial matters, such as the
illegal export of gold from Egypt by Soviet diplomats. But more of
the answer lay in Sadat's desire to haul Egypt out of the morass in
which he found it when he took office. The Soviets were part of the
problem, not part of the solution: They would not deliver the
unlimited weaponry for an all-out assault against Israel, they could
not deliver an acceptable solution at the bargaining table and they
gave other concerns, such as their developing detente with Washington, precedence over the demands of Egypt. And so they had to
go.

In some ways Egypt was an unlikely arena for a struggle for
influence between the superpowers. Only a few miles from central
Cairo, down the bumpy road to Saqqara along a fetid canal, it is still
almost possible to forget the twentieth century.

Peasants bend and squat over their crops. Blindfolded water
buffalo plod endlessly in circles to drive the water wheels, as they
have since the beginning of history. Women in shapeless black
gowns wash kitchen utensils, clothes, animals and children in the
murky water. Ragged little boys and girls with runny noses, lice in
their hair and flies on their faces scamper through the garbage and
donkey dung on the muddy streets.

Men in long blue *galabeyas* of coarse cotton ride by on donkeys. Burping camels plod across the fields. The whole scene is a
cliche, an article from a travel magazine, but it is also reality. Tens of
millions of Egyptians live that way. Most of the villages have
electricity now, and agricultural cooperatives have brought in tractors and mechanical pumps, but the pattern of life is much the same
as it was under the British, the Mameluke sultans and probably
under the Romans. In the bright fields of clover and onions and
peppers, nothing seems more remote than the conflicts of international politics.

But for centuries the accident of Egypt's geography and the
ambitions of empires have made Egypt a playing field for what
Miles Copeland called "The Game of Nations." In his cynical book
about the struggle between Washington and Moscow for a dominant position in Nasser's Egypt, Copeland, who observed the game
from a front-row seat in the American embassy, quotes Zakaria
Mohieddin, vice president under Nasser, as saying that "in the
Game of Nations there are no winners, only losers. The objective of

each player is not so much to win as to avoid loss." At the beginning of the 1970s, however, it appeared that there was indeed a winner, and it was the Soviet Union.

On the day of Nasser's funeral, October 1, 1970, the grief-stricken crowds were still wailing in the streets when Soviet Prime Minister Alexei Kosygin broadcast a statement on Cairo Radio to the people of the "United Arab Republic," as Egypt had been known officially since Nasser's ill-fated merger with Syria. Kosygin delivered a message of strong support in international affairs, which meant in the conflict with Israel. But it was also a message of caution about Egypt's domestic political situation, which had been thrown into turmoil by Nasser's death at the age of 52.

Promising that "our all-around assistance" to Egypt would continue, Kosygin added this elliptical warning: "We are confident that his loss, however grave, will not weaken your ranks, will not create any vacuum that your enemies hope for. President Nasser's departure will increase the unity of the people of the United Arab Republic and all other Arab states upholding progressive gains of their peoples."

His promises of continued aid must have been reassuring to the Egyptians, who looked to the Soviets as their only source of defense against the "deep penetration" bombing raids by Israel that were striking their factories and schools—but it was the Russians who needed reassurance. The Soviet Union had a greater stake in Egypt than in any other country outside the Warsaw Pact as it was the showcase for Soviet policy in the developing world. The Russians did not know what would happen after Nasser.

Nearly 15,000 Soviet military advisers were serving with the Egyptian armed forces, which were Soviet-trained and Soviet-equipped. Soviet pilots were in Egypt flying MiG-21 combat jets, and Soviet missile crews had recently arrived to take over direct manning of the air defense system. The Soviets controlled some of Egypt's air bases. Important military decisions by the Egyptian command had to be coordinated with the Soviet Union.

Russians were stationed in the sensitive civilian ministries, the intelligence service and the police. The Soviet Union had agents promoting "scientific socialism" inside the Arab Socialist Union, the only legal political organization in Egypt. Moscow bought most of Egypt's cotton crop and was Egypt's leading trade partner.

Egyptian factories were equipped with machinery from Soviet satellite countries in Eastern Europe.

For some months after Sadat succeeded Nasser, he gave every sign that he would preserve this relationship as he had inherited it. In fact, he indulged in rhetorical excesses about the friendship between the Egyptians and the Soviets, as he did for example in a well-publicized speech to the People's Assembly, or parliament, on February 4, 1971.

The conflict with Israel, he said, "proved that we had friends, foremost among whom and dearly esteemed are the great people of the Soviet Union. They not only appreciated our viewpoint but also hastened to offer that short of which it would have been difficult to pursue the combat with force and effectiveness."

He went further. "The Soviet Union," he said, "in its attitudes toward us in this crisis, has consolidated one of the major friendships in history and made of it a model and example of world fraternity and unity of the powers averse to imperialism, terrorism and aggression."

He reported that in an attempt to break the diplomatic stalemate that had prevailed since the 1967 war, "I sent a message to President Nixon and I have received the reply to it. I regret to say that America's position remains as it was—complete bias for Israel." By contrast, he said, "the people and leaders of the Soviet Union have stood by us as honest men and militant revolutionaries supporting our right and consolidating our line with honor and determination. Neither our history nor our future generations will forget its honorable stand toward our just cause."

Three months later, on May 25, Sadat and Nikolai Podgorny, the Soviet president, signed a Treaty of Friendship and Cooperation that seemed to put the seal of permanence on this intimate bilateral relationship. Only a few high-ranking insiders knew that there were deep fissures beneath this happy surface and that Sadat and the Soviet leadership were at odds on critical points. The Soviets had been taken by surprise when, in the same February 4 speech in which he praised them so lavishly, Sadat made a unilateral offer to reopen the Suez Canal in exchange for a limited Israeli pullback from its eastern bank; and Moscow had been alarmed when Sadat dismissed and jailed rivals for power who were known to be sympathetic to the Soviet Union. From what was indicated publicly, it would have seemed preposterous to suggest that in less than a decade Sadat would jettison the Soviet Union, make peace with Israel and turn his country into a strategic partner of the United States.

When I first arrived in Cairo, in the middle of the decade and in the middle of this international *volte-face,* nobody, not even Sadat, had any idea how far it would go. Egypt was still technically at war with Israel, and the American view of Egypt as the most dangerous enemy of the Jewish state had hardened over many years. No one imagined that by 1980 American warplanes would be flying out of Egyptian bases and the United States would be supplying Egypt with advanced combat aircraft. Whatever Kissinger's view of Sadat after the Egyptian leader extended *de facto* recognition to Israel by accepting the Sinai disengagement agreements after the 1973 war, Congress would not then have permitted military assistance.

But Sadat was correct in sensing that the United States would reward him for good behavior. Even before he went to Jerusalem, he extracted from the Carter administration a formal commitment to support him and his policies with a complex program of long-term economic assistance. The United States also undertook to persuade American private enterprise to join in the Egyptian development effort, but the results of this were, inevitably, modest. After the dramatic conference among Sadat, Prime Minister Begin and President Carter at Camp David in September 1978, which produced the agreements in principle that would result in a formal peace treaty the following spring, Carter assigned Robert Strauss, a prominent Texas lawyer and political insider, to stimulate American private investment in Egypt. Strauss, renowned for his "can do" approach, hustled over to Egypt and emerged chastened, advising against overoptimism. He said he had a harder job than the diplomats had in negotiating the treaty, and he was right. The Egyptians had long been accustomed to the economic style of the communist countries, in which state policy dictated the decisions: Nobody, for example, would choose to drink Egyptian wine, but Bulgaria imported thousands of cases in a barter deal for live sheep because political policy dictated it. The Egyptians had to learn that free market economies don't operate like Bulgaria's. American corporations go where they can make money, and for most of them that was not Egypt.

The United States, long the bulwark of Israeli security, was reluctant to become a supplier of arms to Egypt. That reluctance faded, however, when the Iranian revolution and the Soviet invasion of Afghanistan in 1979 dramatized the vulnerability of the Persian Gulf oil states. Sadat, stung by their criticism of the peace treaty and the termination of economic aid from the Gulf states, had dismissed the oil sheikhdoms as "jelly-like entities," not countries at all. But he understood their importance to the United States and Europe. He seized the opportunity to offer air and naval "facilities" to the United States and to extract more arms and economic aid in the bargain—that is, he played with the United States the same game of nations that Nasser had played with the Russians, using one superpower's rivalry with the other to obtain material and political support for Egypt.

In the early phase of Egypt's realignment, right after the 1973 war, both Egypt and the United States were sailing through uncharted waters toward an unknown destination. Neither really knew what to expect of the other. But Sadat became a master at charming members of Congress. He received scores of them and was gracious even to the most dense. Diplomatic relations between Egypt and the United States, broken in 1967, were restored after Nixon's visit to Cairo in 1974, a triumphant event in which a tumultuous welcome by the Egyptians revealed a reservoir of pro-American sentiment that had survived the years of official hostility. That trip was the last hurrah of Nixon's presidency, which was soon to be ended by the Watergate scandal, but once the door to good relations had been opened it stayed open.

Economic aid resumed on such a scale that the U.S. Agency for International Development (AID) staff in the American embassy was scrambling to find useful ways to spend the money. That was because the program was set up backward: Kissinger, in a gesture to Sadat, promised the aid, fixed the amount and persuaded Congress to approve it. Only then did work begin on setting up the projects to use the funds. John J. Gilligan, then the director of AID, acknowledged when he visited Egypt in 1977 that the program was out of control. After a talk with Sadat and a tour that fooled nobody—the little village where he was taken to see a health clinic and school said to have been helped by American money was the only one I visited in all Egypt that smelled of fresh paint—he concluded that the nature of the aid program would have to change. It began as a quick injection of cash aimed at rewarding

Sadat for his flexibility after the 1973 war. It evolved into a long-term undertaking by the United States to improve the living conditions of the Egyptian people—an undertaking into which the United States poured nearly $2 billion a year throughout the 1980s, long after Mubarak had restored normal diplomatic and trade relations between Cairo and Moscow.

By the end of 1975, the U.S. navy had earned Sadat's gratitude by helping to clear the Suez Canal of sunken hulls and wrecks so he could reopen it—and by refraining from sending a bill. American technicians were arriving in the Sinai to build and operate monitoring stations that represented a U.S. guarantee of the second disengagement agreement. Chase Manhattan Bank was operating in Cairo, Citibank was about to open, American oil companies were bidding for exploration rights in Egypt and American business executives were coming in to examine the investment climate.

On the other hand, the treaty of friendship with the Soviet Union was still in effect, and although the military advisers had been expelled before the 1973 war, there were residual signs of Russian influence. Dispatches from *Novosti* and *Tass* still appeared occasionally in the Cairo press. The Soviet navy had fueling and repair stations on the Mediterranean coast. Russian technicians worked at Aswan and Helwan. The tourism industry still depended on the groups of Russians and Eastern Europeans who filled the tacky souvenir shops. Some shops in the Zamalek diplomatic quarter still had Cyrillic writing on their signs. And newly arrived foreign correspondents were still being advised to go around to the office of *Tass,* the Soviet news agency, to meet the bureau chief, who had enough inside contacts to dispense informed speculation along with Russian champagne.

Diplomats and journalists who were based in Egypt during the days of the greatest Soviet presence recall that many Egyptians admired the Russians or were at least grateful to them. They had built the Aswan Dam after the Americans refused to do it and had responded to Egypt's military helplessness after the 1967 war by committing their own pilots and missile crews to the defense of Egypt. An entire generation of Egypt's military leadership, including Mubarak, had been trained by the Soviets on Soviet equipment.

But by 1975 the Egyptians were no longer feeling defenseless. Because of their success in the war of 1973—success that was achieved only after Sadat expelled the Soviet advisers—Egypt was

free from Soviet demands for caution and restraint. People generally remembered the Russians as arrogant and parsimonious. Anecdotal evidence abounded that the Russians, while seemingly indispensable, had not been popular.

Fruit vendors recalled that Russian women squeezed every
tomato and mango before buying and kept every *piaster* of the
change they carefully counted. Former military officers spoke with
embarrassment of the years when they had been denied access to
their own air bases because the Russians didn't want them there.

Once the driver of a taxi in which I was riding stopped in front
of the television building on the Nile Corniche and pointed to a
soft-drink vendor's stand beside the river. "One time I had three
Russians as passengers," he said, "and they stopped here for a drink.
The three of them shared a single Pepsi!"

The Egyptians who approached us on downtown streets to try
to sell perfume or souvenirs or black-market currency had reasons
other than politics to be happy to learn we were Americans. Americans were free with their money. I don't mean that the Egyptians
are mercenary people whose allegiance is for sale, though some of
them are. Their wholehearted welcome for the Americans and
Western Europeans who flocked to Egypt after the 1973 war was
more complicated than that. Egyptians are gregarious and outgo-
ing. They find the open American approach congenial. The restoration of Egypt's ties to the United States represented for them not
just a sign that their country was moving toward peace but an
opportunity to reach out for the prosperity that had not been
possible in the previous two decades. It was only natural that
ordinary people whose incomes depended on foreigners would
appreciate the Americans more than they did the stingy, suspicious
Russians. The return of the Americans to the Egyptian playing field
coincided with and was part of an economic awakening that meant
full hotels, higher taxi fares, more sales of souvenirs and artworks,
higher wages for household staff, easier access to foreign currency
and new markets for local products.

A pent-up demand for Western consumer goods exploded
after the war. When we arrived we found the shops stocked with
canned goods, tools and electrical equipment from Eastern Europe,
mostly of inferior quality. The Egyptians' desire for Western goods
was reflected in locally made products that imitated the labels and
names of American counterparts: "Heimz" pickles, "Ale" padlocks

and "Monopol" board games. Those items went on the back shelves as the real things began to appear.

One day I was at the American embassy on a routine errand when I found a long line of young men stretching down the block from the main entrance. They said they had heard on the Voice of America that the cultural affairs office was giving out free instruction books in elementary English. They wanted to learn English because they thought that was the key to opportunity, to a better job, in a way that knowledge of Russian never could have been. A position with Citibank might pay five times the salary of a similar job at the state-owned Bank of Alexandria, and in better working conditions too. A knowledge of English might mean a job at the Hilton or at Mobil Oil or NBC, or as a driver for an American family. Perhaps it would not be necessary to emigrate to Abu Dhabi or Saudi Arabia to bring home extra cash. The Americans were doubly welcome because, unlike the British, they were untainted by colonialism. It wasn't the Americans who had humiliated Egypt by forcing the king to accept a prime minister he did not want; it wasn't the Americans who had invaded Egypt in 1956 in outrage over nationalization of the Suez Canal.

This was an exhilarating atmosphere, and the exhilaration expressed itself in the mass outpouring of support and esteem for Sadat when he returned from Jerusalem. Peace plus American money equaled prosperity. Forgotten for the moment was the fact that only 10 months before, the mob had been in a much different mood: They had attacked shops and nightclubs and burned fancy cars in two days of ugly riots that ended only when the army took over the streets. Those "bread riots" of January 1977 broke out when the government raised the prices of several basic commodities overnight, without warning, in an effort to reduce subsidies that were bankrupting the treasury. Despite the quelling of the riots, Sadat was forced to cancel the price increases. The memory of those events haunts the successor government to this day, accounting for its reluctance to impose austerity measures even when they are clearly needed.

The riots seemed to vindicate the few leftist politicans and disgruntled intellectuals who had stopped to examine the negative implications of Sadat's economic liberalization. These malcontents argued—correctly—that relatively few Egyptians were actually going to benefit from the new commercial enterprises. The opening of the economy was creating a new class of rich opportunists and their spoiled children who were able to buy the luxury goods that were flooding the stores and to purchase the expensive new apartments that were being built. The rest of the country, long accustomed to the "share the poverty" egalitarianism of the Nasser era, looked on with envy and resentment. The growing disparity between the relatively few "haves" and the legions of "have nots" led inevitably to the political disillusionment that haunts the country a decade later.

I watched those 1977 bread riots from start to finish—from the first small gathering of students shouting their anger outside the parliament to the arrival of heavily armed troops to restore order. It was clear to my colleagues and me that they were a spontaneous and popular uprising, the first such challenge to Sadat's regime. But Sadat refused to accept the political implications of this event. He insisted that the riots had been a communist plot. Prime Minister Mustafa Khalil summoned all the foreign correspondents in Cairo, including the Russians, to a meeting at which he scolded us for our refusal to accept the government line on this point. "There is no class struggle in Egypt," he said, ignoring the mounting evidence to the contrary.

But whether the riots were spontaneous or organized, there was no escaping the economic implications—ordinary Egyptians were desperate. This reinforced Sadat's determination to achieve peace and align Egypt with the United States. He had made up his mind that only the United States could provide the capital and the technology to rebuild Egypt's exhausted economy and that only the United States could get the Israelis out of the Sinai peninsula, and there was no force in the country capable of restraining him. No one in Egypt, except for the extremists of the underground religious opposition, opposed peace with Israel as a matter of principle.

When Sadat became president, he was described in the Western press as an obscure leftist politican who had neither the power nor the inclination to reverse his country's course, especially because Egypt was economically and militarily dependent on the Soviet Union. But Egypt's relationship with the Soviets was troubled even before Nasser died. It had not brought victory over Israel, it had led to economic prostration despite the showcase aid projects, and it had eroded the independence of policy and action that was the aim of the 1952 revolution. There were Egyptians who grumbled that the Soviets would be harder to get rid of than the British had been.

Even Nasser, crushed by the rout of 1967, had made cautious gestures toward the United States in an effort to restore some balance in Egypt's international relations. Shortly before his death he spent three weeks in the Soviet Union and upon his return told Sadat, then vice president, that it was a "hopeless case." For lack of any other plan, he announced shortly after he returned to Egypt in July 1970 that he would accept a proposal by Secretary of State Rogers for a three-month cease-fire in the "war of attrition" with Israel and new diplomatic negotiations under United Nations auspices.

This was a surprise, but nothing came of it. The United States was providing sophisticated weapons to Israel and viewed Egypt as an agent of Soviet power. Nasser himself was an exhausted and defeated leader whose dreams of a united Arab world and a prosperous Egypt had been reduced to rubble, and he viewed the Americans as the instruments of this destruction.

Sadat said in his memoirs that the Soviet Union refused an Egyptian request for assistance during the 1956 invasion by Britain and France and "this made me believe, from that moment on, that it was always futile to depend on the Soviet Union." If he actually held that view during the 14 years between the Suez war and Nasser's death, when he was the most loyal of Nasser's acolytes, there is no evidence that he sought to press the argument with the president. But the reasons for his disenchantment and break with Moscow after he took power are well documented.

He believed the Russians had duped him by promising him new weapons that they failed to deliver and that they imposed unacceptable conditions on those they did send, insisting that they not be used without Soviet permission. In his speech of February 4, 1971—the same speech in which he called Egypt's ties to the Soviet Union "one of the great friendships in history"—he reported that he had made a secret trip to Moscow and come away "fully satisfied." This was not true; he was unhappy because the Soviets were holding back on weapons and urging restraint where he felt the need to move boldly.

Anticipating that Moscow would eventually come through with the weapons he believed had been promised, Sadat proclaimed

1971 the "year of decision" in the conflict with Israel, and he was humiliated when nothing happened. Late that year, when he again went to Moscow, the Soviets told him that their arms supplies had been diverted to India for its war with Pakistan and could not be sent to Egypt. Sadat said later that he thought this explanation duplicitous, and it added to the growing anger he felt at the Russians over other issues.

One of those grievances was his belief that the Soviets supported his rivals in an attempted coup d'etat in May 1971. When he rounded up and jailed the conspirators, men who were known to be sympathetic to the Soviet Union, Moscow sent Podgorny to Cairo on a fence-mending mission. That visit resulted in the signature of the friendship treaty, but the document only papered over a split that was to widen more and more rapidly.

Sadat also suspected the Russians of complicity in a communist plot that briefly ousted President Jaafar Nimeiri of the Sudan that July. This incident instilled in Sadat a fear of Soviet intentions in Africa that later became one of the basic determinants of his foreign policy. In a long conversation I had with him in December 1976, he spent much of the time worrying about the new buildup of Soviet weapons in Libya, on Egypt's western border. The simultaneous triumph of a Marxist revolution, aided by Cubans, in Ethiopia added to his conviction that communists were surrounding Egypt and organizing his downfall.

In February 1972, still smarting from the fizzle of his "year of decision," Sadat went to Moscow yet again to ask for arms, only to be put off with excuses about paperwork and red tape that were said to be delaying shipments. "I was beside myself with rage," he wrote in his memoirs. "I realized my patience had run out."

What he did not realize was that the United States and the Soviet Union were playing another game of nations on a bigger playing field. That game was called "detente" and it led them to change the rules of the game in the Middle East without consulting Sadat. He found out about it on May 29, 1972.

After a summit conference between Nixon and Soviet First Secretary Leonid I. Brezhnev, the Soviets and the Americans issued a joint communiqué in which, as part of a long statement on international affairs, they reaffirmed their support for a "peaceful settlement" of the Arab-Israeli conflict in conformity with United Nations Security Council Resolution 242 of 1967. If they had stopped there, that would have been fine with the Egyptians, but they added this: "In the view of the U.S. and the USSR, the achievement of such a settlement would open prospects for the normalization of the Middle East situation and would permit, in particular, consideration of further steps to bring about a military relaxation in that area."

That, Sadat said later, came as a "violent shock," because of the words "military relaxation." The Egyptians, and other Arabs, read that as Soviet acquiescence in the military situation that then prevailed, namely an overpoweringly superior Israel, armed with all the latest American weapons, occupying the Sinai peninsula, the West Bank of the Jordan and other territories seized in 1967, with the Arabs helpless to do anything about it. "It was clear to me that there was to be no war in the Middle East area," Sadat told Mohamed Heikal. "There was to be nothing for us but surrender."

Sadat understood that the Russians had put their desire to avoid a confrontation with the United States ahead of their commitment to help the Arabs. Leading officers in the Egyptian armed forces were seething, complaining to Sadat that the Russians were an obstacle to a renewal of the conflict and demanding that Sadat do something to break the impasse one way or another. On July 18, 1972, Sadat announced that he had told Brezhnev to withdraw all Soviet military advisers from their posts in Egypt.

The following month, he sent Brezhnev a long letter detailing all his grievances about the way Egypt had been treated, about the Soviet Union's failure to deliver weapons, and about the way Soviet actions had "embittered" the Egyptian armed forces. As a result of Soviet policy, Sadat said, "the American claim that the United States and the United States alone is capable of finding a solution has been increasingly vindicated."

With the expulsion of the Soviet advisers, Sadat inaugurated a decade in which Soviet influence in the Middle East would dwindle steadily. But as happened so often during his presidency, outsiders misinterpreted his actions. Once he had thrown out the Russians, the Americans and the Israelis took it for granted that Egypt was even less capable of waging war than before. Only later did it become clear that his action made war possible because the Soviets were no longer holding him back. The end of the Soviet Union's exposure to direct involvement in an Arab-Israeli war, which would surely have resulted if war broke out while thousands of Soviet troops were still on duty with the Egyptian armed forces, freed the Soviets from a fear of direct confrontation with the Americans and allowed them to resume the shipment of weapons that greatly enhanced Egypt's military power. Sadat needed to go to war, both to restore Egyptian self-esteem and to force the Americans, who held the keys to a solution, to pay attention. Now the Soviets could let him do it.

After the war, Sadat no longer needed Soviet assistance. Egypt had achieved all that could be achieved by force of arms. The Soviets had helped Egypt in war, but they would be worse than useless in diplomacy and in economic recovery. Early in 1976 Sadat denounced the friendship treaty as "a worthless piece of paper." In a typically dramatic, late-night speech to parliament, he asked the members to abrogate it and they rose to their feet in applause. The wind of change in Egypt had become a gale. Israel was chastened, the Soviet Union was out of the game, Sadat was an international celebrity and the Egyptians had earned the right to dream of a brighter future. True peace was no longer unthinkable; prosperity was just around the corner. For a brief hour of history, Egypt swelled with promise. Sadat's power over his country seemed beyond challenge.

CHAPTER

2

Exorcising Nasser

Within a year of his accession to the presidency, Sadat's triumph over his rivals for power and his ouster of the Soviet military advisers gave him a free hand to run Egypt as he wished, in domestic policy and foreign affairs. But this was not enough. To enhance his personal stature and political authority, Sadat still had to get rid of Nasser. Nasser was dead, but his spirit had to be exorcised.

Nasser's economic and military failures were manifest. His rule over the country had approached despotism. He had made enemies of the intellectuals, the bourgeoisie, the Muslim Brotherhood, even the communists. But to the masses he remained a hero, the embodiment of Egyptian independence, pride and aspiration. The peasants and the urban proletariat admired him because, as Ambassador Tahseen Basheer put it years later, "only Nasser spoke for the disenfranchised of Egypt." He had a seemingly unassailable place in the national esteem, as the son of Egypt who had thrown off the foreign yoke.

Furthermore, Nasser had a powerful constituency in the new class of officers and technocrats who were interested in perpetuating the system that had given them their opportunities. Nasser's use of military officers to run the government, his commitment to industrialization and his mistrust of everyone associated with the prerevolutionary regime had enabled a growing cadre of colonels and engineers to supplant the landowning pashas and French-trained lawyers who had previously dominated political life under the monarchy.

The Egyptians were also proud of Nasser's international stature, unique in the Arab world, which enhanced the importance and dignity of their country and offered some compensation for its impotence in the conflict with Israel.

Nasser, one of the pioneers of the "nonaligned" movement, had earned the admiration of political leaders of newly independent countries throughout the world by his defiance of the British and French and his refusal to knuckle under to John Foster Dulles. It was Nasser, after all, who organized the overthrow of the monarchy, nationalized the Suez Canal and tamed the Nile with the construction of the Aswan High Dam. He had been taken seriously by Tito and Zhou En-lai. He had left his imprint on events in Arab countries from Iraq to Libya. He represented, at least until the disaster of the 1967 war, an Egypt proud and erect after generations of foreign domination.

Remembering the impact Nasser had on Egyptian history and on two decades of world politics, it is surprising to visit Egypt now and find so little trace of him. There is a Gamal Abdel Nasser Avenue in Alexandria, and the great reservoir behind the Aswan Dam is Lake Nasser. But no city is named for him, there is no Nasser International Airport, his face appears on no coins. In Cairo's public squares there are statues of great Egyptians from Ramses II to Talaat Harb, the first Egyptian in modern times to establish a bank, but the capital has no great memorial to the man who personified the pride of independent Egypt. A few political malcontents claim to carry the banner of Nasserism, but there are more pictures of Nasser on the walls of Beirut than of Cairo.

It is clear now that Sadat, though loyal to Nasser as vice president, had long been uncomfortable with many of Nasser's policies at home and abroad. He began to dismantle the Nasser legend within months of his accession, but in the beginning his position was delicate. Sadat had to move boldly to establish his own authority, but he could not simply repudiate Nasser all at once. Nasser could not be sent away with the stroke of a pen, like the Soviet advisers.

To have challenged all of Nasser's constituencies and purged the country of his legacy directly and immediately would have undercut Sadat's authority as president, rather than reinforcing it. After all, Sadat came to power as an acolyte of Nasser, a creature of the 1952 revolution, and this association was the only source of

Sadat's legitimacy as leader of Egypt. In the power struggle with other cronies of Nasser that unfolded within a few months of Sadat's accession to the presidency, Sadat prevailed because he wielded authority that had been bestowed upon him by Nasser— not because he was repudiating Nasser.

Sadat became president because he was Nasser's dutiful vice president and had stood with him through 30 years of conspiracy, revolution and national tragedy. It was precisely because he had never staked out a position independent of Nasser's that he survived Nasser's chronic suspicion and manipulation of those around him. As president, he could not just jettison the legacy of Nasser as Iran's revolutionaries were to topple statues of the Shah. Even after the 1973 war turned him into the "Hero of the Crossing," the leader who had brought victory in place of defeat, hope in place of despair, Sadat did not repudiate Nasser directly. That was to come later.

His tactic was to embrace the legitimacy of the 1952 revolution and its goals—independence, prosperity, egalitarianism— while dismantling its works—state socialism, futile confrontation, police state government—as aberrations or deviations to be corrected. Sadat took the position that he shared responsibility for the failures of the Nasser era—indeed he could not escape such responsibility—and only after the "bread riots" of January 1977 did Sadat blame Nasser personally for the sorry state Egypt was in when he died.

Wrapped in the mantle of authority bestowed by Nasser and claiming fealty to his policies, Sadat did not wait long to signal that changes were coming. Within a few months of taking office, he ended the practice of sequestration, or seizure of private property from the wealthy and the politically undesirable, and he undertook a diplomatic initiative aimed at inducing Israel to pull its troops out of part of the Sinai.

In doing so, Sadat acted on his own, without consulting the cabinet officials and left-wing political bosses whom he had inherited. Regarding Sadat as a lightweight and themselves as the rightful custodians of the hero's legacy, they wanted to impose a system of collective leadership.

Their challenge nearly ended Sadat's presidency six months after it began. The leader of this cabal was Ali Sabry, an air force intelligence officer. Mohamed Hassanein Heikal, one of Nasser's most intimate confidants, minister of information and editor of *al-Ahram*, Egypt's leading newspaper, said in *The Road to Ramadan*, his account of this crucial period, that although other members

> disagreed with Ali Sabry on a number of matters they had a
> common interest with him in preventing anyone outside their
> group from having any real say in the decision-making process.
> They wanted all power in government, party and army to
> remain in their hands. They were not personally corrupt, but
> they were drunk with power, and after Nasser's death the power
> that they wielded became totally divorced from any social con-
> tent. They echoed the doctrines and sayings of President
> Nasser, but in a blind way. They wanted the dead leader to
> become a fourth pyramid in Egypt and for themselves to be
> installed as permanent and exclusive high priests ministering to
> this shrine.

These conspirators are known collectively as the *marakiz al-quwwa,* or centers of power. The phrase became a building block of Egypt's new political vocabulary under Sadat, as did his term for the power struggle that the group provoked: *thawrat at-tashih,* the "Corrective Revolution."

The "center of power" for Ali Sabry and his allies was the Arab Socialist Union, the only legal political organization in Egypt, which they had virtually taken over since the 1967 war. They considered themselves the guardians of Nasser's essential policies: heavy industrialization, state socialism, strong governmental controls over society, militancy toward Israel and close cooperation with the Soviet Union. The problem with this was that those policies had failed; the country was broke, defeated and spiritually exhausted.

Sadat had liabilities, too. He was an obscure and sometimes clownish figure with no discernible ideology and no personal following. He had been accepted as president by Nasser's entourage because he seemed unlikely to threaten their position. He was, to all appearances, a midget trying to succeed a giant.

But, as Raymond Hinnebusch Jr., an American political scientist, has pointed out in his detailed reconstruction of these events, "The president turned out to be the only one with reliable coercive force at his command." The conspirators overestimated their appeal to groups such as the students and the trade unions, and Sadat held the support of the armed forces by promising to break the impasse with Israel if they would stay out of the political struggle. On May 2, 1971, he announced the dismissal of Ali Sabry from the government. By May 15, all of Sadat's rivals were in prison and he was free to rule as he wished.

During the power struggle, when Sadat discovered that his own office was bugged, he promised to put an end to the indiscriminate wiretapping and eavesdropping that had prevailed for years. He ordered that wiretapping be ended except when a court authorized it. Then he went to the ministry of interior and participated in a public burning of transcripts and tape recordings of telephone conversations that had been made by Nasser's secret police. A few months later, on September 10, Egyptians went to the polls to approve a new 193-article constitution that contained guarantees against arbitrary arrest and seizure of property.

The retreat from Nasserism, in style and substance, was not an abstract political exercise. It was intended to consolidate Sadat's own power, but at the same time it also represented a thorough revision of Egyptian policy, at home and abroad.

Nasser himself had concluded, in the despairing years between the 1967 defeat and his death in 1970, that he would have to make some gestures toward liberalization at home and toward accommodation with the United States. This was the period in which he accepted elements of the so-called Rogers Plan for a diplomatic initiative and offered token gestures of reform to appease rioting students. But he died with his police state apparatus in place and peace a distant goal.

Still, Nasser remained the greatest of heroes to the Egyptian masses. Sadat, in his campaign to redirect Egypt politically and economically, preserved the labels he found useful for what might be called public relations purposes. He talked of Egypt as a "revolutionary" society even as he cultivated the bourgeoisie, as a "socialist" economy even as he opened it to private capital, and as leader of the "Arab nation" even after the League of Arab States moved out of Cairo to protest his peace treaty with Israel. Sadat associated himself with Nasser's achievements and preserved his slogans but otherwise worked relentlessly to dismantle Nasser's heroic image.

In a speech on the ninth anniversary of Nasser's death, Mubarak, then still vice president, said the occasion commemorated

a unique Egyptian and a genuine Arab who, with his companions, carried out a revolution that is considered by all criteria as
one of the prominent revolutions in modern history. The effect
of this revolution did not stop at the boundary of beloved
Egypt but extended to the great Arab homeland and to the
entire Third World. It was enough that Abdel Nasser was the
first Egyptian ruler to come from the soil of this homeland in
two thousand years.

After Nasser, he said, came Sadat's great achievement in the
October war, which

> represents a crossing from despondency to hope and from the
> humiliation of defeat to the honor of victory; the historic peace
> initiative represents a crossing with the Arab cause from the
> phase of lost opportunities and the method of uttering hopes
> and slogans to the phase of true achievement that will liberate
> the Arab lands by deeds and not by words. . . .

This was a grudging encomium. It said Nasser was a patriot
who established Egypt's independence and built Arab pride; he did
that with the help of "his companions"—that is, with the other
"Free Officers," as the group who had led the revolution in 1952
were known, and of whom Sadat was one—but thereafter his
failures led to "despondency" and "lost opportunities" rectified only
by the "crossings" carried out by Sadat.

After the October war, when Sadat had solidified his own
position by leading the Arabs' first successful military confrontation
with Israel, the pace at which Nasser was demythologized and
discredited accelerated. Mubarak, who had no credentials from the
1952 revolution but had performed creditably in the October war,
was made vice president in place of Hussein Shafei, the last of the
Free Officers other than Sadat himself to hold high government
office. This was a symbol of what Sadat sought to make into a
political principle—that Egypt's destiny had passed from the generation of the revolution, in which of course Sadat had a share, to the
"October generation," which Sadat also shared but which excluded
Nasser's cronies.

Having purged or forced into retirement all of Nasser's associ-
ates except himself, Sadat tried unsuccessfully to turn the "October
generation" into a new fount of political legitimacy. He placed
Mubarak, who commanded the air force in the October war, in this

new generation. But Egyptians today don't seem to think of Mubarak as a hero of 1973; they think of him as a military officer like his predecessors, appointed by Sadat as Sadat was appointed by Nasser and deriving his authority ultimately from the same source: the armed forces. Mubarak's military achievements in 1973, when nearly half of today's Egyptians had not yet been born, are irrelevant to the economic and political distress that confronts him now.

In his purge of Nasser's followers, Sadat dismissed Mohamed Heikal as editor of *al-Ahram* and replaced him with Ali Amin, a compliant right-winger. Personalities such as Heikal and Shafei were known to every Egyptian, and the message of their dismissals was unmistakable: Sadat, having overcome the rival group led by Ali Sabry and having engineered the October war, was in charge. Nasser was consigned to history.

Sadat did not encourage attacks on Nasser's personal integrity—he defended Nasser against published allegations that he had pocketed a gift to the Egyptian people from Saudi Arabia—but otherwise it was open season. In the guise of a national debate over the Nasser heritage, in which he was ostensibly neutral, Sadat encouraged Egyptians to purge the myth of Nasser from their culture.

An early landmark of this campaign was the publication of *The Return of Awareness,* by Tawfik al-Hakim, Egypt's greatest dramatist, whose earlier writings were said to have inspired the young Nasser. "The country began to get used to the rule of an individual and trusted and loved him," he wrote in explaining Nasser's grip on the Egyptian imagination.

> The masses, when loving, do not criticize. One by one, the voices that used to criticize were lowered and the beloved leader himself began to be accustomed to a rule in which there was no criticism. The iron curtain began slowly to fall between the people and the actions of the absolute ruler. We loved him but did not know the inside of his thoughts or the real motives for his actions. We only knew of internal or external affairs what he told us, speaking at festival times or other occasions from his high platform. From his isolated position he would make speeches without any trouble lasting for hours in which he made us into heroes under his leadership and made the great states around us into dwarfs. We applauded with wonder and pride.

Newspapers that formerly had used the word *niksa,* or setback, in references to the 1967 war began to use *hezima,* or defeat, enlarging the scope of the catastrophe for which Nasser was now held responsible. Sadat permitted the publication of frontal attacks on Nasser's entire legacy. Individuals prominently associated with the Nasser era, including Heikal and Shafei, were put out to pasture. The remaining members of the Free Officers were forced into retirement. Civilians replaced government officials of military background. Sadat talked more openly about failures and mistakes that were attributable to Nasser himself.

So naked was this campaign of revisionism that it distressed even those masters of revisionism, the Russians. In March 1974, the Soviet newspaper *Pravda* denounced what it saw as Egypt's turn away from socialism and called on Sadat to halt the "vilification" of Nasser, to whom the Soviets had been so close. Sadat responded a month later by announcing that Egypt would end more than 18 years of exclusive reliance on the Soviet Union as its source of arms and would seek diverse suppliers—an announcement seen at the time as a sure sign that he was preparing for a prolonged period of peace.

The first Egyptian film I saw showed how far Sadat was prepared to go in cutting down Nasser's reputation and building up his own.

Most of the films turned out by Egypt's prolific cinema industry are situation comedies and overwrought melodramas that have little appeal to foreigners except as curiosities. But every so often word gets around that some film has political significance and must be seen. *Karnak* was one of these.

Before packed houses, it portrayed Nasser's secret police as sadistic torturers who brutalized innocent people while neglecting the real national interest. Any doubts about the message were erased by a scene that showed prison guards, with a photo of Nasser peering down at them from a wall, beating a patriotic young student to death at the very moment when Israeli jets were bombing a defenseless Egypt during the 1967 war.

That scene brought gasps and murmurs of shock from the audience, because it suggested that Nasser was personally responsible not just for the police abuses but for the rout of 1967, the most grievous national disaster suffered by Egypt in this century.

Karnak was ostensibly fiction, based on a story written in

1971, the year after Nasser's death, by Naguib Mahfouz, perhaps Egypt's most popular novelist. Nasser was never mentioned by name, but no one familiar with the events of the preceding 15 years could have failed to hear the message.

Karnak is the name of the glorious temple at Luxor, in Upper Egypt, but this film had nothing to do with the Pharaohs. In the movie, Karnak is the name of a coffee house frequented by university students in the 1960s. Among them are Zeinab and her fiancé, Ismail, idealistic medical students who fall into the clutches of the secret police when an informer reports on one of their political conversations. Zeinab, we learn, is a girl from a poor family who is getting a free education at a university to which she would not have been admitted before the revolution. This reminds us that the revolution had altruistic aims and brought real benefits, but the scenes depicting brutal injustice show how the revolution went awry when misused by conspirators struggling for power around Nasser. Not coincidentally, this is exactly what Sadat was saying at that time about what had happened to the revolution.

Sadat's version of history was that after Nasser's death he was able to "correct" the course of the revolution; it came as no surprise when at the end of *Karnak* this correction put an end to the torment inflicted on our young students.

In the film, which is not subtle, Zeinab, Ismail and several of their companions are arrested when a casual remark at a student gathering is reported to Nasser's *mukhabarat,* or security police, by an informer. In an effort to extract confessions—confessions to anything—the police subject them to beatings, electric shock torture, attacks by dogs and endless interrogations.

Ismail is first accused of being a member of the Muslim Brotherhood, the fanatical Islamic organization that was suppressed by Nasser in 1954. In a subsequent interrogation he is accused of being a communist. This is depicted as a logical absurdity that makes the intelligence agents look stupid as well as cruel because the Brotherhood and the communists are polar opposites. (But in fact there is a tradition in Egypt of the political right and left merging at the ends of the political spectrum, a tradition revived most recently in the 1987 parliamentary elections.)

In a *Karnak* scene that was well publicized in advance and exploited in garish billboard advertisements, the chief of the intelligence operatives orders that Zeinab be raped on the floor of his office by a silent, impassive thug. Then she is taken to Ismail's cell, where a threat to repeat the rape in his presence induces him to confess that he is a communist.

All this happens between other scenes of prisoners being beaten, agents tapping phones and doctoring tapes, and the chief of the intelligence service luxuriating in his swimming pool—which of course he could not afford on his salary, so he must be corrupt.

Then comes the happy ending. Sadat's "corrective revolution" of 1971 frees the innocent prisoners. The intelligence chief is arrested. Zeinab resumes her medical career. Ismail is a broken man who turns to drink and there seems to be no hope for him, but another of Sadat's accomplishments later saves him, too.

Wandering aimlessly through the streets of Cairo, Ismail notices excited crowds gathering around a television set at a cafe. Joining them, he learns that Egyptian troops have crossed the Suez Canal and driven back the Israelis. It is the start of the 1973 war, the October war, the icon of the Sadat era.

Inspired, he pulls himself together and rushes to a nearby hospital to volunteer to treat the wounded. There, of course, the faithful Zeinab is also working, and they are reunited in love and duty. (Presumably they live happily ever after; the film conveniently forgets that a woman known to have been raped would be considered tainted and unacceptable to an Egyptian man.)

Karnak was scandalously disrespectful of Nasser, but that was the tenor of the times after the 1973 war confirmed Sadat's power. There were no protest demonstrations, no angry rallies by Nasserites trying to suppress the film; the theaters were full. The man who actually had been chief of the intelligence service during the period depicted, Gen. Salah Nasr, filed a court action attempting to block its showing as libelous. He failed when a lawyer arguing against him asked if he saw any similarity between himself and the corrupt, brutal character in the film, and of course he was obliged to say no.

When I saw the film, the audience cheered and applauded when the intelligence chief was shown being put in jail at the same time his victims were being released. In reality, Salah Nasr was imprisoned in 1968, two years before Nasser's death, when Nasser lost confidence in him. It was Sadat who released him along with other political prisoners in 1974, but these details were irrelevant to the exercise in political revisionism that the film represented.

Two years after his release, Salah Nasr was the central figure in another celebrated Cairo legal case that brought out still more stories of false arrest, brutality and torture during the Nasser years. He was tried and sentenced to 10 years' imprisonment at hard labor for having ordered the torture of one of Egypt's most eminent journalists, Mustafa Amin, in 1965. Since Amin was widely known as a supporter of Sadat's policies, and Nasr as one of Nasser's chief goons, it seemed to the public like another victory for the new era over the old, as in fact it was.

Amin, an enormous, jovial figure, is immensely popular with readers, who look for his daily column, "An Idea." His arrest in 1965—the arrest that led to his torture—was on charges of spying for the United States. Thus he and his chief tormentor, Salah Nasr, were both in prison when Nasser died in 1970 and stayed there until Sadat released them. Amin then instigated the legal case against Nasr, accusing him and two junior officers of torturing him mentally and physically. Nasr had written a book saying the spy charges were true, but Amin was vindicated when he prevailed in the court case and Nasr was sent back to prison—not because Sadat wanted him there but because a correct legal proceeding had run its course without political interference.

Sadat claimed that under his regime the independence of the judiciary was at least partially restored. Raymond Hinnebusch concluded that

> the judiciary under Sadat achieved a very substantial measure of autonomy from the executive. Judges became a vigorous force defending the expanding legal rights of citizens against the government. Although he was often annoyed by their rulings in political cases, Sadat, in contrast to Nasser, steered shy of any major purge of independent-minded judges.

It is true that Sadat rarely scoffed at the law, or overrode it. His method was to get parliament to rewrite the law to legalize whatever he wanted to do, including the establishment of special courts for political cases, courts which were not subject to review by the conventional judiciary.

This meant that prominent individuals were not shielded in their professional lives from arbitrary actions by the president, as Mustafa Amin later learned. Sadat's view of the press and his response to constructive criticism were more tolerant than Nasser's, but there were limits to what he would accept. These limits grew progressively narrower, until Sadat finally abandoned restraint and ordered mass arrests of opponents, real and imagined, in September 1981. Amin lost his editor's post at *al-Akhbar* when Sadat decided the press in general was being unpleasant. In 1978 Amin's column was suppressed briefly when he questioned the unseemly rush of members of parliament to join the new political party Sadat was forming without stopping to examine what it stood for. But the column reappeared in a few weeks, and I found Amin in a conciliatory mood when I went to talk to him about what had happened. Not only had Sadat refrained from putting him in prison, as Nasser would have done, he said, but the president had listened to people who criticized the suppression of "An Idea."

"Under Nasser," Amin said, "nobody would have dared to speak out about what happened to me. Now they did speak out and even more than that the president heard them." When Nasser ruled Egypt, he said, "we had the kind of regime that held a ceremony at the Abdin Palace to honor a girl who had informed on her brother."

As a victim of torture, Amin has bitter and deeply personal memories of the Nasser era. He remembers "butchers who slaughtered the lambs . . . who ruined homes and rendered families destitute." His book, *The First Year in Prison,* published in Cairo in 1974, was a landmark of the campaign to tear down Nasser's reputation. In it, he described in detail the torture inflicted on him and other prisoners, and said that Nasser must have known about it.

Most ordinary citizens, of course, never experienced directly the nightmare that befell Amin, but everyone seems to have known what was going on. One of the first jokes I heard was about two men sitting next to each other on a bus. One of them emits a deep, mournful sigh; the other whispers frantically into his ear, "If you don't stop talking politics, I'll have to move."

Another told of the time Nasser reached into a pocket for his gold fountain pen but couldn't find it. He tells his security chief it is missing, whereupon the officer orders a citywide roundup of suspects. An hour later, Nasser calls the security chief and begins to say, "About my pen . . ." when the officer interrupts: "Yes, Mr. President, 23 criminals are now confessing to the nation on television that they stole the pen as part of a terror campaign to over-

throw the government." "Hold it, hold it," Nasser replies. "What I
wanted to tell you was that I found it in my other suit."

Note that in this story, of which there are many versions,
Nasser tolerates and condones torture and arbitrary arrest but he
does not actually order or participate in them. That was more or less
the official line coming from Sadat.

But not all the criticism of Nasser was coming from the right-
wing or from people who were enthusiastic about Sadat. Social
thinkers now found Nasser a man of limited vision and petty
personality who substituted slogans for thought and posture for
principles. Academic leftists began saying that his socialism was
fakery because it was not accountable to the people and served only
to guarantee that his cronies would control the country's economy
as tightly as they controlled its politics.

The magazine *Rose al-Youssef,* then an organ of the respectable
left, invited a prominent philosophy professor, Fuad Zakariya, to
write a series of essays that would assess the Nasser years from a
leftist perspective.

Not only did the professor describe Nasser's economic program as "a socialist experiment in which the abuse of power is the
rule and integrity the exception," but he indicted the Nasser regime
for

> oppression exceeding by far the legal limits for the protection of
> the revolution against minority opposition. Consequently,
> Egyptian man emerged from this experience quite different
> from what he was at its beginning. At first, he felt he could
> speak, discuss and object, and that the country was his country,
> in which his opinion could be heard . . . but after the mass
> arrest, fear crept into him gradually. Fear led to negativism,
> hypocrisy and doubletalk. The Egyptian man lost his ability to
> object, reject and protest, for terror was accompanied by an
> organized propaganda campaign aimed at there being only one
> opinion and one point of view in the country. . . . This inner
> destruction of the Egyptian's soul, personality and mind was
> one of the great disasters of the Nasserite experience.

There were of course commentators who defended the benefits
and achievements of the Nasser years even while they acknowledged the abuses and deficiencies. In their view, restrictions on
personal freedom were understandable in a regime struggling
against real enemies at home and abroad—the Muslim Broth-

erhood, the counterrevolutionary bourgeoisie, the communists, the Israelis, the imperialists—and had to be seen in the context of a revolution that had brought substantial benefits to the country.

Sadat himself said similar things in the beginning, but over time he portrayed his predecessor's regime in ever harsher terms. Those who remember this period can find a delicious irony in Egypt today when the same thing is happening to Sadat's reputation. Mubarak has not encouraged the denigration of Sadat as Sadat did of Nasser, but to listen to Egyptian conversations about Sadat—about his vanity, his laziness, his grandiloquence, his tolerance of corruption, his ultimate sacrifice of everything he said he stood for in the mass arrests of September 1981—is to hear echoes of what the same people were saying about Nasser a decade ago.

Still, Sadat never approached Nasser's extremes of political repression and use of torture and arbitrary arrest. Sadat said that this political repression, combined with the defeat of 1967, did more than send some people to jail and deprive others of their property. It drove the country into spiritual exhaustion and moral inertia, which in turn inhibited development and left the country powerless against its enemies. Whatever Sadat's own failures and weaknesses, it is hard to argue with his assessment of his predecessor.

After the 1973 war, the retreat from repression was accelerated by a gradual elimination of security measures and restrictions on movement that had been motivated as much by the state of war as by internal political considerations. Large areas of the country that had long been off-limits to civilians, such as the Red Sea coast, were reopened. Along the main highways, the military checkpoints manned by red-bereted military police remained in place, as did the signs saying "Foreigners are forbidden to leave the main road," but enforcement slackened. I drove thousands of miles, including trips to industrial towns in the Nile Delta and to the iron mines of the Bahariya oasis in the western desert, and was stopped only once. That was during the brief border war with Libya in 1977, when other journalists and I were unable to get through the Mediterranean coastal town of Mersa Matrouh on our way to the Libyan frontier.

Military officials authorized me to be present at the Cairo West military airfield for the arrival of the first shipment of American-built F-5 combat jets. That was the same airfield to which even

Egyptian officers had been denied access during the years when Soviet advisers were there. Granting me permission to go there was emblematic of both the new openness in the society and Sadat's policy of courting American public opinion. (The planes, however, were never actually delivered because Saudi Arabia, angered by the peace agreement with Israel, backed out of a commitment to pay for them.)

Still, whatever the guidance from the top, old habits die hard, especially in a society such as Egypt's, where entrenched officials throughout the bureaucracy can ignore policy directives. When a military plane crashed at an airfield in Aswan in 1978, everyone knew what had happened because obituary notices for half a dozen air force officers and men appeared in the newspapers. But no announcement was ever made and nothing appeared in the form of a news story on the radio or in the daily press. As late as 1975, two students from the American University were arrested for conducting unauthorized interviews with students on the campus of Cairo University—work among students was still suspect. At the state-owned Gianaclis winery, I was allowed to see whatever I wanted and to lunch in the executives' canteen; the managers answered all my questions. But because I did not have a permit from the ministry of information, they would not allow me to photograph their obsolete East German processing and bottling equipment, on the grounds that it was "industrial" and therefore a potential enemy target. Permits, when sought, were usually easy to obtain. I received permission to visit and photograph an installation that really is a potential target, the Bahariya iron mines, but once I got there nobody asked for the papers.

It remained generally more difficult to work with cameras than without because for many years every bridge, police post, pier and factory in the country was marked "No Photo." But gradually, throughout the 1970s, as Egypt left war, suspicion and the influence of the Soviet Union farther behind, these restrictions were relaxed. On a visit in 1987, I watched tourists take pictures without hindrance at the Israeli border, the Suez Canal, Cairo Airport and an oil refinery near Alexandria. This represents a complete psychological turnaround in 10 years from the era when armed soldiers behind piled sandbags enforced security regulations at every public building.

Access to government officials, except for the military, became progressively easier throughout the 1970s and remains routinely easy under Mubarak. In terms of foreign press access, Egypt today is the most wide open Arab country. By the late 1970s, to the amazement and envy of our predecessors who had covered Egypt in the Nasser era, my press-corps colleagues and I were talking regularly to officials in the ministries of economy, health, agriculture, tourism, finance and education who would grant appointments without clearance from the State Information Service and who spoke on the record. Leading officials of the foreign ministry were available to us whenever they had time, and we were on a first-name basis with many of them. Sadat's personal entourage was more difficult to penetrate, but access to this group was less necessary because the president himself saw the press more often than any other world leader.

Nor was there any real restriction on what we wrote; censorship of the foreign press came to an end. (The domestic press was another matter; it was uncensored, and certainly had more room to probe and criticize than under Nasser, but it was hardly unrestricted.) Shortly after my tour as a resident correspondent began, I wrote a long article dealing with the problems that the Egyptian armed forces faced because of the shortage of spare parts for their Soviet-made equipment. This was no secret—Sadat himself had told the nation that those planes and tanks would soon be little more than "scrap iron" because of maintenance problems. But the Egyptian editor on duty at the Reuter news agency, where I usually filed my copy, was nervous about it and asked me to clear it with the censor. So I went to the office near the American embassy where the censors worked. They were surprised to see me, they said, because their function had been abolished. They still had their office and their desks, but they no longer had their official stamps, and an Egyptian bureaucrat without his wooden-handled, purple-inked official stamp is a bureaucrat without a function.

It was still customary, when sending copy abroad on the telex machines at the government press center, to write across the bottom the phrase, "Contains no military information," and to attest to that with a signature. But at a time when Sadat was appealing directly to Western nations for new arms supplies, a lot of our copy did contain military information and it was pointless to maintain the fiction that the condition of Egypt's armed forces was a deep secret. Besides, the state of war was over, in spirit if not yet in fact.

None of this means that the enormous, ubiquitous security network built up by Nasser has been dismantled. Mubarak still uses it to control domestic dissent, as did Sadat. The targets generally are the same as they were under Nasser: the extreme religious right, communists or suspected communists, disaffected military officers and those whose criticisms of the leadership are expressed in forums or in language that the president considers irresponsible or likely to provoke demonstrations. The arbitrary secret arrests, incarceration without charge or trial, internment camps and routine torture that characterized the Nasser regime have been curtailed. They represent no threat to anyone who stays out of organized groups clearly identified with extralegal tactics, but that does not mean the government has surrendered its ability to keep track of who is doing what.

During President Jimmy Carter's visit to Egypt in March 1978, he and Sadat traveled by rail from Cairo to Alexandria, waving from an open-sided car. It was a trip of about 130 miles on tracks that paralleled the main road. The route passed through heavily populated towns where hundreds of thousands of people were massed within a few feet of the slow-moving train. It would have strained the resources of the police to secure the entire route, but they had help.

Every 50 yards or so, there appeared at trackside an ordinary *fellah,* or peasant farmer, in *galabeya* and turban, the Egyptian Everyman, but with one difference: each was armed with a shotgun. They were part of a nationwide force of security deputies, a sort of village auxiliary, who reported to the local police and could be pressed into duty on special occasions. This was the rural equivalent of what Miles Copeland called

the famous 'city-eye' system which Nasser inherited from the previous regime, and which has probably existed in Egypt for centuries. It is entirely unobtrusive. A CIA officer, formerly an FBI man, who had undergone the most sophisticated modern training in surveillance, once went from one end of Cairo to the other and was prepared to swear that he had not been under surveillance for one moment, only to learn later from the smiling chief of security that every move he made had been observed, every telephone call monitored, and every contact identified and recorded. The secret is simple: doormen, taxicab drivers, telephone operators, beggars, street vendors and hordes of other people know that they may be rewarded by a few *piasters* should they be able to give helpful answers to some security officer coming by to ask questions about a foreigner who has just passed.

In April 1979, after an outbreak of religious demonstrations and fights between Muslims and Christians at the university in Asyut, in Upper Egypt, Sadat gave the country an impressive reminder of the effectiveness of this information network.

"On February 18," he said in a meeting with the faculty,

> student Najih Ibrahim of the Asyut school of medicine, the leader of the Islamic group in it, confronted Sayyid Rashid, Amir Abdel Halim and Maryam Tinaji while sitting in the garden next to the Omar Makram mosque in Asyut. He asked them to leave, but an argument took place between them which ended with Sayyid Rashid attacking the student. Some of the Islamic group members gathered and accompanied the Christian girl and the other citizen to the university city building. Then about 600 students living in the city got out and crossed the public road and destroyed an-Naqara cafe opposite the university city building, repeating some Islamic slogans.

The president knew that Nasr Abu Aynayn beat up Murad Adli; that Hassan Shawki attacked Bassam Aziz Doss for leaving a building through an exit reserved for women; that Husam Eddin Abdel Razak attacked Ashraf Adib for dropping food on him from his balcony.

The very omnipresence of the network that sends up this kind of detail explains why Sadat had the confidence to ride through Cairo in an open car at night upon his return from Jerusalem and why terrorist agents of the Palestinians, Iraqis, Libyans and other Arab opponents of the Egyptian regime have been able to cause so little trouble.

The security forces' remarkable record of preventing trouble has of course been marred by a few spectacular failures, of which the successful plot to assassinate Sadat was the greatest. The Egyptians were mortified when, on one occasion in the late 1970s, three Libyans armed with automatic weapons, on a mission to kill or capture a prominent Libyan dissident who lived in Egypt, were allowed to board a Rome-bound airliner at Cairo Airport. The police knew about a group of religious fanatics who were planning a murder and an uprising against the government in 1977 but failed to act because they were concentrating on supposed plots among various leftists. The chief of Sadat's personal security detail, Taha Zaki, was quietly fired in 1978 because he failed to detect regular contacts between a mechanic in the presidential motor pool and an administrative officer in the Iraqi consulate.

In the mid-1980s, under Mubarak, the security forces have sometimes shown themselves more effective at tracking alleged plots and conspiracies than at apprehending the perpetrators of actual crimes. As under Sadat, they have a tendency to carry out the famous command from *Casablanca:* Round up the usual suspects. Mubarak's interior minister, Zaki Badr, has acknowledged that they "have not managed to treat the disease in the body of society that can produce these [terrorist] elements." Taking his cue from Mubarak, who insists on stability above all, Badr is unabashed in talking about "the force and oppression of the law" to be used against violence-prone organizations and individuals. But the whole security apparatus is used much more selectively than under Nasser, when it was allowed, even encouraged, to go out of control, inhibiting the freedom of ordinary Egyptians to talk, travel, write and organize.

Nor was arrest the only penalty to be feared by those who incurred Nasser's suspicion. They also faced the loss of their property. Sadat moved quickly to put an end to this. On December 28, 1970, in one of his earliest frontal attacks on his predecessor's policies, he issued a decree abolishing sequestration, the practice of arbitrary seizure of property for political offenses, real or imagined. Not only did Sadat impose strict legal requirements for state seizure of private property, he also ordered the return of property that had been wrongly taken by the Nasser government. This was a clear signal that the war against the bourgeoisie was over and that there was a place in Sadat's scheme of things, as there had not been in Nasser's, for a prosperous entrepreneurial and merchant class.

Sequestration was not the same as land reform, which involved breaking up the great rural estates that controlled agriculture, limiting the acreage individuals could own and distributing the rest to the peasants. Nor was sequestration part of the nationalization of trade and industry. Sequestration meant seizure by the state of the property of individuals who were politically out of favor or accused of being counterrevolutionaries. Property meant not only land but houses, apartment buildings, works of art, race horses—anything of value.

Talaat Badrawi, a member of one of the hardest hit families, told me that jewels were taken from his grandfather's vault and even his grandfather's Rolls-Royce was seized. Michael Youssef, a scholar who was a high school student at the time, says in his book *Revolt Against Modernity,* "As one who lived through all this, I vividly recall the humiliation and mistreatment of the wealthy as the police took over their palaces and companies." In speeches at the time, Nasser denounced "the feudalists, the traitors and the collaborators with imperialism," which meant the wealthy and the bourgeoisie. "The revolutionary leaders," Youssef said, "began to refer to their revolution in terms of 'social democracy' instead of just plain democracy. This gave them the necessary excuse to destroy the class distinction between the wealthy and the underprivileged."

These "feudalists, traitors and collaborators with imperialism" were the targets of sequestration—being the relatively few people who had any property of substantial value. Having lost their estates to land reform and their businesses to nationalization, they were considered politically unreliable. That made them natural victims for the notorious "antifeudalism committee," headed by Abdel Hakim Amer, who was Nasser's right-hand man until he committed suicide after the 1967 war. When Sadat became president, he did not undo land reform or give the nationalized department stores and insurance companies back to their original owners, but he did order that arbitrary extralegal seizures of personal property be halted, that property be returned where possible and that compensation be paid for what could not be returned.

The property that could not be returned included some of the best-known landmarks in Cairo, which had been converted to public use while under state control. Among them were the splendid palace that is now the centerpiece of the Marriott Omar Khayyam Hotel, the president's official residence on the Nile in Giza, and the majestic villa opposite the British embassy that houses the U.S. government information center and library. That villa was given to the United States by the Egyptian government; obviously it was not available to be returned to the family that had owned it, the Sednaouis, whose name still appears on the department store they used to own. So the government offered a compensation payment of 18,000 pounds. That was a tiny fraction of what it would be worth on the open market but the amount did not lessen the political benefits Sadat received from the compensation program. It helped his effort to build investor confidence and lure private capital back into the marketplace, and it buttressed his claim to have restored the "rule of law" in place of arbitrary state action.

Saad Abu Oaf, the lawyer who presided over the return of property and the distribution of compensation, told me that the sequestration laws had had a basis in legitimacy when they were first imposed during World War II. Then the property seized was that of Germans and Italians, he said. After the war of Israeli independence in 1948, the property of Egyptian Jews was sequestered; then, at the time of the "tripartite aggression"—as Egypt calls the Suez war of 1956—the property of British and French residents was taken. A case could be made for all those, Abu Oaf said, but after the nationalization laws of 1961, the sequestration decrees "were applied for the first time to the property of [non-Jewish] Egyptians. The problem was that it was done without any legal procedures. Anyone could go to the government and denounce you, and you would lose your property."

By the end of Sadat's tenure, more than 400 apartment buildings, mostly in Cairo, and about 20,000 *feddans* of farmland had been returned to their original owners, out of a total of some 1,000 buildings and 40,000 *feddans* that had been sequestered. (A *feddan* is 1.04 acres.) The state-owned insurance companies that had had control of the apartment buildings had the option of keeping them in exchange for a negotiated compensation payment, Abu Oaf said, but these buildings were subject to the same rent controls as any others, and were no longer profitable, so they were being returned to private ownership.

The end of sequestration was part of Sadat's effort to rehabilitate the entrepreneurial classes. This campaign, which included the liberalization of the economy, the lifting of currency restrictions and the reappearance of the private sector in commerce and industry, invigorated the Western-oriented bankers, traders, merchants and industrialists who found opportunity restored to them. These people felt no nostalgia for the Nasser era.

Not long after our arrival in Egypt in 1975, my wife and I sat one night on the penthouse terrace of a fashionable apartment building in Zamalek, one of Cairo's best neighborhoods. The building had been restored to the Badrawi family after the end of sequestration. The occasion was a sumptuous dinner party that featured imported wine—an expensive luxury. The hostess was a multilingual young woman, her low-cut gown an import from Europe and the tint of her hair the work of one of Cairo's finest salons. Her husband was related to one of Sadat's confidants, and his business card said "Commercial Consultant."

She was speaking scornfully of the Libyan leader, Muammar Qaddafi, and she dismissed him as "absolutely crazy." And the symptoms? "He must be crazy. In Libya, they still show Nasser's old speeches on television." So much for the man who led the revolution.

While it was clear at the time of the "Corrective Revolution" that Sadat had taken charge and that he, not some surrogate of Nasser, was running the country, it was not clear what he would do with his power. He had revealed no comprehensive version of his program, he had not codified his objectives. When he did so, after the 1973 war, it was apparent that those objectives required a rejection of most of what remained of Nasser's legacy. The Arab Socialist Union was to give way to multiple political parties; the burden of economic development would be carried by private capital; and Egypt was going to free itself from the foreign policy shackles that had been imposed on the country by Nasser's dream of Arab leadership.

On the fifth anniversary of Nasser's death, Sadat said in a speech that

> Abdel Nasser was a human being, so it is not belittling him to say that he did right things and he did wrong things. There were goals which he achieved and others which he did not achieve. The July 23 revolution [of 1952, which ended the monarchy] had its negative aspects. I am exercising self-criticism from a position of responsibility. Yes, there have been deviations and there have also been prisons and detention camps. And though exceptional measures are naturally adopted by any revolution, those of the July 23 revolution remained longer than they should have and were extended to fields where they should not have reached.

It was a measure of how far the purge of Nasser and Nasserism had already come that those words hardly made news. In five years, Sadat had gotten rid of Nasser's cronies, restrained the police, ended the dependence on the Soviet Union, proclaimed the liberalization of the economy, fought a successful war against Israel, split with the other Arabs over the Sinai disengagement agreements and reestablished Egypt's ties to the United States. However Nasserism was defined, Sadat had certainly jettisoned it.

Sadat has now been dead longer than Nasser had been when Sadat gave that speech. Sadat's reputation, tarnished in life by his own miscalculations and excesses, has been further diminished by the ridicule and scorn that it is fashionable to heap upon him. Heikal caught the tone in *Autumn of Fury:* "The saddest thing about Sadat's death was that none of his dreams came to anything. As I heard someone say of him soon after I had been released from prison: 'He died when he died'. . . . Sadat made Egypt the center of nowhere."

This is effective writing, but inaccurate. Most of Sadat's policies remain in place—unlike Nasser's, which Egypt was happy to abandon as soon as he was dead. Sadat freed Egypt from the prison of ideology and began to break the state's grip on economic initiative. He turned Egypt, however haltingly, toward greater personal and political freedom, economic liberalization, alliance with the United States and independence in foreign policy. Mubarak, though less flamboyant and less given to extremes of rhetoric and impetuous decision-making, has followed the course Sadat charted.

But without the drama that stirred the country for three decades, progress now is measured by improvements at the margins here and there; political stability is more important than sweeping change. Egypt's economic and social conditions leave Mubarak little room for the dazzling initiatives of his predecessors. Pulling back from Sadat's excesses, especially in relations with other countries, he has adopted cautious, balanced policies aimed at keeping the treaty with Israel intact, American aid flowing and the caldron of domestic dissent from boiling over. Mubarak is not given to drama for its own sake. Survival, not triumph, is the objective, for the regime and for the nation.

The dreams of prosperity that were inspired first by the revolution and then by peace have been overtaken by a sense of realism.

No one is more insistent than the Egyptians themselves on the need to discipline their society and concentrate their energies on efficiency, productivity and realistic, if mundane, planning. But achievement of the attitudinal transformation that Egyptians know they need will be difficult and time-consuming, if it can be accomplished at all. Economic progress is hostage to history and to the idiosyncrasies of Egyptian society.

3

The Tyranny of the Falcon

In his famous nineteenth-century treatise on Egyptian life and culture, Edward Lane said that the Egyptians are by nature admirable but that religion, politics, environment and climate corrupt their personalities as they go through life. The result, in Lane's assessment, was that the list of the society's vices exceeded that of its virtues.

He said that the Egyptians "are endowed, in a higher degree than most other people, with some of the more important mental qualities, particularly quickness of apprehenson, a ready wit and a retentive memory." Among their many good qualities, he listed affability, cheerfulness, "filial piety," respect for the aged, love of country, hospitality and "temperance and moderation with regard to diet."

But he also found the Egyptians "equally remarkable for generosity and cupidity." He concluded that they were "honest in payment of debts," but that "constant veracity is a virtue extremely rare." He noted that "the higher and middle orders of Muslims in Egypt are scrupulously cleanly, and the lower orders more so than in most other countries," but their children run about dirty, ragged and covered with flies.

Lane, an Englishman who mastered Arabic and knew the Egyptians with an intimacy equaled by few outsiders, found that

> indolence pervades all classes of the Egyptians excepting those
> who are obliged to earn their livelihood by severe manual labor

> . . . even the mechanics, who are extremely greedy of gain, will
> generally spend two days in a work which they might easily
> accomplish in one, and will leave the most lucrative employ-
> ment to idle away their time with the [hashish] pipe.

He said it is "seldom that an Egyptian workman can be induced to
make a thing exactly to order. He will generally follow his own
opinion in preference to that of his employer, and will scarcely ever
finish his work by the time he has promised"—a characteristic, he
said, that makes the Egyptians "extremely obstinate and difficult to
govern, though very obsequious in their manners." (It does not
seem to have occurred to him that a people forced to live under
foreign domination, as the Egyptians were in Lane's time, can be
expected to be both obstinate and obsequious.)

Lane did not admire the Egyptians' social conduct. He said
they were given to "the indulgence of libidinous passions" that
earned their country its appellation, "abode of the wicked." He
deplored what he thought of as their insulting and obnoxious
behavior, leading sometimes to violence, in their quarrels. "The
generality of Egyptians," he said,

> are easily excited to quarrel, particularly those of the lower
> orders, who when enraged curse each other's fathers, mothers,
> beards, etc.; and lavish upon each other a variety of op-
> probrious epithets such as "son of the dog, pimp, pig," and an
> appellation which they still think worse than any of these—
> namely, 'Jews.'

Lane's book was published in 1836, but much of it might have
been written yesterday. The colonialist arrogance of his observa-
tions was tempered by affection, and even now Egypt is a blend of
the charming and the infuriating. It is as difficult now as it was in
Lane's time to write about the collective behavior of the Egyptians
without sounding condescending, even when the comments are
intended constructively. The difference is that the Egyptians in
their independence no longer feel obliged to defend patterns of
behavior that inhibit their national development, as they were when
those patterns represented a culture to be shielded against aliens.
One need not be an imperialist, a snob or a racist to render
unflattering verdicts on Egyptian attitudes and organizations, because in the aggregate they form a major obstacle to fulfillment of

the country's ambitions for itself, and the Egyptians know it. Aspiring to match the economic, social and political standards of the West, the Egyptians invite judgment by Western standards of performance. They are sensitive to criticism from outsiders but vigorous in criticism of themselves. Among the secular and educated classes and the technocrats, there is a recognition that the country can no longer afford its own eccentricities.

The first time I met Tahseen Basheer, a prominent diplomat who was then Sadat's press secretary and later ambassador to the Arab League, he clucked disapprovingly when I told him I was temporarily serving on the faculty of the American University in Cairo. He had a low opinion of that institution, he said, because it had not brought to the Egyptians the qualities they needed to learn from the Americans. "We don't need American instruction in mathematics or history," he said. "We have had those for centuries. What the Americans should be instilling in the students there is that unique American quality that we do not have—the love of work."

An Egyptian who does love work is Elhamy el-Zayat, president of a fast-growing travel agency that leaped to do business with Israel when the border was opened. He says he prefers graduates of the American University to graduates of the large state universities because "at least they have learned to do things in a straight line. The others are like all the Egyptians, I put them behind the counter to serve customers and they try to be nice to everyone so they never finish taking care of the person who is standing before them. They talk to everyone who comes up behind." Anyone who has ever stood in a line for a service in Egypt, at a bank, say, or at the motor vehicle offices, knows exactly what el-Zayat is talking about. Trying to talk to a dozen people at once, the person behind the window accomplishes nothing. And the people in line for any service know that if they don't push and shove and shout, they won't get what they need, so they all join the fray.

"I have to ask myself, are we lazy?" said a young Egyptian diplomat who returned in the late 1980s from four years in Australia and was dismayed by the contrast. "Sure, we had war, and that was our excuse for a long time, but what about Japan?"

Well, what about Japan? Why can't Egypt, which at the beginning of this century was at least Japan's equal in economic and educational development, marshal the discipline and energy to keep pace today? It isn't that the people are lazy by nature; farmers and

factory hands are quite industrious. But a system that added repression and bureaucratic complexity to behavior patterns learned
under foreign occupation stifled initiative among the white-collar
classes. Sadat and Mubarak have only begun to chip away at the
glacial inertia that had overtaken the country by the time of Nasser's
death.

Anis Mansour, a prominent journalist who often served as a
conduit for Sadat's opinions, wrote in 1978, "Nothing will improve unless people learn to distinguish between the bed and the
desk: when they leave the bed they must forget it and when they get
to the office they must forget everything except work, production
and creativity." He noted that the legions who "sit at their desks in
the office, doing nothing but drinking coffee, smoking and reading
newspapers are to all purposes still in bed. . . . This is the essential
problem of life in Egypt, and it determines the real future of the
country."

There are innumerable examples of Egyptians making that
kind of assessment; they know what's wrong. Sadat talked often of
the need to improve quality, increase productivity and bring some
sort of order and discipline to the streets and offices; Mubarak has
emphasized hard work and quality control. But attitudes and patterns of thought and work habits built up over generations cannot
be changed overnight, especially when the structure of the government and the economy perpetuate them. They cannot be sent away,
like the Soviet military advisers, or overcome by an act of individual
will, like the state of war with Israel. The vast, bloated structure of
state-owned industry built up under Nasser, and his policy of
guaranteeing a government job to every university graduate, ensured that every factory and office would be filled to overflowing
with people who do not have enough to do and little incentive to
do well at what tasks they do have. No wonder the legions of
supernumeraries who populate every office appear to be lazy. There
was a great deal of amused commentary in the spring of 1987 about
a study purporting to show that the average Egyptian does only 27
minutes of actual work each day. It was an exaggeration to make a
point, but it was a point that everyone already understood. Egypt
has only begun to attack the attitudinal and organizational liabilities
that match its paucity of resources as a drag on progress.

The Egyptians lived for thousands of years at high levels of
creativity and accomplishment in art, science and craftsmanship,

and their experience of running a unified state predates that of their neighbors by centuries. But today their achievements are often lost in a morass of confusion and ineptitude that holds back the entire country. The heavy hand of the bureaucracy and the pervasiveness of the welfare state snuff out initiative; the chaos in public services and the insatiable demands for paperwork perpetuate the class of messengers, agents and hangers-on who profit from manipulating the system but contribute nothing to national productivity.

At the time *infitah,* the open door, was proclaimed and foreigners began pouring into the country in search of business opportunity, the most acute and immediate difficulties were mechanical, such as the collapse of the telephone system. This excuse no longer obtains; the telecommunications network is adequate. The larger problems lie in habit, bureaucratic regulation, social tradition and personal style. Every diplomat, journalist and businessman who has worked in Egypt has his favorite tales about how difficult it is to get things done in Egypt and how erratic Egyptian behavior can be. Here are some of mine.

Seeking an interview with Hilmy Murad, a prominent political figure since Nasser's time, I went to the offices of the Socialist Labor Party, with which he is affiliated. He was not there, but a courteous party functionary made several telephone calls to track him down. The result, I was told, was that Murad would see at 6 PM at his home in the suburb of Heliopolis. When I arrived, I was greeted by a baffled servant who said Murad was out of town and that he had told this to the person at party headquarters who had called on my behalf. Explanation? None. This was in 1987, when the improvements in telephone service made such calls possible, as they had not been 10 years earlier. In this case, the better telephone service only compounded the inconvenience.

About to run out of business cards, I went to Weinstein's stationery store in downtown Cairo—no longer owned by any Weinsteins, of course—to order a new supply. I asked for 250 cards printed in English on one side and Arabic on the other. It should have been easy since they had already made a batch of these for me and kept the plates, but I was told it would take 10 days.

Knowing that "10 days" means perhaps 10 days, perhaps 3 weeks, I waited 15 days before going to see if the cards were ready.

I handed my receipt to the clerk on duty, an aged and nearly toothless gentleman with whom I had not previously dealt, and I watched him fumble among the boxes of printed cards on the dusty shelf behind him. I knew right away that mine were not among them.

"Not ready yet," he said. No offer to go back to the print shop and inquire, no apology, no explanation and no suggestions.

Irritated, I said exactly the wrong thing. "They were supposed to be ready a week ago. No wonder your country is in such a mess if you can't even get 250 cards printed in two weeks."

"And you, what country are you from?" the clerk demanded of me in return. "What's your nationality?"

"I'm an American," I said.

"Ha!" he snorted, throwing my receipt back at me. "America, two hundred years. Egypt, seven thousand years."

Preparing to leave the country for a few weeks to report on events elsewhere in the region, I was trying to set up appointments with people I would need to see when I returned. At the Cairo press center, where officials of the State Information Service attempt to arrange trips and interviews for foreign journalists, I asked that an appointment with Mustafa Khalil, then prime minister, be set for any time after the 16th of the month, that being the date on which I would return.

I did return to Cairo late on the 16th, long after the press center staff had left for the day, so I went there the next morning to check on the appointment. It had indeed been set up—for the morning of the 16th. Of course I had missed the interview. But worse than that, the prime minister of the country had blocked out 45 minutes to talk to *The Washington Post,* not a trivial matter in a country vigorously courting congressional favor, and had been left with a hole in his calendar when nobody appeared. The staff assistant at the press center was chagrined, but she said it wasn't her fault. "I told them you said it should be after the 16th but this is what they gave me," she said. The next time I wanted to talk to Khalil, I just called him at home.

I was visiting the Gianaclis winery in the Delta, south of Alexandria. All wineries and distilleries were nationalized under Nasser; Gianaclis, though still operated by some of the people who worked there when it was owned by a Greek family, is now the generic name for the products of Egypt's alcohol industry. The company makes white, red and rosé wines characterized by harsh texture and chemical taste. We sometimes drank them because imported wine was extremely expensive, but I wanted to find out why Egypt, whose wines had inspired the poetic imagination of Virgil, was now making wines that ranged in quality from tolerable to dreadful.

How come, I asked the marketing manager, the quality of the wine was so uneven, to put it politely? Why was it that two identical bottles of, say, Omar Khayyam red or Cleopatra white would vary so widely in taste and texture when the weather was always the same and the wines were blended anyway?

"Well," he said, "it's like your favorite meal that your wife makes at home for dinner. One night it's excellent, the next time it's not so good. What can you do?" This was at a time when the Egyptians were miffed at the discovery that Egyptian-made products were difficult to export to the free markets of the West because of a reputation for poor quality control.

Thomas P. F. Hoving, then the director of New York's Metropolitan Museum of Art, organized the exhibition of artifacts from the tomb of the Pharaoh Tutankhamen that toured the United States. As a related project, intended to raise money for the renovation of the Egyptian Museum in Cairo, American craftsmen made reproductions of several of the most stunning items from the boy-king's hoard. These were to be sold in the museums in the United States where the exhibition was to be presented. When the reproductions were ready, Hoving flew to Egypt to meet Sadat and present some samples as a gift. He had his meeting with the president, but he did not present the samples. Customs officials refused to allow them into the country.

One day the telephone at our house went dead. This had happened before and I had worked out a regular procedure. First I went up to the roof to see if the wire coming in from the pole on the street was intact. It was, so I moved on to step two.

I sent the gardener's son across the street to ask Fuad the Pepsi-Cola vendor to ask his friend at the embassy of Niger down the block to find out what was wrong. (I never did learn what mysterious connection the man from the embassy had with the telephone service people, but he seemed to get results when no amount of discussion with the clerks at the telephone office nearby produced any, so we were happy to use this informal channel.) The answer came back that service had been shut off because we had not paid the bill. Of course, no bill had come; that was because the telecommunications authorities had instituted a new procedure. Instead of sending out statements they inserted notices in the newspapers and read announcements on the radio from time to time saying that bills were due and subscribers should go in and settle up. I had missed the announcement. Now I paid the bill and service was restored. Two weeks later, however, a man came to the house and announced that he was taking the phones out altogether because of another unpaid bill: 49 pounds, then more than $70, for international calls.

My wife and I had not made any international calls for many months. We tried to, but we hadn't even been able to get the international operators to come on the line. So I went to the ministry of telecommunications to inquire. The calls in question, it seemed, had been made more than 18 months earlier. The bills had been put in the mail (international calls are billed separately from local service) but for some reason never delivered. They were returned to the ministry and put in a file, and when they popped up through some unexplained process all those months later they led to the order to terminate service. Naturally, nobody telephoned the number to which the calls were billed to ask for payment. That would have required the very kind of initiative Egyptian civil servants have learned not to demonstrate, and in any case, in those days not even employees of the ministry would have been able to get through on the phone from their part of town to ours.

Reluctant to pay without being certain that those calls really had been made from our phone, I had to find the person in charge of this operation. The building of the telecommunications ministry where these things are handled consists of several floors of overcrowded, ill-lighted offices, piled high with dusty records and ledger books in which clerks make entries by hand between the coffee stains. Inquiries at a few doors led to Madame Khadiga, chief of the international section. Her staff knew by heart which telephone numbers belonged to which subscribers because there were so few subscribers to the international service. So when I gave my number to Mme. Khadiga, they knew without looking it up who the subscriber was: Dr. Tewfik Ramzi, the owner of our villa. Mme. Khadiga dug out the records on which the bills were based. I went down to the ground floor to the cashier's office and paid, and returned with my receipt.

She then took me out to the corridor and led me, weaving between mats spread for midday prayer, to see her boss, a man who had a private office, a secretary and the power to suspend the order to take out the telephone. He was not there and the secretary was dozing with her head on the desk, but Mme. Khadiga scrawled a note and left it under the boss's blotter and assured me it was all taken care of.

Nowadays, of course, the telephone service is much better. It is possible to obtain a telephone without waiting years, and business executives and correspondents routinely dial calls all over town and all over the world. But the government system and the civil service attitudes reflected in that episode are still in place.

Muslim leaders in Turkey invited an Egyptian delegation to participate in an important conference to discuss standardization of the starting times for holy days and religious feasts. (These vary because they depend on sighting the moon with the naked eye, not on astronomical calculations.)

Three leaders of Egypt's religious hierarchy, including the Grand Sheikh of al-Azhar, the highest-ranking religious dignitary in the country, accepted the invitation. The Turkish embassy in Cairo went to work on arrangements for their travel, and purchased airline tickets. Two days before the Egyptians' scheduled departure, a Turkish embassy official telephoned the office of the Grand Sheikh to ask that someone come and pick up the tickets. He was told that the Egyptians had forgotten all about it, and now could not go because there was not enough time remaining before the conference for them to get themselves organized.

There is no end to these tales. Their content varies according to the occupation and contacts of whoever is telling them, but their import is similar—the country is at once disorganized and stiflingly bureaucratic, its systems and services are maddeningly erratic, and its people, while amiable, are also frequently inefficient, un-disciplined, opportunistic, unproductive, vain and occasionally venal.

Mubarak has worked diligently to overcome the inertia that crippled Egypt's public services. More hospitals are under construction in Egypt now, for example, than were built in all the previous years since the 1952 revolution. But he seems to have no illusions about the magnitude of the task still ahead if Egypt's level of performance is ever going to match the needs of the population. Newcomers to Egypt in the "Open Door" years noticed quickly that the most efficient organizations in Egypt were those that operated autonomously, outside the structure of government ministries and the public sector industries, such as the Suez Canal Authority. A decade later, the number of efficient organizations has increased because responsibility for economic growth has largely been transferred to the private sector, but the government and the state industries have been unable to keep pace.

"Bureaucracy exists in all countries," Mubarak said in a speech to Egyptian expatriate workers.

> Because of our need for greater activity in the investment, trade and export fields, we are trying to eliminate as much of this bureaucracy as possible. [But] we are dealing with humans. We cannot just touch a button and end bureaucracy. . . . There are many examples of bureaucratic behavior. In some cases, an employee is afraid to make a decision and wants an order from a [cabinet] minister. He is afraid he will get into trouble. We want to end this. The state is exerting enormous efforts in this regard.

He had been president nearly six years when he said that.

Sadat always insisted that the country he ruled was not corrupt. In his talk with the professors at Asyut University in April 1979, he was emphatic: "There is no corruption or anything of the sort. There is always the good and the bad in every country and in every place on Earth, but when one talks about corruption this means the state is corrupt. Not at all. By God, no one could go through what we have gone through and emerge standing up, as we are standing today" if the state were corrupt.

It is now well-established that Sadat, if not corrupt himself, tolerated corruption that enriched his cronies and sometimes besmirched the honor of the country, such as a deal that would have allowed foreign developers to build what they called a "Palm Springs for the Arabs" right at the feet of the Great Pyramids. But in the larger sense Sadat was correct. Egypt is not corrupt as Iran was corrupt under the Shah, or as Lebanon is corrupt. The occasional cabinet official taking money to influence a contract, or the teacher charging money to give his pupils privately the lessons he was supposed to be giving them in school, or the watermelon vendor injecting water into the melons to make them heavier cannot be likened to the flagrant siphoning of the national wealth that was going on in Iran or to the grasping selfishness of the factional leaders in Lebanon, who were willing to pull down the entire edifice of the state to protect their power bases.

But Egypt is afflicted with other forms of corruption that are perhaps even more pernicious, and more difficult to root out. Sadat made frequent references to a "crisis of morals and ethics" that required enactment of a "code of ethics" to regulate social conduct. He was speaking less of graft than of the inertia and selfishness that inhibit progress: bureaucrats sabotaging policies to protect their own interests, workers and managers loafing on the job knowing that they cannot be fired or racketeers selling Egyptian girls to rich Gulf Arabs. On a more mundane level, petty graft is inevitable in a country unable to deliver either public services or economic advancement. The payoff, the personal favor, the appeal to connections and the gratuity are indispensable lubricants of the system—a system, ironically, that was largely set up to implement the egalitarian ideals of Nasser.

Shortly after our arrival as residents in 1975, my wife and I went to the Cairo traffic department to apply for drivers' licenses. We were staggered by the noise, the confusion, and the inability of the harassed clerks to meet the demand for their services (especially because, as Elhamy el-Zayat noticed at his travel agency, they seemed terminally unable to concentrate on one task at a time). We had just begun to study Arabic, but even if we had been fluent we could not have coped with that maze of shouting, pushing men and jumbled ledger books.

But because I was on the American University faculty, we were accompanied by the university's traffic fixer. (The university, like all major organizations, also has a customs fixer, an airport fixer, a passport fixer and a fixer for every other transaction.) At the fixer's instruction, we stood in the quietest corner we could find and shelled out small change as he requested it, 20 *piasters* here, 15 there, while he darted from line to line.

In an hour, without moving, we had "passed" our written tests and our road tests, and we had our licenses. It was a useful lesson: The Egyptians understood that we had more money than they did, and that the grief that would come from trying to do something by the rules, without spreading around a little happiness, was not worth it. It is easy to understand why the clerks or workers tend first to those who contribute to their welfare. Their salaries are so low that they cannot feed their families. Besides, the demand for services is greater than the supply, so bidding is inevitable. Whether it is a cigarette to the cop on the corner for permission to park or thousands of dollars to the hustlers trafficking in telex machines, the payoff is a form of defense against all the others seeking the same service.

This is the *baksheesh* system. It implies that a favor bestowed or a service rendered—telephone repair, authorization for legal goods to clear customs, permission to park, delivery of a message—merits a favor in return. In routine low-level transactions, where the *baksheesh* is a few pennies, the system is tolerated, even honored, and nobody is ashamed of it.

But it breeds parasites, like the man at the airport who demands a tip for moving a suitcase from scale to conveyor belt or the "gatekeeper" who extracts a fee for admitting visitors to the minaret of Ibn Tulun mosque. And it erodes public confidence in the state, because services that are ostensibly available to all are purveyed more quickly and in better quality to those who can afford a little extra. At first we were baffled by the apparent inability of Egypt's political and economic elite, from Sadat down, to comprehend the appalling condition of the nation's public services, but the explanation was simple: they never come in contact with these public services. Their wealth and position insulate them. They don't ride the buses or use Egyptian hospitals or shop at the subsidized groceries; they don't go to the motor vehicle bureau or check their own bags at the airport or go to the post office—they hire people to do those things.

Well, many Egyptians argue, what's wrong with that? It saves time for important people and provides employment for people who need jobs. Perhaps, but it breeds resentment among the vast numbers of honest citizens who can barely make ends meet and who see services that had been promised to them, such as education, being sold to the highest bidder. And at higher levels, the system is yet another hindrance to national development.

When the Xerox Corporation opened its first office in Cairo, it represented one of the great early accomplishments of the "Open Door" policy—a high technology American concern investing capital in Egypt. Xerox announced its arrival with full-page advertisements in Cairo's newspapers; the ads gave the address of the office, but they did not give the telephone number. That was because Xerox had been unable to obtain telephone service. It would clearly have been in the national interest to move an applicant such as Xerox to the top of the long waiting list for telephone service, but the company refused to make payoffs to any of the officials who had the authority to make such a decision, so no phones had been installed by the time of opening. Other companies, less determined than Xerox, took their business elsewhere.

At the first Cairo International Film Festival, in 1976, the "Nefertiti" award for the best Egyptian film was presented to *The Guilty Ones,* which portrayed the entire society as corrupt and decadent.

In that film, a famous movie star, who clearly achieved much of her success on the casting couch, is found murdered in her bedroom the morning after a party attended by friends and admirers. All the male guests, who are ostensibly respectable government officials and professionals, are able to give the police solid alibis. Those alibis are the real story of the film: Each of the men, in order to prove his innocence of the murder, is obliged to tell the police what he was actually doing at the time of the killing—in each case, committing a different crime somewhere else. All of them end up behind bars, jailed with the common thieves.

This film, denounced as scandalous by conservative Egyptians even as audiences were standing in line to see it, invited contempt for personalities who appear to be dignified and respectable gentlemen in prominent positions, just the kind of people Egyptians are taught to emulate. One after another, in ascending order of rank and wealth, they are exposed in the movie as shabby frauds.

One guest, the authoritarian headmaster of an exclusive school, was in his office at the time of the murder, 2:30 AM. He was taking examination questions out of a safe to sell to rich students, his way of obtaining the funds needed to cultivate companions like the famous actress.

Another partygoer is a distributor of merchandise to the state-owned cooperative grocery stores. He owns a Mercedes and wears European clothes because he steals subsidized food from the coop-

eratives and sells it on the black market. At the time of the murder,
he was smoking hashish in a narcotics den.

A distinguished gynecologist was in his clinic, performing an
illegal abortion. Another man at the party, an engineer at the
housing ministry, who cultivated the actress's favor by providing
state-owned building materials for her new house, was seducing the
gynecologist's wife. Not one of the dozen potential suspects was
doing anything lawful or respectable at the time of the killing. The
culprit, it turns out, is a young man from a good family who has
given up his ideals in his desperate love for the actress, believing her
promises to reform her life and marry him. He killed her when he
learned she was deceiving him.

Except for the two detectives who conduct the investigation,
there is hardly an honorable character in the film. Not only are all
the men corrupt but, according to a member of the film censors
board, the absence of any chaste woman from a movie that has
women in almost every scene made the censors hesitate before
approving the film for release, even after all the most suggestive sex
scenes had been trimmed out.

The script for *The Guilty Ones* was written by Naguib Mahfouz, the same man who wrote *Karnak*. He had been equally
unsparing of the lower classes of Egyptian society in his famous
novel *Midaq Alley,* written in the early 1940s. All the denizens of
his alley are given to violence, greed and sexual perversion, and
among them the lowest of the low is Zaita, a filthy rascal whose
profession it is to

> create cripples, not the usual, natural cripples but artificial
> cripples of a new type. People came to him who wanted to
> become beggars and, with his extraordinary craft, the tools of
> which were piled on the shelf, he would cripple each customer
> in a manner appropriate to his body. They came to him whole
> and left blind, rickety, hunchbacked, pigeon-breasted, or with
> arms or legs cut off short.

Even the beggars are corrupt.

Under Mubarak, Egypt's moral affliction appears to be less one
of official corruption than one of a decline in social responsibility
among certain groups of young people. The absence of any threat
of war, combined with the sudden affluence of those who profited
from the "Open Door" and the oil boom, has bred a generation of

wealthy but undisciplined young people whose vulgarity and materialism have become an issue for political opponents of the government. Their behavior flaunts the glaring inequities of wealth that were the inevitable result of Sadat's economic policy.

If the charge of official corruption cannot be leveled against Mubarak, it clearly bulked large in the dossier of public grievance against Sadat, even if few would go so far as Heikal: "Not since the days of Khedive Ismail had Egypt been the scene of looting on such a massive and organized scale as it was during the last years of President Sadat. Corruption spread from the top of the pyramid of Egyptian society to the bottom." This is suspect testimony. Heikal acquired immense wealth and power as an insider under Nasser and he despised Sadat. Not everyone who suddenly got rich when Sadat opened up the economy acquired his wealth by illicit means, as Heikal seems to think. But his indictment of Sadat was not without grounds.

Even as Sadat railed against corruption, evidence mounted that his government was riddled with it. He declared that corruption would not be tolerated, and announced that Mustafa Khalil, as prime minister, had been instructed to root it out. "Any foreign company that pays commissions to any Egyptian official will be blacklisted and we will stop dealing with it," he said.

That was in October 1978, when potentates throughout the Middle East were loudly proclaiming their civic virtue in a collective effort not to resemble the corrupt Shah of Iran, who was about to be toppled from the Peacock Throne. And there were, in fact, several highly publicized cases in which cabinet ministers and former cabinet ministers who took payments to influence contracts were prosecuted.

When the People's Assembly wanted to know who had authorized and who benefited from the decision by a state-owned bank to lay out millions of dollars in hard currency to finance a new privately owned textile plant that was not part of the government's development plan and would compete with the state-owned factories, the project was suspended and the minister of industry was allowed to resign.

When former Deputy Prime Minister Ahmed Sultan Ismail was identified in an American legal case as the Egyptian who allegedly took $322,000 from Westinghouse to arrange a contract, Khalil quickly opened an Egyptian investigation and stripped Sul-

tan of his parliamentary immunity to prosecution. In that incident
the prime minister had little choice because the scandal was international and the Egyptians could not afford a backlash in Congress.
On strictly domestic matters, where there were no such pressures,
the old ways reasserted themselves a few days later when Sadat
selected Dr. Sufi Abu Taleb, president of Cairo University, to be
speaker of the People's Assembly.

That post, which confers immense status, some power and
good benefits, such as travel abroad at government expense, is filled
by vote of Assembly members, but of course the president's party
had more than enough votes to install his candidate. The job had
been held by Sayed Marei, a rich agronomist who was one of
Sadat's intimate confidants. Egyptians saw the appointment of Abu
Taleb as more of the same. While he was president of the university,
Sadat's wife had received the highest possible grades in her courses
there. A professor who was dismissed from the faculty claimed to
have lost his post because had given Sadat's son a failing grade in an
engineering course. And Abu Taleb, a poor boy from the provinces,
was widely believed to have more money than he could have earned
from his academic pursuits.

Abu Taleb may have been a man of integrity, but that was not
the issue. His appointment reinforced the belief of Sadat's critics
and of ordinary citizens that there was less than met the eye to the
president's egalitarian pronouncements and his preaching about
democracy. Egyptians were disgusted, but not surprised, by Abu
Taleb's appointment, just as they were never surprised when the
biggest public construction contracts were awarded to The Arab
Contractors, a company run by Sadat's millionaire friend and pa-
tron, Osman Ahmed Osman.

Sadat's appeals for a return to the ideals and values of the
Egyptian village—part of his relentless campaign to portray himself
as a simple *fellah*—implied that farm folks are somehow nobler than
city dwellers. But there was evidence that the centralized bureaucratic system of government held as much potential for corrupt
manipulation in the provinces as it did in Cairo or Alexandria.

In the Nasser years, for example, it was decided to put the
poorest peasants in position to control the boards of directors of
the agricultural cooperatives, because it was assumed that the richer
peasants must be corrupt. The poor peasants promptly took advantage of the opportunity handed them by the government, helped

themselves to the fertilizers, seed grains and pesticides controlled by the cooperatives and collaborated with clerks of the local agricultural credit banks to steal public funds intended for rural development.

In fairness to these farmers, it must be said that the cooperative system, which was designed in Cairo and aimed at controlling agriculture on behalf of the national treasury, did not work in their interest. They had no real control over an organization that decided what they would plant and how much they could charge for their crops. Mostly illiterate, and defenseless against officials who were demanding "commissions" on sales, they had more incentive to circumvent the system and operate on the black market than to obey the regulations. (In some sectors of the agricultural economy, this is still true.)

As for the petty official, whether his job is to distribute pesticide to farmers or issue ration books to factory hands, he has both strong incentive and limitless opportunity to take unauthorized payments. His salary is paltry, his family large and his food bill rising; his control over whatever function it is enables him to reward those supplicants who are properly grateful and deferential. The system is so rigidly centralized and inflexibly organized that his control over the function assigned to him is a monopoly, at least for that neighborhood or district. If he does not issue the paper or stamp the document, nobody else has the authority to do it. He is in a position to say yes or to come up with a reason to say no—the usual excuse being the absence of some other document that he deems necessary.

Ahmed Ragab, a popular humorist, told the following story in a newspaper column: An official of Ideal, the state-owned appliance and office furniture company, went to the ministry of foreign affairs for an endorsement on his marriage certificate that would enable his wife to accompany him on a trip abroad.

"The procedures are very simple," Ragab wrote.

The document has to be stamped with the state falcon seal at the civil status court concerned in Shubra [a neighborhood of Cairo]. Later it has to be stamped with the state falcon seal at the Ministry of Justice. When that is done it has to be stamped with the state falcon seal at the Foreign Ministry office in the government building in Tahrir Square, and finally it has to be

stamped with the state falcon seal at the headquarters of the
Foreign Ministry.

These "simple" procedures were much more complicated before the "administrative revolution" proclaimed by Sadat to cut
paperwork, Ragab said. In the old days, "the Foreign Ministry used
to insist that the marriage certificate be accompanied by a living
falcon you had to bring from the zoo."

The "government building in Tahrir Square" to which he
referred is the notorious *Mugamma,* the grand temple of Egyptian
bureaucracy, a reeking 12-story warren of filthy, crowded government offices where citizens wait for hours, even days, to execute
the minor paperwork functions of life. This place is the same
under Mubarak as it was under Nasser, except that now there
is a fleet of taxis parked outside—waiting not for passengers
but for their owners, who work in the building but often depart
after a token appearance to take up the much more lucrative job
of cabdriver.

Frustrating and inefficient as it is, the system provides employment for tens of thousands of people—the people who print the
forms, the people who stamp them, the people who carry them
around, the people who bring them tea while they work—and the
economy does not provide any alternative source of employment.
However much Mubarak's economic planners may hope that
growth of the private sector will alleviate the government's burden
as employer of last resort, that has not happened, and the tyranny of
the falcon stamp remains a chronic hindrance to national development. (Mubarak is of course well aware of this. In a speech to the
nation in the spring of 1987, he said, "The entire revenues of the
state, some of which go to subsidies and to buy food, amount to 12
billion pounds. Of this sum, 5 billion pounds go to pay salaries. No
state in the world, other than those that do not know what to do
with their money, can match this.")

During the oil boom years, I used to watch Egyptian workers
at Cairo Airport going off to jobs in the Persian Gulf states or in
Libya. They were simple men, often from the countryside, absurdly
dignified in their turbans and the woolen overcoats they wore over
their *galabeyas.* Many were illiterate; almost all were unfamiliar with
international air travel. They clutched in a firm grip every piece of
paper that was handed to them at every step of the proceedings—

ticket envelope, currency exchange receipt, work permit, health card, identity card, passport—and handed them all in at every point. Arriving at their destinations, they continued to hold on to their boarding cards even after disembarking from the plane, knowing that a document thrown away is a document that will be asked for by the next official down the line.

Whatever his other failings, Nasser is not entirely to blame for the development of this paper morass. He just took advantage of it for his own purposes, namely political control and full employment. Its roots are deep in Egyptian history, which has always been characterized by a centralization of power in the ruling authority, whether it be the Pharaoh or the Mameluke sultan or Napoleon or the British High Commissioner or Hosni Mubarak. Provincial governments have been extensions of the central authority, not rival claimants to authority, as in the United States. So is the People's Assembly. Egypt has no industrial empires to challenge the state's power, no dissident tribes or regional claimants to autonomy, no linguistic minorities. Even Islamic leaders such as the Grand Sheikh are employees of the state.

The government under Mustafa Khalil undertook a campaign of decentralization in the late 1970s, but cynics recalled that a similar campaign had been announced in 1960. Cairo remains the seat of all power. Each governorate, as the provinces are called, issues its own license plates, but the rules for doing so are set in Cairo. The police are a national force, headquartered in Cairo. Cropland allocations are made in Cairo. Tax collection procedures are set in Cairo. School curricula are written in Cairo. And the officials in Cairo, as often as not, are more concerned about holding onto their places in the capital and at the center of control than about expediting the delivery of services.

In the nineteenth century, Muhammad Ali introduced secular and technical education, but this was, as Morroe Berger wrote in a study of the Egyptian bureaucracy 30 years ago, only "for the specific purpose of training government employees and advisers," a policy that was "instrumental in encouraging generations of Egyptians to think of nonreligious education only as a means to civil service appointment."

The British, under Lord Cromer, added a requirement that employees of the government, at least those in white-collar jobs, have school-completion certificates. That was intended to encour-

age the spread of education, but instead it reinforced the idea that
the purpose of education was to get a government job. It created an
atmosphere in which those who had government jobs thought
themselves superior to the citizenry they were supposed to be
serving.

"When an Egyptian goes to the post office or police station or
even to a railroad ticket office," Berger noted, "he is almost certain
to meet government officials who earn more than he does and are
better educated. In the West the situation is more likely to be just
the opposite." That is, the man behind the desk (or now, sometimes, the woman) is accustomed to being able to push people
around and to command a deference out of proportion to his ability
or his real authority. Since Berger's study, the gaps in literacy and
income between official and ordinary citizen have lessened; in fact a
good carpenter or mason can now make considerably more money
than a middle-level bureaucrat. It is part of Egypt's current discontent that the legions of government functionaries with university
degrees find themselves earning less than artisans and private-sector
factory hands to whom they consider themselves superior. But the
power these officials wield over the country is basically intact—and
it is almost impossible for the ordinary citizen, after reaching
adulthood, to acquire the education and status that would put him
behind the desk of authority. There is no way, for example, that a
plumber could go to law school at night, no way to become
"doctor" or "engineer," the titles that command respect.

Under Nasser, nationalization of the banks, insurance companies and industries absorbed the workers in those enterprises into
a centralized state system in which everyone drew the same pay
regardless of performance, and promotion was based on seniority.
The imposition in 1962 of a rule guaranteeing a job to all university
graduates required that system to take on tens of thousands of
workers who were entirely redundant.

By the time Sadat became president, the government and the
public-sector industries had grown into a bloated, self-serving apparatus that wallowed in inertia, abused its authority and reinforced
the belief that desk jobs in the government were the most desirable
socially even if they entailed no duties.

"A quarter of a million employees at the time of the revolution," Raymond William Baker noted in his study of the Sadat
years,

had grown to over a million by the early seventies. While this inflation reflects in part the expanded role of the government in all fields of economic and social activity, it also measures the failure of the Egyptian economy to grow rapidly enough to absorb its more educated manpower. With that failure, irresistible pressures mounted for the regime to create jobs in an already bloated bureaucracy.

Mubarak put the total number of government employees in 1987 at 3.2 million, observing ruefully that this is "a huge figure for any country."

The resuscitation of the private sector was intended to relieve those pressures by providing new opportunities in the private economy, but by the end of the 1970s its chief effect had been to divert into the private sector a relative handful of talented and energetic managers who could meet the more stringent standards of private enterprise and who spoke foreign languages. The most promising of them, such as the graduates of the American University's management program, were happy to forgo the lifetime job security and meager pensions offered by government jobs and take the higher salaries, better working conditions and opportunities for promotion offered by the private sector.

The Mubarak government's five-year economic plan for 1987–92 anticipates that half the investment capital in that period will come from the private sector, but of course the very efficiency of profit-driven enterprises restrains them from absorbing surplus labor. That burden continues to fall upon the state, where inefficiency is a corollary of the bloated labor force.

In 1977, for example, statistics compiled by *Middle East* magazine showed that Egyptair, the notoriously inefficient national airline, had 8,000 employees for its fleet of 15 aircraft. By comparison, the Turkish airline THY had 5,000 for 21 planes; El Al, the Israeli state airline, had 4,000 for 14 jets. Many of those Egyptair workers, of course, are low-level supernumeraries who stand around check-in counters and luggage claim areas at the airports, performing unnecessary services for reluctant clients.

The time-wasting potential of the Egyptian system is limitless, even though improvements in telephone service have made it easier to find out in advance who is the right person to see and when he might be in his office.

On one occasion, preparing an article about the tourist business, I wanted to find out exactly how many hotels were under construction or planned. I went to the ministry of tourism to see Dr. Mohammed Shafik, the director of information and public relations. (Note the doctorate. The grander the bureaucrat's title, the more likely he is to possess a doctorate, though not necessarily in a subject related to his work. Conversely, possession of a doctorate, in whatever field, enhances the opportunities to gain a good safe position.)

Shafik was an engaging fellow, a big florid-faced man who parlayed his charm and his position at the ministry into a good life of full social calendars and frequent travel. Naturally, therefore, he was not in Cairo when I wanted to see him. Nobody on his staff knew when he would return, and none of them had access to the information I wanted. The offices around his, and indeed the corridor outside, were full of people drinking coffee and reading the morning papers, but none of them was authorized to dig out the comprehensive list of hotel projects—assuming Shafik had told them where it was. That was to be expected in a system where information belongs to its holder and he consolidates his position by limiting access to it.

Or consider the task of transferring title to the office car to my successor. The car was an Egyptian-built Fiat. Since it was made in Egypt, there was no question of its customs status—no import duty was owed. Nor was any hard currency to change hands; the *Washington Post* had paid for the car and I was simply putting title to it in my successor's name. We began the process 10 days before I was to leave the country; we did not complete it before my departure.

This operation tied up three *Washington Post* employees: myself, a hardened veteran of the Cairo bureaucratic wars; my successor, who was new in Egypt but spoke excellent Arabic; and my driver, an Egyptian who had been dealing with automobiles for a living for all of his adult life.

At the traffic department, we learned that under the law a car is not actually a car but is considered capital, as if it were a suitcase full of cash, and the registration of its transfer therefore requires the approval of an appropriate official in the finance establishment. Which official? Somebody at the Banque du Caire, downtown. We went to the Banque du Caire, one of the big state-owned banks, looking for the man with the falcon stamp.

Bafflement, consultations, obligatory cups of coffee, and finally the discovery of an official who understands this transaction and tell us we are at the wrong bank. It isn't Banque du Caire we want, it's the Central Bank, up the street, and the person we have to see is the director of the foreign exchange control department.

This was hard to believe. We could not understand how the central bank's director of foreign exchange controls—one of the most critical jobs in the country—could be involved in so trivial a transaction, especially since the transaction didn't involve any foreign exchange. But having no choice we went to his office. He was present, and he was indeed the right person. He had a form letter ready for just such occasions. He signed it and put the falcon stamp on it, on the spot.

Why did he have to do this himself? What if he had been on vacation? What if we were not in Cairo but in some remote province? He had no answers; it was just the system he had taken on with the job.

But that was not the end of the story. More trips to the traffic department followed, to fill out all the irrelevant data about the parties to the transaction (including our religions) and complete the paperwork. At last it was midday on a Thursday. I was to leave at dawn Saturday, and government offices are closed Fridays, so we were out of time, but all that remained was to pay a few cents in fees for stamps and clerical services.

We underestimated the system's capacity for failure. The finance clerk at the traffic department, the only person authorized to collect these fees, was out sick. We could pay, but only at another government office a mile or so away, where another clerk could receive the money and issue the final recept. So we dashed down there. Alas, it is the custom to close early on Thursdays, the start of the weekend, and no money would be accepted after noon. It was 12:15, and the clerk in question was still there, but the books were closed. We considered offering him an appropriate inducement to reopen them, but by that time our collective irritation at the whole process left us disinclined to reward any of the participants in it. Several months later, I finally paid the fees and filled out one last paper at the Egyptian consulate in New York.

Having gone through that, I was not surprised to hear from a prominent American industrialist in 1980 that he had had no response to a proposal for an agribusiness project that he had

submitted to the Egyptian government two and a half years before—a project for which he had personally obtained a letter of
endorsement from Sadat. It is no wonder that the clock above the
main entrance to the Central Bank of Egypt has no hands; the
country has not yet understood that in the modern world, time is
money.

Throughout Sadat's presidency, every analysis of Egypt's economic, industrial, agricultural and organizational liabilities dwelled
at length on this bureaucratic morass and its paralyzing effect on
development. Chided by the Americans, warned by foreign businessmen that red tape was driving them away, and compelled by a
shortage of cash to confront reality, the government in the late
1970s announced some reform measures. University graduates
seeking government jobs were obliged to wait several years, in the
hope that they would find something else in the meantime, though
the payroll continued to grow. Section chiefs in the ministries were
authorized to grant 10 percent of their promotions each year on the
basis of merit instead of seniority. And Prime Minister Khalil began
his attempt at decentralization, in which some routine functions
were transferred out of Cairo, eliminating the need to bring every
dossier to the capital for action.

But all important decisions regarding economic policy, agriculture, transportation, education and security are still made in
Cairo. And in any case, the obstacles to greater efficiency and
productivity are as much attitudinal as organizational. Mubarak has
struggled valiantly to break the psychological reliance on the government and the public sector, and Egyptians say they detect signs
that people are more willing now to take initiatives, to go outside
the established decision-making networks, to take economic risks in
the pursuit of gain. But the universities continue to churn out
thousands of unemployable graduates every year and Egypt cannot
risk the political liability that would be posed by armies of unemployed, overeducated young people, so jobs continue to be made
for them.

Dr. Abdel Meguid al-Abd, deputy minister of labor in the
1970s, once said to me that "your country is different. You have
appreciated the importance of competing in excellence. Like all
developing nations, we copied the educational system of advanced
nations, and what happened? A lot of striving for certificates and
diplomas that mean nothing in the world of work and experience."
He said that Egypt has

plenty of institutions that could develop more skilled labor, but the whole system has to be reformed. If I pay an auto mechanic 18 pounds a month, he has to take another job to support his family and when he is offered a job outside Egypt that pay 10 times that, he takes it. We have to meet the challenge of getting away from the snob appeal of university education. We must stress the importance of attitude training.

He was promoting the idea that a skilled worker—an elevator installer, say, or a bus mechanic—should not only get more money than some ministry clerk but also be regarded by the society as a more valuable asset, respected and emulated even if his hands were dirty. Al-Abd could not have foreseen what actually happened: Thousands of Egypt's best craftsmen and artisans did migrate to the oil states, where they made good salaries and were paid in dollars. When the construction boom ended and oil prices fell in the early 1980s, these people returned to Egypt, where they traded their dollars for Egyptian pounds at the black market rate and used their wealth to buy the automobiles and appliances and good apartments that their compatriots in the civil service and the state industries could not afford. But this prosperity did not necessarily bring them social status. On the contrary, they are widely regarded by the educated classes as vulgar parvenus who have earned more than they are worth. The irony of this is that now it is most often the civil servants and teachers who have to take second jobs to support their families, not the electricians or plumbers. That is why those petty officials in the *Mugamma* have their taxis parked outside.

It is also the chief cause of a long-running scandal in which schoolteachers, unable to live on their salaries, have taken to selling on the side the lessons they are supposed to deliver free in the classrooms. Because students must pass their examinations in order to stay on track toward admission to a university, they are at the mercy of their teachers, and the teachers have taken advantage of this by giving "private" lessons at home or by taping their lectures and selling the tapes. The students have responded by wide-scale cheating on the examinations.

Sadat's style of government was similar to Ronald Reagan's, in that he tried to lead by exhortation and image but paid little attention to the nuts and bolts of running the country. This was appropriate, even essential, for a decade of grand gestures, first in war, then in peace. But Sadat, for all his rhetoric, accomplished little in the way of reforming the system and overcoming the attitudes that crippled Egypt's effort to develop. Mubarak, who is as cautious and attentive to detail as Sadat was impetuous, has tried to energize, segment by segment, a nation dragged down by opportunism, indifference, indiscipline and neglect. But the state still carries, and will continue to carry, the burden of untold thousands of employees from whom it does not, cannot, get its money's worth.

At a cocktail party I once met a man named Mounir Labib Moussa, whose business card bore the impresive titles, "minister plenipotentiary, commercial," and "director, American department, Ministry of Commerce." He asked me to come see him at his office, and of course I did, happy to know someone in his lofty position. I thought he wanted to talk about U.S.-Egyptian trade. When I went to the ministry, however, I found that his title was much grander than his duties. He occupied the typical office of a middle-level government official, filled with battered metal furniture and yawning cabinets containing bound volumes of dusty files, and what he wanted was an opportunity to make money on the side. He asked me if I knew of any businessmen in the United States who could use his services as a "commercial consultant"—that is, go-between or agent—in their attempts to penetrate the Egyptian market. Acceptance of such an assignment, if offered, would not of course imply resignation from his job in the ministry. I said I would let him know if I came up with anything.

On an Egyptair flight from Nairobi, I watched the purser disappear into the lavatory as we approached Cairo Airport. He emerged a few minutes later in a civilian suit and tie, his uniform packed away in his briefcase. The business suit, he said, was the correct dress for what he considered his "real job," which was to attempt to establish himself as a "business consultant" for foreign films coming to Egypt. After all, he was a business graduate of Cairo University, and he might as well put his free education to use.

There was nothing inherently wrong, of course, about reaching out for new opportunities to make money; that was what the "Open Door" was all about. But what these men and legions of others like them were proposing was to make money for themselves by manipulating the system on behalf of foreigners, not by reforming or energizing it to produce on behalf of the country. Mubarak has had to chip away at this attitude piece by piece; there has been no collective national response to his appeals to abandon the old ways and concentrate seriously on work and production. Outside of the army, there are few Egyptians who can be identified as having made sacrifices or taken risks for the collective good, and it is not clear how much they could accomplish were they to do so.

Take, for example, the cooking range story, as related by the well-known columnist Mohsen Mohamed in *al-Gomhouria*. The state-owned Helwan Company for Metallurgical Industries, which manufactures a basic gas cooking stove, raised its price in 1986 by 92 percent, to 1,200 Egyptian pounds, attributing the increase to the rise in the dollar against the Egyptian currency and increased customs duties, which had driven up the price of imported parts. However, Mohamed noted,

> local markets are now flooded by cooking ranges imported from an Arab country under the so-called "barter deals." [Egypt encourages barter trade because it permits the import of goods without an outlay of foreign currency.] No customs duties are paid on that type of imported cooking range since this is stipulated by the barter deal system. It is for this reason that the range is sold for less than 700 Egyptian pounds. This means that the imported range is sold for about half the price of the locally made one, and because it is imported, it is usually thought to be of a better quality and hence preferred by the consumers. The result is that locally made products cannot compete with products of foreign makes even in Egypt.

The state-owned Egyptian company is thus in a position where it cannot sell its stoves, cannot lay off its workers because they have no other jobs, and is facing pressure from the government to turn a profit so it will no longer have to be subsidized. Mubarak's government has attempted to limit the import of nonessential goods, especially where they compete with locally made products, but of course cancellation of the barter deal would take away the market for whatever Egyptian product was being exported in the trade. The Egyptian system consists of anomalies such as this multiplied a thousandfold.

It is not as if Egypt were some sleepy tropical backwater where there is no work to be done. By six in the morning, the bus stops and train stations of all the big cities are crowded with students, factory hands, soldiers, clerks and salesgirls setting off for their daily duties, vendors' carts are rolling, farmers are going into the fields, airliners are departing for every country of Europe and the Middle

East, convoys are lining up to go through the Suez Canal, oil is flowing through the Sumed pipeline, trucks are rolling out of the port of Alexandria.

But much of that energy is vitiated by a maddening slovenliness, incompetence and indifference that no ministerial decrees have been able to overcome. A tour guide arrives at a hotel only to discover that nobody ordered the bus; the factory hand arrives at his post only to discover that some shortage of parts has shut down the assembly line; clerks report to their offices only to find that there are not enough desks for all members of the bloated staff, let alone enough work, and there is really nothing to do but have tea; the messenger and secretary arrive at the scheduled hour only to learn that there is no sign of their boss, who may or may not be along later.

The customs of a proud people command respect, and if the riders of an Egyptian bus are content to wait while the driver pulls over and leaves them sitting as he goes for tea, it is no business of ours—except that the United States is paying more and more of the bill for Egypt's way of life. Besides, the Egyptians themselves recognize that their attitudinal eccentricities impede their progress, and they do not hesitate to criticize themselves.

When Mamdouh Salem was prime minister, in the mid-1970s, he began dropping in unannounced on offices and public facilities, accompanied by reporters, who gave these forays extensive coverage. At Cairo's main railroad station, he found some workers dozing atop piles of used linen from dining and sleeping cars. He also find piles of old rails that had been marked for sale as scrap in 1910 and were still there. That brought a new round of clucking from editorial writers, but there was no systematic follow-up and these adventures soon ended.

On another occasion, a newspaper was complaining about neglect of language and culture by the manufacturers of toys. "An Egyptian toy company does manufacture, very cheaply, a set of cardboard building blocks depicting on each face an animal with its initial letter underneath," the paper noted. "That is the good news. The bad news is that the initial does not always correspond to the name of the animal above it, the animal has been drawn very often by a man who has never seen the beast and the beast is very often one which has become extinct or near to it in its Antarctic or equatorial jungle hideout." Conclusion: A country that cannot match up the initial letters with the correct animals on childrens' blocks is not ready for high technology industrial competition.

The Egyptians are capable of great, if infrequent, feats of organization and logistics. It was their workers who built the Aswan Dam. Their meticulous preparations for the 1973 war and the precision with which they carried out their plans for crossing the Suez Canal are admired by all military analysts. At the time of the "Geneva Preparatory Conference" in December 1977, where the first direct Egyptian-Israeli negotiations took place at a hotel in Cairo, the government organized hotel rooms, press facilities, security protection, communications and even kosher food for hundreds of participants and journalists almost overnight. Those accomplishments are remembered with pride because they were so far above the standard level of performance.

Nearly 30 years have passed since Don Peretz, an American scholar examining the social impact of the 1952 revolution, reported on a conversation with an agricultural official who

> told me of his difficulties with Egyptian teachers and government workers who were supposed to be undergoing training for rural construction work. To begin with, his students resist even the idea of visiting nearby villages during their training period. They prefer to listen to lectures on rural problems rather than observe them in the raw. Once they are "forced" into the villages, they insist on maintaining their "dignity"—which means they refuse to wear work clothes, open necked shirts and overalls or khaki trousers. Instead they must wear their business or office suits and sport a necktie and jacket so as to "maintain the proper distance" from the peasants. "They are afraid," he said, "to get their hands down into their native soil . . . They are ashamed of dirt and disease and of the peasants among whom they will work in the future."

Peretz concluded that the new attitudes required to get those students down into the soil

> cannot be imposed. They must come from a sense of mission and dedication to a cause . . . Nationalist fervor has infected most middle class youth, but it is more a fervor "against" than "for" something—against "imperialism," "Zionism," "oppression," "foreign occupation" and the like. Not until there is an ardent desire to *work* for reform, to sacrifice not only on the field

of battle, but in the muddy fields along the Nile, will reform as hoped for by the Revolution have a pervasive effect in Egypt.

Those lines, like many of Edward Lane's, might have been written yesterday; they sound like an echo of Mubarak's speeches.

Mubarak is a practical man, a doer, a patient man who likes to undertake useful projects and see them through to conclusion. He seems to have liberated Egypt from the "Japanese monorail syndrome." This malady, of which the country suffered an epidemic in the mid-1970s, consists of the belief among a gullible public, encouraged by an undiscriminating press, that the Japanese will soon build a monorail to solve the transportation problem—or that the equivalent unlikely development will soon solve some other problem. Mubarak says there are no Japanese monorails; there is only hard work.

Egypt under Mubarak seems to be turning this psychological corner. Egyptians say they have begun to recognize that the state cannot be all things to all people, that initiative and hard work can be rewarding, and that they can lead better lives outside of Cairo than in the capital. Fewer Egyptians are looking for lifetime sinecures in the bureaucracy; more are looking for challenging jobs in private enterprise. Mubarak has urged the education establishment to emphasize technical and vocational instruction instead of turning out more unemployable liberal arts graduates. (The government's 1987–92 development plan calls for establishment of 100 industrial, agricultural and commercial secondary schools, although there is a nationwide shortage of vocational and technical instructors, since there never has been any demand for them.) Mubarak has also begun to attack the traditional rote-learning system.

> The aim should not be to concentrate the largest volume of information in the students' brains in an automatic and dumb way, and to measure their ability to retain and memorize this information; rather, the emphasis should be on developing their talent for inventiveness and creativeness and on polishing their character and training them to think and debate in an objective manner

he said in a 1987 speech. In the industrialized countries, he said, examinations emphasize thought and analysis, not repetition of undigested facts. "Our system should be like this."

That sounds encouraging, but it has to be understood in context: Sadat was saying similar things as long ago as 1974. In the "October Working Paper" he issued that year, the key policy document of his administration, Sadat demanded a change not just in curriculum but in attitude about education that would "eliminate the theory of the social difference between one form of education and another." He denounced the "overwhelming disease whereby many consider education as the instrument for acquiring a special social privilege, while the principal target for some educated people has become office jobs, irrespective of their value in the movement of society."

Mubarak has flailed away relentlessly at the attitude Sadat was describing, always emphasizing production and competence rather than status as the objective of education. But even as these changes are occurring, the gains they might imply for the nation are being outpaced by the inexorable and apparently uncontrollable increase in the population, and by the systemic maladies of the economy.

CHAPTER

4

A Rube Goldberg Economy

I f Egypt's economy could be reduced to a theoretical model, the designer would be neither Adam Smith nor Karl Marx, but Rube Goldberg.

Unlike many developing countries, where the economic system is based on the export of a single commodity—oil, bananas, copper—Egypt has an economy of awesome complexity, a baffling contrivance of odd angles and irrelevant protuberances, an assemblage of gadgets, a zany mixture of mismatched systems, of rich resources and inept management.

And yet the basic situation is easily comprehended: Egypt cannot feed, house or employ its fast-growing population. Promises of prosperity for most Egyptians are fraudulent, whether they are based on Nasser's egalitarian vision, Sadat's theatrical gestures or Mubarak's dogged appeals for greater output. Sadat, Mubarak and a long parade of highly skilled cabinet ministers have struggled against this reality for nearly two decades, and they have brought about salutary changes in the structure of the economy. But for every step forward there has been a step back; bad luck, bad management, conflicting demands on a shaky economic structure and the ever-accelerating growth of the population have left the economic morass almost as sticky as it was when Nasser died. The Egyptians who celebrated in the streets when they thought peace was imminent and prosperity not far behind were doomed to disappointment because the systemic flaws that undermined economic progress were too deep to be rooted out.

About 96 percent of Egypt's land is desert. There is not much more arable land for the population of 50 million than there was for a population of 10 million. Egypt must import food and distribute it at subsidized prices, because its citizens don't have enough money to pay market prices. Egypt cannot pay for these imports in Egyptian pounds, which are worthless outside Egypt. The country's hard currency resources are insufficient to meet the bill for the imports. And it lacks the capital to modernize and develop its industries so Egyptian products will be competitive in foreign markets and earn hard currency—that is, Egypt cannot become Japan, or even South Korea. Besides, a large portion of Egypt's foreign exchange earnings is committed to the payment of interest on an ever-increasing foreign debt.

Egypt has six major sources of the foreign currency it needs to finance its food imports and its debt. These are Suez Canal transit fees, oil, tourism, cotton, foreign aid and remittances from Egyptians working abroad. The early 1980s, the first years of Mubarak's presidency, were relatively good times as all six of these sources produced at high levels and allowed Egypt to paper over the inadequacies of the domestic economy.

But the oil component of this package fell apart with the worldwide decline in oil prices. Egypt's earnings from crude oil exports fell from $2.63 billion in 1985 to $686 million just a year later. Hundreds of thousands, perhaps millions, of Egyptians working in the major oil states—Saudi Arabia, Libya, Kuwait, the United Arab Emirates—lost their jobs as those economies contracted too. Not only did these Egyptians stop sending home dollars, they went home themselves, looking for jobs and houses.

At the same time, the bottom dropped out of the tourism business. Terrorists hijacked a cruise ship in the Mediterranean and an American airliner, frightening tourists away from the Middle East. Just as that scare was receding, the Egyptian security police rioted over pay and working conditions, burning down tourist hotels near the Pyramids. Hotel rooms, tour buses and restaurant seats went begging. Foreign aid leveled off; the U.S. commitment, which grew from zero to about $2 billion a year while Sadat was president, now is increasing only marginally.

The results can be found in one paragraph of the United States embassy's "Economic Trends Report" of September 1987:

Egypt in 1987 has been facing problems that are more serious than ever before. Egypt's fundamental problem is low productivity and inefficient allocation of resources resulting from excessive government regulation of economic decision-making, combined with a very rapid rate of population growth. It has also suffered from declining earnings from its principal exports. Low productivity has produced a growing balance-of-payments deficit as demand for imports has grown and exports have fallen, and as Egypt has borrowed abroad and then faced the need to service the debts. By early 1987, the Egyptian government was experiencing very serious liquidity problems [that is, the government didn't have any cash], with resulting delays in public-sector imports of both consumer and capital goods and accumulated arrearages in foreign debt repayment in excess of $5 billion.

Virtually every phrase of that gloomy assessment has a complicated background all its own. "Low productivity"—of course productivity is low in factories where the machinery, acquired from Eastern Europe in the Nasser era, is obsolete, where production quotas are irrelevant to market demand, and where employment rolls are swollen because of pressure on every enterprise to absorb as much manpower as possible. The obsolete machinery can't be replaced because of the shortage of hard currency required to import spare parts and new equipment. And the factories can't export enough to earn that hard currency, partly because their output is of low quality and relatively high cost, and partly because the Egyptians, in two decades of state control of the economy and negotiated barter trade with the socialist countries, completely forgot the concept of marketing, if they ever understood it. Why should the can of mango juice sold at a snack bar in Kuwait come from Taiwan instead of Egypt, a fraternal Arab state? Egypt has a big canned-food industry, and produces all the ingredients: mangoes, sugar, water and the aluminum for the can. The answer is that the Taiwanese, who have to sell to survive, hustled into Kuwait and signed a deal with a distributor. The Egyptian enterprise, owned by the state, never made a bid.

It does not require a profound knowledge of economics to look at the ledger sheet and understand the magnitude of Egypt's difficulties. The domestic budget deficit for the 1986–87 fiscal year was 7.2 billion Egyptian pounds. Total state revenues were 12.4 billion pounds, which means the budget was in deficit by 58 percent. The deficit figures were similar for several preceding years. According to World Bank figures, the Egyptian economy grew at a real average annual rate of 6.4 percent from 1973, the year of the October war, through 1983—one of the best economic performances in the developing world. But by 1987 the growth rate of the economy was negative, by at least 1.5 percent. The 1987 foreign trade deficit was $5.5 billion; it had been at least $6.3 billion in each of the three preceding years. Hard-currency foreign debt, which was virtually nil at the time of the 1952 revolution, had reached $44.1 billion by 1987; even after an agreement with the International Monetary Fund led to a rescheduling of payment on that debt and a reduction in interest rates, Egypt remained $5 billion in arrears on debt service. The consumer price increase was officially calculated at 25 percent, up from 20 percent in 1986, putting a tight squeeze on millions of workers in the government and publicly owned industries whose incomes are fixed.

Of course, those figures do not reflect the activity of a vigorous off-the-books economy. The country is poor, but many of its citizens are not; even a superficial look at the flashy shops and restaurants in Cairo and the expensive beach clubs of Alexandria and the demand for appliances such as refrigerators and color television sets confirms the presence of an abundance of cash. But besides being inefficient, the Egyptian economy is now ludicrously out of balance. To understand what this means to ordinary citizens, it is necessary to see the economy as they see it, not as the bankers and theoreticians and World Bank economists see it.

For more than two decades, under three presidents, the exchange value of the Egyptian pound was determined by what George Bush might call "voodoo economics." The rate was controlled by the government, but varied according to type of transaction and affiliation of the parties making the exchange. The official rate was different from the tourist rate, which was of course different from the black market rate. Through most of the Sadat years and well into the 1980s, the most common rate was that given to tourists and foreign residents when they exchanged dollars at a bank: one Egyptian pound equaled about $1.43. In the spring of 1987, the government engineered an overnight devaluation, aimed at bringing the exchange rate into line with the "parallel" or black market; the value of the pound dropped to 48 cents.

For an American tourist, this meant that a dinner that cost $25 on Monday cost only about $10 two nights later. But most Egyptians don't conduct economic dealings in dollars. They live within the domestic economy; they are paid in Egyptian money and they make their purchases in Egyptian money—pounds and *piasters,* 100 *piasters* to the pound. The value of the dollar is significant only to the extent that they buy imported goods, which most Egyptians rarely do. In this domestic context, the economy is irrational and a constant political irritant. There appears to be less and less correlation between education or productivity and income, and no correlation between income and price structure. The result is social dislocation and political discontent.

Here is how the marketplace looked to Egyptian consumers in mid-1987.

Sample incomes:

Primary school teacher: 54 pounds a month to start.

Police recruit: 13 pounds a month; his officer, a career captain: about 200.

Car parker on a Cairo street: 500 pounds a month (estimated, of course).

Shirt folder in a privately owned clothing factory: 110 pounds a month.

Museum guard: 58 pounds a month.

Assembly-line worker in a private sector refrigerator factory: 275 pounds a month; in a nearby plumbing fixture factory: 150 to 400 pounds, on a piecework basis.

Suffragi or housekeeper for an Egyptian family: 200 pounds a month; for a foreign family, considerably more, depending on experience and knowledge of English.

Ticket clerk in a privately owned travel agency: about 150 pounds a month.

The purchasing power of those incomes can be judged from this sampling of prices:

Factory-made cotton dress shirt: 18.9 pounds.

Tomatoes: 30 *piasters* per kilogram at the Tewfikiya Street vegetable market in downtown Cairo; less in the countryside.

Bananas: one Egyptian pound per kilogram; dates: two pounds; potatoes: 35 *piasters.*

Mutton: eight pounds per kilogram; camel meat: four pounds.

Box of "Carmen" brand tissues: one pound.

Locally assembled small car: 10,000 pounds.

Refrigerator, 10.5 cubic feet: 398 pounds for the Egyptian-made model, 675 pounds for a foreign model made in Egypt under license.

Visit to doctor in private clinic: 20 pounds.

Two room apartment in Tenth of Ramadan City, northeast of Cairo: 5,000 pounds.

Bottle of locally made Pepsi-Cola: 10 *piasters*.

These numbers mean that the ragged illiterate who controls curbside parking on a downtown Cairo block can buy a refrigerator but the schoolteacher cannot; they mean that working-class Egyptians rarely eat meat; they mean that prenatal care is beyond the reach of most pregnant women. The significance of the prices is magnified by the context. Nasser nationalized Egypt's banks, insurance companies and major industries. He also instituted a policy of guaranteeing a government job to every university graduate, which led inevitably to absurdly bloated payrolls in the civil service and the state-owned industries. The result was that by the time Mubarak became president, about 3.7 million workers in a total labor force of just under 13 million were employed by the state, either in the civil service or in a publicly owned enterprise. About half the labor force is employed in agriculture, which means that more than half of all non-agricultural workers are on the public payroll. Those workers on the public payroll, whose salaries the state cannot afford to increase, are the people most affected by inflation, the high cost of housing and the gap between aspiration and fulfillment.

Consider, for example, the schoolteacher, a university graduate, now employed at a starting salary of 54 pounds a month. It's unlikely that he or she can afford an apartment in Cairo or Alexandria, where there is a chronic housing shortage. If mutton costs eight pounds a kilo, how often can the teacher buy it? A factory-made shirt costs a third of a month's salary. And as for a car, which every urban Egyptian dreams of owning, where is the schoolteacher going to get 10,000 pounds? And what is the teacher to make of his or her contemporaries whose parents were able to cash in on the economic liberalization under Sadat and are now driving around in Mercedes-Benzes?

Egypt's economic distress did not develop overnight, or for any one reason. The economy is as complex as it is feeble. The World Bank's "country economic report" on Egypt, published in

1980, is 444 pages long. But in essence, Egypt's problem is one of too many people on not enough land, combined with misguided leadership, flawed policy and the effects of three decades of war.

Before the 1952 revolution, and even for a few years after it, Egypt had a laissez-faire economy built on cotton and textiles and dominated by powerful landowning "pashas," the rich bourgeoisie and foreigners. The country fed itself on cereal grains, rice and vegetables. Industrialization had begun under Muhammad Ali in the nineteenth century; by World War II, Egypt had passed the "import substitution" phase of development, diversifying into products for export such as furniture. Telegraph lines and railways came to Egypt not long after they were developed in Europe, and there was a sophisticated network of financial institutions. The condition of the masses was abject, but Egypt was still far ahead of its Arab and African neighbors.

Nasser and the other military officers who deposed the king had no economic program and no collective ideology beyond their nationalism and a general desire to improve conditions. They adopted a land-reform program that broke up the hereditary estates, but otherwise their economic policies in the beginning were conservative and traditional. Encouraging the leaders of business and reassuring the middle class, they offered tax exemptions to new corporations, and other business incentives. They raised tariffs, supported an industrial development bank and welcomed foreign private investors.

The Suez war of 1956 began a series of events that were to reverse that economic alignment and precipitate a chain of misfortunes and mistakes that left the country virtually bankrupt by the time Nasser died. Nasser responded to the "tripartite aggression" of Britain, France and Israel by seizing British, French and Jewish assets and placing them under state control. That roundup began an assault on the primacy of private enterprise that was to end in a total victory for state power over the economy.

Nationalization of the Bank Misr and the National Bank of Egypt in 1960 was followed by the comprehensive nationalization laws of 1961, under which the state took over virtually every commercial and industrial enterprise with 50 or more employees. Nasser's government did not collectivize agriculture or seize the property and businesses of small shopkeepers or artisans. But his war against the bourgeoisie, whom he considered politically unreliable, and his determination to channel the country's resources into industrialization—at the expense of agriculture—led to state domination of every important sector of the economy. By the time Sadat became president, the state owned not only the banks and insurance companies but all energy and utility organizations, the metallurgical and textile plants, the airline, the railroads and most maritime transport, the film studios and distributors, the newspapers, all major construction companies, the oil refineries, the fertilizer industry and even the department stores, though these bore and still bear the names of the families that once owned them. The state controlled the Suez Canal, all ports and airports, the High Dam, agricultural credit and food distribution, and all allocations of foreign currency. In addition, through its control of credit, export services and food distribution, the state was able to force farmers to accept below-market prices for their exportable output, especially cotton, so that money raised from the sale of these commodities abroad could be directed into industrial development. As John Waterbury, an American scholar who lived in Egypt for many years, has observed, "few developing countries other than those that are professedly Marxist ever cut so deeply into their private sectors as Egypt."

Nasser's government also committed itself ever more heavily to government spending to improve conditions for the impoverished peasants and urban workers. Social welfare programs, health clinics and primary schools were extended to the villages, and the state set up a nationwide chain of cooperative grocery stores that sold basic foodstuffs and rationed commodities such as meat and rice at subsidized prices. These commitments were undertaken just as external events were combining to limit the government's resources.

Egypt's intervention in the civil war in Yemen, which kept more than 50,000 troops tied down at the end of a long supply line, was as costly economically as it was futile militarily. Then came the 1967 rout by Israel, which not only closed the Suez Canal and cut off its revenues, but also forced hundreds of thousands of residents of Ismailia, Port Said and Suez City to flee; they became refugees in their own country, and the state was obliged to care for them. Tourism dwindled, as did investment, because of the ever-present threat of war. The cutoff of American aid that followed the break in relations forced the government to buy wheat for cash on the world

market. Military debts to the Soviet Union, payable in hard currency, mounted swiftly.

By the early years of Sadat's rule, the country's hard currency
external debt exceeded the value of the gross national product. The
national budget showed chronic deficits. And the country was
unable to meet its short-term debt service obligations. At the time
of the October war in 1973, Egypt was unable to pay anything on
its debts or to buy any more wheat to feed its people.

The Egyptian pound then had a nominal official value of
$2.50, but this was an artificial rate used for bookkeeping purposes
in international transactions; its actual value was far less. Individual
Egyptians were prohibited from possessing foreign currency, so the
exchange rate and the external value of the pound mattered little to
them, but the government, shopping abroad for food, weapons and
industrial supplies and parts, was obliged either to pay in hard
currency—which it lacked—or to negotiate barter deals, usually
with communist countries. (In a typical arrangement, Bulgaria
accepted a shipload of Egyptian wine in exchange for 10,000 live
sheep.) The availability of goods in Egyptian markets often depended upon what the ministry of supply could find in the way of
foreign manufacturers and trading companies that were willing to
sell to Egypt on credit or make barter deals; as a result, the markets
in Egypt were poorly stocked with inferior merchandise—Czech
light bulbs, for example, medical instruments from Poland and jam
from Romania.

As Sadat was fond of saying, Egypt was "below zero" economically when he became president, and the economic conditions
shaped his agenda. Peace with Israel, the resuscitation of private
enterprise and the turn to the West for capital and technology were
to be instruments of an economic revival that he perceived as
essential to the preservation of order and the restoration of dignity
in a desperate country. It is easy to say now, as Sadat's many critics
do, that he shamed the country by making a separate peace with
Israel and that his economic policies succeeded only in enriching a
parasite class of middlemen and opportunists, not in bringing
prosperity. After all, the country is still unable to meet its debt
service obligations, the budget is still in deficit and investment
capital is still scarce, in spite of all the changes Sadat made. But his
policies had the approval of the nation until it became clear they
would not succeed; no one wanted to continue on the course that

Nasser had set. And if Sadat and his government failed to wrestle the economy into prosperity, the reasons lie at least as much in the conditions they inherited as in their own inadequacy.

"Planning for Economic Development in Egypt," a summary of the ministry of planning's comprehensive development plan for the years 1978 to 1982, said that

> political wisdom and simple justice call for the alleviation of the burdens of the masses. They deserve respite, for they have given much when Egypt has required it of them, socially, politically and militarily. Political wisdom further recognizes the inherent danger in allowing the standard of living of the majority to continue to deteriorate, when they can see around them luxurious consumption and special privileges. It is only human that they should feel discontent, fear and envy.

Those are unexceptionable sentiments; the words are still applicable, and they show that the Sadat government was not blind to the political volatility of the economic situation. But the economic planners were, in effect, starting so far behind their own goal line that they could not win the game.

Nasser's industrialization was unplanned and haphazard; Egypt lacked the technological base and complex infrastructure required to support heavy industry and the management capability to operate it. Ostracism of the bourgeoisie and the managerial class had stripped the factories of people who knew how to run them; the imposition of political watchdogs sent in by the Arab Socialist Union to ensure the political reliability of the new managers inhibited their power, and their willingness, to make decisions.

Because only those citizens with incomes of more than 1,000 pounds a year—that is, only a handful of people—were taxed, industry was expected to provide the funds to pay for the expanding social welfare commitments. But negative balance sheets were virtually built in as the industries grew. The shortage of raw materials made it necessary to import the commodities needed to keep the factories running. When a dearth of hard currency cut those imports, production lines slowed or stopped. Labor laws aimed at protecting the workers from dismissal and at raising their incomes resulted, inevitably, in redundant staffing and low productivity. Military requirements drained off funds that should have been used for maintenance, new equipment and technical training, with the result that some plants were obsolete almost as soon as they were built. (Military expenditures were not regularly disclosed, but in 1976 the finance minister, Ahmed Abu Ismail, put the figure at 1.3 billion pounds, exclusive of debt repayment to the Soviet Union. At the time, Egypt's gross domestic product was 6.2 billion pounds.)

Sadat, in liberalizing the economy and encouraging the re-development of private enterprise, still proclaimed his adherence to the "socialist solution" as the foundation of the economy, which in practice means that almost all major industrial enterprises and economic institutions are state-owned and state-run. As analyzed in the 1978 five-year plan, Egypt is

> a socialist society which thinks with a capitalist mind, which takes from socialism and communism the concepts of public ownership, dominance of the public sector, guaranteed employment, education and social security, but neglects to take firm enforcement of civil authority or condemn the carelessness which decreases productivity. Similarly, the government has taken from capitalism the features of consumption and inter-class mobility, the concept of the importance of the individual and of his historical tradition. But it has not adopted from the capitalist system the stringency of market competition or the responsibility of the firm for quality control, upon which stands the success or failure of the firm. Nor has it gone so far as to endorse the idea that the right to work and earn is for those who produce and not necessarily for all. The end result is a society lacking in discipline or supervision: distribution without production, promises without obligations, freedom without responsibility.

That document was refreshingly free of the palliatives and false hopes customarily dispensed by the Cairo press. It described the inevitable result of years in which the state assumed all responsibility and controlled all initiative: a coddled and selfish society, reaping benefits to which it had come to believe it was entitled, forfeiting responsibility to the government and unmotivated by the slogans that substituted for political leadership.

"The characteristic ineptitude of popular political organizations," the planning document said,

> has led to the assumption by the government of more and more public responsibility. Thus it has come about that the government's domestic responsibilities exceed its capabilities and avail-

able resources . . . a summary of the government's present
duties toward the people looks like this:
1. The government guarantees unconditional employment
and earnings to all.
2. It provides social welfare through housing, health, education and other services.
3. It protects the consumer from the increase in the cost of
living (through subsidies.)
4. It administers all public utilities and most units of national production.
5. It provides the public with both necessities and luxuries, from bread to motion picture films.

The cost of maintaining those services far exceeded the revenue
available to pay for them, as it still does a decade later. In 1979, the
state budget of 6.7 billion pounds projected a deficit of 2.46 billion;
by 1987, the projected deficit was 7.2 billion. The difference, of
course, must be borrowed from abroad—increasing the debt the
country cannot pay—or borrowed from the central bank—that is,
printed, which only aggravates inflationary trends. Mubarak, like
Sadat, has struggled with this quandary: the measures that would
bring the budget under control cannot be reconciled with the
commitment to maintain and even increase the level of benefits
bestowed on the public. The widespread "bread riots" of January
1977, which presented a dangerous challenge to Sadat's regime,
were touched off by sudden increases in food prices. They demonstrated the political impracticality of any abrupt or serious curtailment of the benefits Egypt's people have come to rely on. And
while state revenues have risen dramatically since 1974, the need to
rebuild basic public facilities such as sewer lines that were neglected
under Nasser, combined with the relentless growth of the population, has soaked up resources faster than the state can generate
them.
　　In theory the Sadat government committed itself to tax increases and structural tax reform that would raise domestic revenues, but the actual potential of taxation is limited. Relatively few
individuals have substantial cash incomes. Major state-owned businesses are subject to taxation, but only on their profits, if any, and in
any case that form of taxation amounts to robbing Peter to pay
Paul. New enterprises established with foreign capital since 1974
have been granted tax concessions. A proposal to impose a European-style value-added tax, floated by the finance ministry in 1978,

was ridiculed because such a tax would require accurate records, organized inventories and the cooperation of wholesalers, none of which was available. Besides, the tax administration system would have been unable to monitor and collect such a tax. World Bank analysts who studied the taxation system at the end of the 1970s concluded that "the inadequacy of tax administration is an important issue that stems from traditional causes: insufficient staff, a lack of office space and equipment, and corruption among the poorly-paid tax officials who often deal with large amounts of tax money."

Attempts to improve the tax collection system included an offer of incentives to tax workers who brought in additional revenue, but there was a ceiling on these payments of four times the monthly salary, still not enough to discourage corruption. Overall, the World Bank team concluded,

> the recent changes in the tax structure, especially the inclusion of agricultural income in the general income tax and the creation of the tax on some capital transactions, will place an additional burden on the tax administration. This burden will become even greater when general sales taxes are introduced and the tariff structure is reformed. In other words, the future problems of tax administration will certainly be more complicated than the present ones.

State revenue would have been increased if the state-owned industries had been able to increase their prices to realistic levels, but this was not possible for the same reason it was not possible to eliminate direct government subsidy of food prices: the public could not afford to pay. Farm prices were controlled by the government, as were industrial and civil-service wages. Egyptians dependent on those sources of income, which means most Egyptians, simply did not have the cash to absorb the price increases for basic products—fruit juice, batteries, soap, cigarettes—that would have been necessary to increase revenues in the state-owned factories that produced them. For the most part, they still do not, and the price structure remains unrealistic, a form of subsidy that cannot be eliminated.

Another way to cut the deficit, which Mubarak stresses in all his public discussions of the economy, just as Sadat did, would be to increase industrial productivity, output and quality. That would make manufactured goods available for export, satisfy domestic demand for finished products and reduce the drain on the treasury caused by the need to subsidize money-losing industries. Some important steps in this direction have been taken. American aid funds, for example, were used to reequip and modernize the main textile mills at Mahalla el-Kobra. But some of the largest industrial enterprises probably can never be transformed into productive components of the economy.

Sadat was often accused by the left-wing opposition of trying to dismantle the enormous, clumsy apparatus of the state-owned industries. But he could not have done so even if he had wanted to, at least not directly or in the short term. It was not possible politically or economically, even though the publicly owned industries turned out to be a constant drain on the state's resources. The state owned and supported an industrial base that it could not afford but could not dismantle because it employed about 12 percent of the civilian labor force and, as Waterbury argues, was an indispensable "instrument of political and economic control."

I had been in Egypt only a few weeks when I first heard the joke about two Israeli pilots who flew over Egypt and bombed the Helwan Iron and Steel plant, halting its operations. When they got home, they were court-martialed for helping the Egyptian economy.

The giant steel mill at Helwan, south of Cairo, is a classic Third-World white elephant; it has never shown a profit, even though Egypt is self-sufficient in iron ore. Through one agency or another, the state provided the steel mill with subsidized energy, cheap labor, subsidized transportation and a guaranteed market for some products. Added to the cost of imported coking coal, these subsidies ensured that steel made at Helwan would be more expensive for Egypt than imported steel.

But the plant could not be sold—who would buy it? And it could not be closed—who would employ the 20,000 workers who depended on it for a living? The plant was a showcase of Nasser's commitment to industrialization and of Soviet aid to Egypt. It is the biggest industrial enterprise in the country and one of the largest in the Middle East. Unfortunately, it was obsolete almost as soon as it was built in its present form, a Soviet-financed expansion atop the original German-built plant. It was one of the last integrated steel mills in the world to be constructed without computers.

Even with a reliable supply of domestic iron ore, it cost more to produce steel at Helwan than it would to import it. By the mid-1970s production was at little more than half of theoretical capacity, and what was being produced was of erratic and unreliable quality. Export sales in 1975 brought in $21 million in foreign currency, but it cost more than that to import the coking coal, spare parts and vehicles needed to operate the plant.

When I asked Abu Bakr Mourad, the chairman of the Iron and Steel Company, what was wrong, he replied, "We need help. We need help in the seven big Ms of industry—management, manpower, machines, money, method, materials and marketing."

Accustomed to being told how well things were going, I said, "You are being unusually frank."

"How can I hide this?" he said. "I'm leaving tomorrow for the United States to ask for help." He said he wanted technical and design assistance to enable the plant to build its own replacement equipment and the basic machinery for other industries. "Anybody can buy a plant abroad," he said, "but you can never say you are industrialized unless you can make your own means of production."

Mourad, a British-trained engineer who typified the management of state-owned industries, said there was "nothing to be ashamed of" in the steel mill's performance because "steel industries in all countries have long gestation periods." In the West, he said, "there has been a revolution in management, the second industrial revolution. If we can adopt your Western management systems, we will get good results."

Of course, "Western management systems" would have required the dismissal of a great number of the plant's employees. Mourad, like all industrial administrators in the state enterprises, had to live with labor laws that make such dismissals impossible.

There were still 500 Soviet technicians at Helwan even after the abrogation of the friendship treaty. Their job was to install new equipment and show the Egyptians how to use it, but Mourad was more concerned with how to keep the equipment he already had operable. With a grant of $835,575 from the United Nations Industrial Development Organization, he brought in a team from United States Steel to look over the plant and make recommendations to improve its efficiency.

The Americans found that the plant, though obsolete, was

basically sound in design and well-constructed. The problems lay in operation and management. For example, they discovered that while the Iron and Steel Company has its own plant at Helwan for converting imported coal into coke for the furnaces, backlogs and delays in the port of Alexandria sometimes interrupted the coal shipments, cutting back operations at the steel plant.

While the plant as a whole was overstaffed, there was a shortage of technicians and middle-level managers; because salaries were so low, they left for better opportunities elsewhere. In the four preceding years, about 3,500 had left, mostly for other Arab countries that were developing steel industries of their own. Their absence, and the tendency of senior engineers to spend their time at their desks instead of on the shop floor, left workers unsupervised and invited corruption among purchasing clerks that left gaps in supply lines. Improper use of equipment caused extensive breakage, so much so that key units of the plant were operating at only 20 percent of capacity. One American told me of an expensive piece of imported gear that would have had a life expectancy of 10 years in an American or Japanese plant but lasted only four days at Helwan.

Most serious of all, the consultants found, were the shortcomings in maintenance and spare parts supply. A modern steel mill, they said, should have a system for predicting parts failures, setting up a preventive maintenance schedule and manufacturing and storing the parts. Helwan did not, so the plant was plagued by unexpected breakdowns that could not be repaired quickly because the necessary parts were not on hand.

Operations at another major industrial complex in Helwan, the Nasr [Victory] Automotive Co., were hindered by a different, but equally intractable, set of constraints and problems. Nasr Automotive produces tractors, buses, trucks and passenger cars, mostly foreign models built under license with a high percentage of imported parts.

Entering the era of peace in the mid-1970s, Egypt had a limitless need for buses, both to replace the battered, exhausted vehicles then on the roads and to meet the growing demand for mass transit. The ministry of transportation arranged to purchase several hundred from the Iranian subsidiary of Mercedes; when the American aid program was reestablished, the United States provided 1,600 more. Egypt would have saved many millions of dollars if the Nasr plant had been able to supply those buses, but it could not. Its capacity was 50 buses a month.

I asked Salah Abdel Fattah, the director of the truck and bus plant, why he did not just put his bus assembly line on double shifts and the workers on overtime. The reason it could not be done, he said, was that the plant's suppliers could not deliver the components and materials needed to run the assembly line for those extra hours. Egyptian industry had progressed to the point where most of the parts for the buses—engine blocks, window glass, tires, batteries, seats, crankshafts, paint, axles—were manufactured domestically. It had not progressed to the point where the output of all those components could be orchestrated to increase the production of the vehicles in which they were to be combined.

Besides, Abdel Fattah said, a bus produced in the Nasr plant, even though made mostly from domestic components, was more expensive than an imported bus. "A private enterprise can beat our price," he said, "because here we have maybe 10 persons to do the work of one over there. We are not liberated from the economic rules of the country, you know."

The fact that it cost more to produce a bus in Helwan, where workers then were paid about 65 pounds a month, was not the full measure of the inefficiency built into the operation. Like all industrial enterprises in Egypt, the Nasr plant benefited (and still benefits) from cheap electricity, and from the ability to purchase domestic components such as cloth at controlled, subsidized prices. If the company had to pay world market prices for energy and components, to say nothing of labor, it would be even less competitive than it is. The power plant and factories that are supplying the components and energy at below-market prices can do so because they in turn are subsidized by the government. This accounted for the nominal profitability of the public sector. But the combination of subsidies and a captive market meant that the Nasr plant, like most of the public industries, was never subject to the discipline of the competitive marketplace, and it showed.

The Iron and Steel Company and Nasr Automotive were among the largest and most visibly inefficient of the state industries, but they were hardly isolated examples. No one was surprised when World Bank analysts found systemic inefficiency, misallocation of resources and raw materials, and underutilized plant capacity throughout this sector of the economy.

Inefficient industries, onerous subsidies, an empty treasury, stagnant agricultural production, minimal private investment—such was the situation after the October war when Sadat, still the "Hero of the Crossing," set out to transform the domestic economy.

"Our national responsibility does not permit us to miss such an opportunity," he said in the "October Working Paper," the basic policy document of his administration, which was presented to the People's Assembly in April 1974 and approved in a referendum the next month. The economy would have to be opened to financial and technical participation from abroad, he said. Egypt would actively seek investment from the Arab oil countries with their skyrocketing revenues, and would "accept unconditional aid and loans, as well as direct investment in such fields of modern development as require world expertise."

The "public sector" would remain the cornerstone of the economy, the "basic instrument of expressing the national will in shaping our national economy." But the relative roles of the public and private economies should be redefined, with the public sector relieved of "annexed" responsibilities for which it was ill-suited. Within a planned framework, foreign investment would be welcomed. Priority would be given to modernized industry, tourism, oil and energy development and intensive agriculture—the last through what he later came to call the "green revolution."

This was the new industrial and economic policy known as *infitah,* the opening or "Open Door." Its most important element was Law 43, enacted by the People's Assembly in 1974. On paper, if not immediately in practice, it transformed the country's economic—and, by extension, political—landscape. It allowed the creation of private companies that were not subject to profit-sharing formulae or salary ceilings. These companies were not required to have worker representation on their boards of directors and were exempted from the compulsory employment of university graduates. Foreign investment was encouraged; an Investment Authority, established by Law 43 to designate which projects would be approved, would give priority to those that could export enough to become self-sufficient in foreign exchange, bring in advanced technology or substitute for imports. The state's banking monopoly was abolished. The law provided that in joint ventures between private companies and the public sector, private-sector rules would apply. Enterprises established under Law 43 were to receive liberal exemptions from taxes and customs duties on imported equipment.

What this meant in practice was that market forces were to be allowed to supersede state planning in shaping the future of the economy. Sadat and his planners wanted to leave the public sector in place but rely on private investment for economic expansion and absorption of growth in the labor force. A hybrid was to be created—a market economy with a greater public-sector component than was to be found in any other market economy. Entrepreneurism was to replace egalitarianism as the engine driving economic expansion.

This would have been a difficult feat to manage in the most orderly and efficient of societies; in Egypt it seems to have brought political grief and economic distortion without much of the progress—the "trickle-down benefits," so to speak—that was envisioned.

It quickly became a joke, then a cliché, that the door to Egypt was open but nobody would go through it. Imported influence in the marketplace became visible almost overnight as consumer goods flooded the country, feeding a pent-up demand, but imported investment capital was much slower to arrive. The political and psychological climate for foreign investment was favorable, but investors wanted to know if they could make money. Those who explored Egypt for investment opportunities found a depressing list of disincentives.

The country's physical plant was utterly unprepared to accommodate foreign-financed industrial expansion. The years of neglected and underfinanced maintenance under Nasser now extracted their revenge. Telephone service was among the world's worst, and no new lines were available. International communications such as telex were scarce and unreliable. Cairo Airport, the only international airport, was overwhelmed. Traffic on the urban roads was at a standstill. Sewer and water lines, where they existed, were antiquated and overloaded. Modern office space was nonexistent. Warehouses were scarce. The port of Alexandria was notorious for inefficiency, delays and corruption among its customs officials.

The bureaucracy resisted change. Different departments of the government often worked at cross-purposes. The Investment Authority was undermanned and incompetent.

Fear of war was receding and the new laws provided guarantees against expropriation of investments, but at the same time the other Arab nations, which were flush with oil cash and had been expected to be a prime source of investment capital, had cut off investment in Egypt because of their opposition to Egypt's agreements with Israel.

Egypt's domestic market, though vast, was economically weak: the people did not have much money to spend, and they certainly did not have any convertible currency. This meant that foreign investors would have to convert their Egyptian profits, if any, into foreign currency to repatriate them, but unrealistic exchange rates wiped out their gains. Nor could foreign investors expect to make hard-currency profits by exporting manufactured goods from Egypt. In a paper known as the "Suter Report," a cold-eyed analysis of *infitah* issued by the Egypt-U.S. Business Council, New York banker Lauren J. Suter wrote that investors were unlikely to put their money into Egyptian ventures that required export of their products.

"With some exceptions, such as cotton and textiles," he wrote, Egypt "suffers from a reputation—as it does within Egypt itself—for producing inferior goods. This is a strong deterrent to many potential investors, one of whom said that he could not risk the reputation of his company or his markets in other countries by exporting Egyptian-made products under his name." Suter and the Business Council recommended that the Egyptians drop their insistence on manufacturing for export and allow foreign firms to manufacture consumer goods for the domestic market, liberalizing currency exchange rules to permit the repatriation of profits. The Egyptians did do that in industries where domestic output was of insufficient quantity or quality to meet domestic demand, such as soft drinks, razor blades and batteries. Union Carbide Corporation, for example, was an early entrant and now produces a full line of its Eveready household batteries in Egypt. But the venture lost money for five years because rising world prices for raw materials forced Union Carbide to raise its prices while its Egyptian competitors, public-sector companies, did not. Their hidden subsidies from the state allowed them to absorb the price increases, leaving price differentials of up to 130 percent between their products and Eveready. Union Carbide executives say their marketing and distribution expertise, and their flexibility in adjusting product line to changing demand, finally enabled them to overcome the price disadvantage, but how many other potential investors dropped out rather than go through a similar experience?

Mubarak has often said that he is not interested in theoretical or political debate over whether the public or private sectors should dominate the Egyptian economy. His view is that both are essential and the balancing act must continue. In a 1987 speech he said:

> The equipment being used in a certain public sector factories dates back to 1938. You can imagine the output of these factories. The previous [five-year development] plan called for the modernization of factories in order to increase the production of the public sector and, consequently, to promote revenues. While most factories recorded losses in the past, now only 11 percent of them do. Although this figure is still high, we should not seek to get rid of the public sector. Anyway, I will not allow this, because it is the sole guarantee allowing the poor people to purchase their basic needs.

But the private economy is also essential, he said.

> My interest in the private sector is similar to my interest in the public sector. This is because the public sector can never meet all of the needs of the citizens. The private sector bears the brunt in meeting those needs which the public sector cannot. It is a sound concept that the two sectors are two sides of one coin, and that there are vast opportunities for each one to expand. . . . It is unacceptable to arouse this controversy at a time when all states in the East and West are pursuing a practical course that does not adhere to rigid ideological molds.

The five-year economic development plan approved in 1987 sets a goal of nearly equal public and private participation in economic development. But both sectors face insuperable obstacles in carrying the burdens that the country is placing upon them.

It is too late now to debate whether large-scale industrialization was appropriate for Egypt in the first place. In the postcolonial context, it was a political necessity: industry was understood to be the key to modernization and economic independence. But Nasser imposed on the industrial operations conditions that made it impossible for them to function efficiently or productively.

Factory managers were selected as much for political reliability as for competence. They operated under the eye of suspicious

cadres from the Arab Socialist Union, without any clear understanding of their objectives: make a profit, meet production quotas,
employ as many workers as possible, substitute for imports, or all of
those. Shortages of foreign currency and hostile relations with the
West led to an increasing reliance on Eastern European and Soviet
machinery and design. Because marketing policies were set by the
dictates of politics, not economics, and because there was no competition, nobody worried about marketing the products or backing
them up with service.

Labor laws mandated overstaffing by ratios as high as six to
one, and undercut managerial authority. Under a 1963 decree, four
of the nine directors of each major industrial establishment were
selected from the ranks of the workers; managers naturally complained that those delegates were interested only in higher wages
and less work. They could be outvoted, but their obstructionist
potential was guaranteed.

"In each large factory," Raymond Baker wrote,

> there existed: a labor union, a joint labor-management con-
> sultative committee, worker members of the board of directors,
> and the Arab Socialist Union Committee. All four groups acted
> as "popular" restraints on the managers, while their mutual
> rivalry prevented any one of them from assuming a too power-
> ful role in the institutional framework.

The Americans, planning their long-range aid program in the
mid-1970s, commissioned the consulting firm of Arthur D. Little
Inc. to make a comprehensive assessment of Egyptian industry. The
Little report, "An Assessment of Egypt's Industrial Sector," published in January 1978, found managerial failures to be even greater
than technological shortcomings; the managerial and administrative handicaps imposed on the industries by Nasser had not
been corrected under Sadat. The report said:

> The wealth of trained technological talent produced in
> Egypt's universities has tended to flow to other countries
> through emigration in the face of limited economic and career
> opportunities for Egyptian technologists at home and the high
> pay offered in Arab petroleum exporting countries. The condi-
> tions have been made more constraining over the last 20 years
> by shortages in Egypt of foreign exchange needed to maintain
> or acquire equipment, to finance international travel and educa-

tion, and to secure specialized technical assistance from abroad
(except through United Nations channels).

In fact, those engineers and technologists who had gone
abroad were sending home an abundance of the very hard currency
Egypt needed; but because of the unrealistic exchange rates these
funds were mostly converted into Egyptian pounds on
the black market, which diverted the hard currency away from the
public-sector banks and state industries. This was not fully corrected until the devaluation of 1987, but by that time much of the
flow of cash from the oil states had dried up.

The Little report also found that after nationalization,

> very few managers raised in a competitive business environment
> were left in Egypt. Many of the businesses had been run by
> foreigners who left. . . . Nationalized companies depleted of
> management were generally taken over by military or university
> personnel who often learned management by trial and error. In
> addition to the initial large-scale loss of trained management,
> the lack of a competitive environment in Egypt after na-
> tionalization led to a virtual lost generation trained in manage-
> ment decision-making under uncertainty, a shortage of indus-
> trial entrepreneurism, the disappearance of salesmen, and
> neglect of financial management as a profession.

These were not deficiencies that could be corrected by Law 43.

One of the great ironies of modern Egyptian history is that
Nasser, who claimed leadership of the entire Arab world, forfeited
Egypt's opportunity to establish a dominant economic position
within it. When oil wealth began to stimulate development in Saudi
Arabia, Kuwait, Iraq and Libya, Egypt might have entered the
competition to supply them with farm equipment, steel, trucks,
canned food, communications equipment, electrical gear, coastal
ships, textiles and fertilizers, all of which they needed and
Egypt produced. But Nasser's industrial policies ensured that
Egypt would be cut out of those markets.

Had the Egyptians been functioning in a competitive environment, they would have been well-positioned to make advantageous
contracts in the oil states because of nationalist sentiment, prox-
imity, and the fact that tens of thousands of Egyptians worked in
the banks, ministries and trading houses of those nations, whose

leaders were often Egyptian-educated. Now those opportunities have evaporated. The oil states have built up their own industrial sectors, and they leapfrogged over Egypt to establish supply and technology contracts with Europe and the Far Eastern countries. That is why the mango juice in Kuwait comes from Taiwan, not Egypt; it is why the Saudis, looking for a supplier of airfreighted lunches for 200,000 schoolchildren, bypassed Egypt, going all the way to France to get them; it is why the fabrics in the *souks* of Dubai and Jeddah come from Japan, Korea and Europe, not Egypt.

The Egyptians were of course well aware of the deficiencies of their industrial network. They have committed hundreds of millions of pounds to new equipment and plants and to the infrastructure of utilities, roads, pipelines and water supply needed to support them; and for more than a decade they have tried to correct the organizational deficiencies. A law approved in 1978 allowed public-sector companies greater flexibility in organizing their work forces and authorized payment of incentive bonuses to encourage productivity. Companies were allowed to invest up to 750,000 pounds without approval of the ministry of industry. Some industrial commodities were removed from the list of items covered by price controls, and export restrictions have been loosened to encourage sales to foreign customers. But lack of marketing expertise has been a crucial handicap.

An American public relations consultant, for example, received an inquiry from Egypt's perfume establishment about the possibility of promoting Egyptian perfume in the United States. The American wanted to know whether any market research had been done here, whether prices would be competitive and whether delivery schedules would be met if there were any orders. But first he asked how much money would be available to undertake the promotional campaign. The answer was $10,000—negligible—so he dropped it.

The marketing director of the state wineries told me he was having great difficulty in finding any sales outlets in Europe, where he thought Egyptian wines could compete with those of Lebanon, Algeria, Cyprus and Israel. He blamed unfair competitive practices by wine distributors on the continent. It did not seem to have dawned on him that nobody who had a choice would ever buy Egyptian wine, because it is dreadful. He simply did not know his customers.

Egypt has been far from stagnant in the era of *infitah*. Gross Domestic Product per capita grew from 189 pounds in 1978 to 581 pounds in 1986, despite the increase in population—an impressive gain, but a gain that still left Egypt's per capita output behind those of such nations as Thailand, Costa Rica and the People's Republic of the Congo. The government's participation in overall economic activity has declined rapidly. But it is far from certain that private investment will be sufficient to generate the growth in output and employment that the Mubarak government is counting on, or that the bulk of the population will benefit from it.

The current five-year plan projects the creation of 2.1 million jobs by 1992, mostly in the private economy. Even if successful, this policy is not without risk. Samir Toubar, the economic theoretician of Mubarak's ruling party, who participated in the preparation of the plan, acknowledged when I talked to him in the summer of 1987 that "to buttress the private sector has negative effects too. It undermines the public sector where they compete. It increases wage disparity if private business thrives and gives raises. And it absorbs a lot of the economy without creating a lot of jobs because it's so much more efficient and driven by the profit motive."

Nowhere is this last point more obvious than in Tenth of Ramadan, a new city in the desert, about 35 miles east of Cairo on the road to Ismailia. (Tenth of Ramadan was the date on the Muslim calendar on which Egyptian troops crossed the Suez Canal in the 1973 war.) Tenth of Ramadan is a planned city of the type that was briefly in vogue in the United States 20 years ago: created from scratch according to a master plan, integrating industrial, commercial and residential development.

In the late 1980s, the city is thriving. Already there are factories producing carpets, paint, clothing, pumps, electric cable, refrigerators, plumbing fixtures, canned food and a score of other products. Most of these have been financed entirely with private capital; a few are joint ventures between private and public-sector partners. Wages are good; here an unskilled young woman can earn 110 pounds a month folding shirts for packing, or an assembly-line factory worker can make 400 pounds a month or more. And the quality of the products is good, precisely because the equipment is new and supervisors are driven by the need to be profitable in order to survive. By the year 2000, according to the master plan, Tenth of

Ramadan will be a city of 500,000 residents, with 68,000 employed in its industries.

But at what cost? The government created the community. The state built the roads, the water lines and sewage treatment facilities, the schools and mosques, the hospital and the shopping center, the bus station, the police station and the subsidized housing—all while giving tax and customs exemptions to the private corporations setting up shop. This is development that Egypt needs but cannot afford.

There is no doubt that *infitah*, combined with peace and the participation of Egyptian workers in the oil boom of the late 1970s, energized Egypt's stagnant economy. No one who visits Egypt today after being there in the 1970s could fail to see the difference—new factories, hotels, transport facilities and housing developments are everywhere. But there is also no doubt that the opening of the economy and the lifting of currency restrictions on individuals touched off a riot of consumerism and consumption that channeled funds away from investment. This is not just an economic concern; it has become Egypt's most intractable political problem as well. Faced with the growing discontent of the legions of Egyptians whose limited incomes prevent them from participating in the new consumer economy, Mubarak has listed "reducing consumption and increasing savings for use in productive investment" as the country's highest economic priority.

The greatest stimulus to consumption was not the policy known as *infitah;* it was the coincidental influx of cash and goods brought home by Egyptians working in other countries. The Sadat government was opening up the country's economy at exactly the same time as the Organization of Petroleum Exporting Countries was reaching the height of its price-fixing power, creating a surge of development and a vast market for Egyptian manpower in such countries as Saudi Arabia, Iraq and Libya.

Hundreds of thousands, then more than a million, Egyptians went to those countries to work. They were paid in dollars and sent the money back to their families or brought it home with them. In the Nasser years, individuals had not been permitted to possess foreign currency. Now, "worker remittances" became a crucial component of Egypt's foreign exchange earnings; they were calculated at about $2 billion a year in the late 1970s, a figure that included only the money sent through official channels and exchanged in the state-owned banks. It did not include millions more brought home in cash or exchanged on the private market, nor did it include the value of goods purchased abroad in such consumer paradises as Kuwait and carried home by the Egyptian workers.

It was only necessary to be in the customs hall at Cairo Airport when a planeload of migrant workers came in from the Gulf to see what was happening: Huge mounds of stereo equipment, clothing, electric appliances, toys, watches and cigarettes, purchased in countries where customs duties were minimal, were being brought in for use, or resale, in Egypt.

Even if the full legal duty had been imposed on those goods—which was unlikely once the travelers had concluded their negotiations with the customs inspectors, who needed a few dollars themselves—the goods were still cheaper than they would have been if purchased in Cairo—assuming they were available in Cairo—and of course they were superior in quality to goods made in Egypt. Workers who brought back goods for resale in Egypt formed a new class of "suitcase millionaires," who cashed in on the demand for consumer products.

The government encouraged the migration of workers because it brought dollars into Egypt and reduced domestic unemployment. The 1976 census found 1.5 million unemployed workers in a labor force of about 12.8 million. That figure did not take account of the armies of people who are nominally employed but whose jobs exist only because there are bodies available to fill them, such as tea boys, messengers, shoe shine men, streetside car guards, hawkers of cheap jewelry, taxi-finders at the airport, sweet-potato vendors and other supernumeraries. The man whose job it is to sit outside the office of the minister of manpower and training and summon the elevator for departing visitors by pounding on the shaft door and yelling "Eight! Eight!" to the operator is not counted as unemployed.

But the gains to Egypt from worker migration were balanced by negative effects. Many of those who left were common laborers, but others were exactly the people most needed by the expanding domestic economy: middle-level managers and technicians, skilled workers and craftsmen. And the money they brought or sent back was converted into possessions—automobiles, apartments, land, appliances—that hardly anyone had been able to afford for a generation. Virtually overnight, the migrant workers, educated or not, became a new privileged class, a privileged class based entirely on money.

During that period, I attended a luncheon at which General Motors was introducing its latest models to the Egyptian market, air-conditioned Buicks and Pontiacs. With customs duties included, they would cost more than $20,000 in Egypt. Seated beside me was an Egyptian journalist who covered economic affairs for the Middle East News Agency. I asked him who could afford such cars.

He said there were four groups of potential purchasers. "First, thieves and smugglers. Second, butchers. Third, doctors. And fourth, anyone who owns an apartment." All were getting rich: the smugglers by evading customs duties and selling at inflated mark-ups; the butchers, or more accurately the meat producers, by using subsidized bread, which was one-third the price of hay, as cattle fodder; the doctors by raising their fees to private patients eager to escape the dirty, crowded public clinics; and the apartment owners by filling their flats with cheap, tacky furniture (in the style known as "Louis Farouk") and leasing them at uncontrolled rents to foreigners. Unfurnished flats were subject to rent control, furnished flats were not, so naturally nobody would lease a flat unfurnished.

It was unfairly cynical of my colleague to suggest that the only people making money were corrupt or opportunistic; there was plenty of legitimate cash floating around. And it was naive, as well as futile, to blame ordinary Egyptians for the frenzy of consumer spending. Demand had been pent up for more than a decade. Egypt was an austere country in the 1960s and early 1970s; Egyptians did without for so long that they were like children on Christmas when the restrictions were lifted. If some of their fellow children found nothing under their trees, that was unfortunate, but there was no reason for those who could afford to indulge themselves to hold back in the interest of some abstract economic or social principle. When Sadat's youngest daughter was married to the son of one of Egypt's richest men in late 1976, the newspapers reported that only tea and sandwiches were served to the guests. Ordinary Egyptians, unrestrained by political considerations, found no need for such symbolic restraint.

To understand why they were so eager to spend instead of save, buy instead of invest, it was only necessary to go to the corner grocery store—not the state-run cooperative grocery, which served the poor, but the private grocery, which existed to provide greater choice and higher quality to those who could afford to pay more. From the outside this store might appear well-stocked, but it was not. Beyond the tins of olives and pickled vegetables floating in brine that stood on the sawdust-covered floor, the merchandise declined in quality and appeal.

Eggs, when available, were the size of ping-pong balls. Tea was rationed, available only in the cooperatives. Locally made luncheon meat and cheese were tolerable, but the butter, distinguished by its rancid taste and greasy consistency, was inedible.

Shelves were piled high with canned goods, but most of them were either fruit juice or jam bearing the Kaha label of the state-owned processing plant. There was no reason to buy them because fresh fruit was abundant and cheap, and individual confectionery shops sold jam superior to the Kaha products. Some shops in the most expensive neighborhoods offered imported canned goods, but the imports were mostly from Romania and Bulgaria and the cans had been around for some time—many bore suspicious bulges and stains. Besides, they were very expensive. At the exchange rate of that time, a can of peaches cost more than a dollar.

Spices were plentiful, but locally produced condiments such as prepared mustard were watery and bland. The locally made detergent and cleansers left a gray film on everything.

Egyptians were fed up with inferior goods and periodic shortages and dull inventories; one day there was no soap, the next day no beer, the next day no eggs, and the next day no toilet paper. And it was not just groceries: locally made clothing was shoddy, the shoes were ugly and uncomfortable, toys were uninspired and the appliances, when available, were expensive and unreliable. Even hardware was a problem. I once roamed the hardware stalls near Ataba Square searching for a pair of pliers, a hammer and some nails. I never found any pliers; I bought a hammer from which the head fell off the first time I used it; and the nails invariably bent as they were being driven.

The only photographic equipment available was film made in Czechoslovakia. The light-bulb supply was sporadic. Auto parts for cars other than Egyptian-assembled Fiats were virtually unobtainable. Even during the worst days of the Lebanese civil war, I went shopping in Beirut for staples and delicacies that were unavailable in Cairo.

When the interest rate on domestic savings was 6 to 8 percent and the inflation rate was 25 percent, it should not have been surprising that Egyptians were willing, even eager, to spend their cash on imported goods displayed in attractive shops. It is no wonder that Egyptians today enjoy browsing in the three-story Safeway store that has opened in Cairo, complete with audio equipment and escalators. Many of the products sold in that store are locally made, but at least they are attractively displayed, and quality has improved because of joint manufacturing ventures with foreign companies.

The inevitability of the consumer boom did not lessen its political sensitivity. Government officials have been trying for more than 10 years now to defend and rationalize a policy that may well produce long-term benefits but in the interim appears to stimulate inflation and enrich a few at the expense of the many. Prime Minister Mustafa Khalil went on the radio in October 1979 to say that of 2.11 billion pounds invested in 655 "Open Door" projects,

> only 30 million were allocated to consumer projects. Consumer projects represent only 19 companies. Our open door policy is not consumer openness but production and services openness. The companies we describe as consumers—can I say that a macaroni company is a consumer? It is providing the people with a basic commodity. The same applies to the canned food companies.

Shortly before, Khalil had promulgated a rule known as "Decree 600" requiring that import duties on some consumer goods be paid in dollars, an attempt to discourage imports. This kind of tinkering continues under Mubarak. His prime minister, Atef Sidki, told parliament in his presentation of the new five-year plan in 1987 that "in the allocation of new investments, care should be taken to ensure that a balance is achieved between industries that produce consumer goods and those making production goods, in order to guarantee stability for development efforts and increase the returns on them."

The consumption issue, however, is as much political as economic. Almost from the day the "Open Door" policy was proclaimed, some Egyptians have taken advantage of it not just to make money but to flaunt their wealth. They devoted their energies not to improving the conditions of the nation but to taking care of themselves. This, too, was probably inevitable among people who had known nothing but war and sacrifice for a generation, but its political effects were serious. It provided ammunition for critics on the left and the unreconstructed Nasserists, and it obliged the government to hand out bonuses, subsidies and wage increases it could not afford to the masses who might otherwise be even more resentful than they are of the growing gap between themselves and the opportunistic few.

As early as the winter of 1976, Sadat and his ministers were infuriated by an article in the *New York Times* that carried the headline, "New Millionaires Flourishing in Egypt's Liberalized Economy." Henry Tanner, the veteran *Times* correspondent in Cairo, reported the emergence of a new class of "fat cats" and "new pashas" who were getting rich on consumer imports and real estate speculation. He wrote of tax evasion and fur coats, of black marketeering and imported cars. Citing comments from politicians and newspapers, Tanner said that "there are now 500 millionaires in Egypt."

It was all true. Sadat could not deny it. But he was incensed because his critics, not just in Egypt but around the Arab world, seized upon that story to attack him for what they saw as an abandonment of Nasser's egalitarian principles and a return to the prerevolutionary days of domination by the "pashas" and the bourgeoisie. The "500 millionaires" cropped up in conversations in Damascus and Beirut and slipped into the verbal arsenal of Sadat's domestic opponents.

Khaled Mohieddin, a "Free Officer" with Nasser and Sadat and later the leader of the Egyptian left, referred to the "500 millionaires" when I talked to him that summer of 1976. He alleged that Sadat's policies had benefited only the "parasite classes and land speculators." Egypt under Sadat, he said, had become "a society where you can find Gruyere cheese in the shops but you can't find beans or lentils." Nearly a decade later, in 1984, the opposition newspaper *al-Shaab* was complaining that the existence of "dwellings made out of straw, fabric and cartons" was a "disgrace to Egypt's other face, the city of freedom, the city of jeans and videos."

No one disputes this. Every observer of the economic evolution in Egypt since the October war has noted that a relative handful of the more fortunate or the more enterprising are making money and flaunting it, while everyone else is losing ground.

It became fashionable for the rich to spend thousands of pounds on lavish weddings. These events, held at expensive hotels, have become tourist attractions. Guests gather on the stairs above the lobby of the Nile Hilton or the Meridien to watch the spectacle unfold like scenes in a Hollywood musical—long lines of women in new gowns, young girls in specially made dresses bearing gilt candelabra on their heads, orchestras, entertainers, abundant food and drink for big crowds of guests. Such a wedding costs far more than a schoolteacher makes in a year.

It is also fashionable for the prosperous to celebrate holidays by taking suites of rooms at the most expensive hotels, such as the Marriott Omar Khayyam, where they have access to the swimming pools, bars and tennis courts that are light-years beyond the reach of most of their compatriots.

I once attended a reception given by the manager of the Cairo Sheraton and his wife, the famous belly dancer Nagwa Fuad, to celebrate the eighth anniversary of the hotel's opening. Every inch of wall space in the grand ballroom was lined with tables bearing roast beef, smoked salmon, shrimp, and such local delicacies as *shawarma*, which is marinated sliced lamb grilled on a vertical spit and served on bread with sesame sauce. There must have been 400 guests, Egyptian and foreign, but the food did not run out, nor did the liquor. (The retail price of a fifth of Scotch or gin nearly equaled the monthly salary of a policeman, but the hotel did not have to pay the retail price. Duty-free to those with duty-free privileges, Scotch was only three dollars a fifth.)

The opulence of that event was heightened by the contrast to what was then happening in the rest of Cairo and in Alexandria: the food distribution system had broken down. Staples such as tomatoes and oranges had disappeared from the markets and a shortage of bread, the principal source of nourishment for the masses, had prompted a parliamentary inquiry. In the Sheraton ballroom, there were no shortages, and no talk of any; the conversation was about vacations in Europe and furnished apartments for the season at the seashore.

Taking their cue from Sadat, whose personal lifestyle became more and more lavish, the newly rich Egyptians were unable to restrain themselves. Two parties in 1979 touched off gossip all over town because it was said they had featured topless go-go dancers. When the ministry of culture organized a soireé for the participants, guests and hangers-on at the Cairo International Film Festival, it engaged Nagwa Fuad to entertain, and laid on a handsome buffet beside a hotel swimming pool, charging 35 pounds a ticket.

Frank Sinatra was welcomed in Cairo to sing at an invitation-

only concert. Sadat personally went to Ismailia to receive Elizabeth
Taylor. The Grateful Dead rock band took over the sound-and-light
theater at the Great Pyramids for a series of concerts; tickets were
priced at four pounds, a week's wages for many Egyptians. As we
sat in the darkness at one of those concerts, I became aware of
stirrings and movement beyond the ends of the rows of seats, out
on the sand. Inhabitants of nearby villages, attracted by the noise,
had stolen up to the edge of the theater and were lined up against
the fence, peering in at the incomprehensible spectacle of young
Egyptians, male and female, in T-shirts and tight pants, dancing in
the aisles. The gap between those inside and those outside,
culturally and economically, seemed unbridgeable.

These elite events, vulgar and unseemly as they often were,
represented only the most visible and provocative manifestation of
the growing gap between Egypt's economic classes. The overcrowded masses of Cairo and Alexandria could only watch with
envy as new shops with names like Playboy and Riviera opened to
display European jeans, stereo equipment, imported wine, trendy
furniture and imported refrigerators, all as far beyond their reach as
the Sheraton's buffet table.

"It was not intended," wrote the authors of the 1978 five-year
plan,

> that the private sector use the Open Door policy as a means to
> import luxury consumption goods, but this is in fact what has
> happened. Nor did the Open Door policy encourage the private
> sector to bid on land and buildings, but it has done so, with
> huge support from foreign capital. Finally, the Open Door
> policy was not intended to promote class divisions, but this has
> happened. . . . There are indications of a societal trend toward
> class division in Egypt now, which can only mean a weakening
> of national solidarity.

That was a prescient analysis.

As inflation soared under the pressures of new money and
deficit spending—the consumer price index in 1978 was 212 percent of what it was in 1967—some disgruntlement was inevitable
among those excluded from the bonanza. The political pressure to
assuage that resentment forced Sadat and Khalil to bestow wage
increases and bonuses upon workers whose production was not
increasing, and to keep the subsidized prices of basic commodities

at their unrealistically low levels. That in turn further widened the budget deficit, partly because the prices of imported goods were going up and partly because quirks in the tax structure ensured that government revenue would not rise as prices rose. Taxes on specific items in Egypt are often set in fixed amounts, rather than in percentages, so inflation does not increase tax revenues.

The subsidy system is what enables most Egyptians to eat regularly and to clothe themselves. The country produces far less food than it consumes; the balance must be imported. The majority of people cannot afford to buy imported food at market prices, so the government makes up the difference. Cooking gas, usually butane, is also subsidized. So are some domestically produced items such as textiles, and even some food staples in which Egypt is self-sufficient, such as rice.

By the end of the 1970s, these direct subsidies were costing the treasury more than a billion pounds a year. The subsidies accounted for nearly half of the 2.5 billion pound deficit in a 1979 state budget of 6.7 billion pounds. By the end of 1986, the cost of direct subsidies had risen to 3.8 billion pounds, or about one-tenth of GDP.

Those figures do not include the cost of indirect subsidies. The prices of gasoline, electricity, bus rides, books and other domestic goods and services have been maintained at artificially low levels, with the government making up the balance of the true cost. Mubarak, in a 1987 speech, said that "the total cost of state subsidies comes to about 5.502 billion pounds. This includes subsidies for goods, textiles, medicines, dairies, housing, railroads and potable water." The annual cost to the government, he said, amounts to 583 pounds per family.

This burden is one that all economic analysts, Egyptian and foreign, have recognized as insupportable. There have been reductions in direct subsidies on nonessential goods such as tobacco, and in indirect subsidies on energy; the 1987–88 state budget projected a decline in total subsidy outlays for the third straight year. But the basic system has remained intact because of one great traumatic event, the riots of January 1977.

On the morning of January 18, 1977, Egyptians read in their newspapers and heard on the radio that in an effort to reduce the cost of subsidies, the government had raised prices overnight by as much as 31 percent on flour, rice, soap, cigarettes, gasoline, butane gas, some textiles and other basic commodities. By midafternoon, the country was paralyzed by the worst riots since the revolution.

Sadat always insisted that the "Uprising of the Thieves," as he called it, was a communist plot, not a spontaneous protest. It is true that the appearance on the streets of skillful agitators bearing professionally lettered signs indicated that there were at least some organized groups ready to seize upon an explosive situation to challenge the government. But it was also clear that tens of thousands of workers and students were genuinely shocked at the sudden assault on their pocketbooks, for which there had been no political preparation. Their esteem for the "Hero of the Crossing" did not survive this clumsy attempt to reduce the budget deficit at their expense. Sadat's journey to Jerusalem, 10 months later, would refurbish his image, but only so long as it led Egyptians to believe that the conditions against which they rose in anger that January would improve.

The riots built rapidly. I watched on the fringe of a mob that gathered outside the People's Assembly as the mood shifted from outraged to sullen to destructive. "Down with the Khedive," the mob shouted, insulting the president by likening him to the ruler who had fawned over European culture and led the country to bankruptcy a century earlier. "Your daughter is living in splendor and we are 10 to a room," they yelled. And there were the inevitable cries of "Nasser! Nasser!"

Getting no response at the parliament, the crowd moved toward Tahrir Square, the heart of the city, defying the police who fired canisters of tear gas—canisters marked "Made in U.S.A.," as the demonstrators quickly pointed out to each other and to the press.

Meanwhile violence was erupting among factory hands in Helwan. The rail line linking Helwan to Cairo was closed, apparently a move by the police to keep the Helwan protesters from linking up with those in the capital. Cars were stoned on the riverside road linking Helwan and Cairo where it passes through the upper-income suburb of Maadi, home to many Americans. In Alexandria, demonstrators ransacked the downtown headquarters of the Arab Socialist Union and pillaged the home of Mubarak. Sadat, who was at his winter residence in Aswan ("You are living it up in Aswan while we eat stones!"), returned to Cairo.

By the next morning, the situation was out of control. Roaming bands of men smashed windows and attacked government buildings. Demonstrators burned and looted the nightclubs on the road to the Pyramids, carrying off the liquor—a sure sign that members of the religious opposition were participating. Other demonstrators attacked Shepheard's Hotel, the newspaper *al-Akhbar,* buses and tramcars, the science building of the American University and several police stations. Alexandria, Suez and Cairo and its suburbs were placed under curfew. The official death toll rose to 43. Sadat called out the army to halt the violence, and troops soon appeared at all major intersections, took up positions on bridges, and assumed control of government installations, including Sadat's residence. Driving around from one point of disturbance to another, I felt little sense of danger; the riot was not directed at foreigners. It was an outburst of wrath against Sadat and his government.

Mohamed Heikal says that Sadat and his family had a plane ready to take them to exile in Iran if the army could not restore order, but in retrospect it can be seen that while the riots challenged the regime and frightened Sadat and his ministers, they did not come close to bringing down the government. For every person who participated, thousands did not. The police followed orders and the army, when summoned, responded promptly and with restraint. But the rioters got what they wanted: Mamdouh Salem, then prime minister, not only rescinded the price increases but also left in place substantial salary increases for government employees and workers in the public sector industries, increases that had been intended to help compensate for the new, higher cost of basic foods. The memory of those riots and the fear of igniting a similar outburst have shaped economic decision making in Egypt ever since.

To meet the new wage obligations, Egypt appealed for foreign assistance. The United States and some of the Arab oil countries stepped up their infusions of cash. Even the Sudan pledged $5 million in food aid and sent several thousand camels—a shock to Egyptians accustomed to thinking of the Sudan as an impoverished outpost dependent on Egypt for support. This aid enabled the government to surmount the immediate crisis, but capitulation to the mob on the price issue scuttled its efforts to convince the international financial community that Egypt was prepared to undertake long-range systemic reform.

Some months before the riots, Sadat, under pressure from major aid donors and the International Monetary Fund, had shaken up his team of economic ministers and had installed a respected economic technician, Abdel Moneim Kaissouni, as deputy prime minister in change of economic policy. Kaissouni was determined to cut the budget deficit, to demonstrate to potential investors and lenders that Egypt was fiscally responsible. But military spending, capital investment and debt service were virtually irreducible components of the budget, so the only target for his paring knife was the subsidy system.

It had been clear for some time that the subsidy system was out of control. Wagih Shindy, then deputy minister of the economy, told me that senior officials began to review it when "we discovered that the cake eaten by rich tourists at the Hilton was made with subsidized flour, subsidized sugar and subsidized shortening." The principle of trimming the subsidies might have been acceptable to the public if cast in the light of eliminating abuses. But Kaissouni and his economic team were, as they later admitted, politically tone deaf, and their drastic proposals, when included in the proposed budget, failed to elicit any warnings from the People's Assembly committee that reviewed them. The result was that the subsidy reductions were sprung upon an unprepared public, which saw them only as soak-the-poor price increases that they could not afford.

Kaissouni offered his resignation. Salem declined to accept it, but Kaissouni's credibility had evaporated and he soon drifted out of the government, leaving the budgetary imbalance as he found it and the subsidy system flourishing. Since then, economic policy has concentrated more on increasing revenue and production than on cutting the subsidies. When the Mubarak government finally reached a debt-rescheduling agreement with the International Monetary Fund in 1987, it again came under IMF pressure to reduce the budget deficit. Electricity prices were raised for large users, but Prime Minister Sidki assured the public that the government "has no plans to lift subsidies, and will endeavor to ensure that all those eligible will benefit from these subsidies." Egyptians were well aware that the basic loaf of coarse bread, while not increasing in price, diminished in size, which was the same thing in different form, but Mubarak insisted that "we are committed to maintaining and subsidizing the prices of basic foodstuffs. . . . We are lifting subsidies only on some commodities that the able can afford. The able must pay. The problem is that it is the able who tend to make a fuss."

Before the riots, the subsidy system created by Nasser attracted little attention. It was out of control, rife with abuse, but Egyptians had long since come to think of it as an entitlement. No one was excluded from the government's largesse. Even my family and I, as legal residents, were entitled to a family ration card, and our house-keeper used it to obtain subsidized rice, cooking oil and tea at our neighborhood cooperative grocery store. Since we of course had enough money to shop on the free market for meat, vegetables, coffee and whatever else was available, we were not dependent on the cooperatives and I gave no thought to how the system actually worked. When the riots prompted me to inquire, it was not difficult to comprehend the government's problem.

At 1977 exchange rates, I found sugar selling in the state cooperative groceries for seven cents a pound; rice was three and a half cents a pound; a loaf of coarse bread cost less than a penny; boneless beef from Uruguay was 45 cents a pound; a yard of cotton broadcloth shirting cost 26 cents. The prices, set by the govern-ment, were the same throughout the country.

Anyone willing to wait in line, regardless of income, was entitled to purchase subsidized goods. In an effort to control costs and halt diversion of subsidized commodities into private grocery stores, the government rationed tea, cooking oil, meat, sugar and rice. Each household had a ration book that allowed the purchase of, for example, a kilogram (2.2 pounds) of rice per month at the subsidized price. Those who had the money were free to buy more on the open market, where prices were higher.

Other subsidized goods, such as cooking gas, baby formula, imported soap, sesame oil and beans were not rationed. Nor was *baladi* bread, the rough, round loaf made with coarse flour that is the staple of the Egyptian diet. Its weight and price were fixed by law and there was no limit to how much anyone could buy, which led to spectacular abuses that the government was unable to con-trol.

Some bakers cheated by short-weighting their loaves and using the extra flour to make higher profit items such as pastries. In rural communities, peasants who had always baked their own bread in home ovens were buying it at the state bakeries because it was cheaper. The greatest distortion of the system, however, was in the use of this cheap bread as cattle fodder.

This practice was no secret. A newspaper cartoon depicted a herd of barnyard cows munching the round loaves as one of them told the others, "This people food isn't any good unless it's washed down with 7-Up." Thus the subsidy to the Egyptian working man became a subsidy to wealthy cattle breeders.

Subsidized groceries other than bread are sold at the state-run cooperative grocery stores, called *gaameyas*. These can be found in every village and every urban neighborhood. It used to be easy to spot them because of the crowds that formed outside before they opened each morning, but the Mubarak government has expanded the network as a public service. This reduced the lines, but also increased consumption of subsidized goods.

These stores sell subsidized commodities imported and distributed to them by the ministry of supply. They also sell local produce. On this the *gaameyas* are theoretically able to hold down prices by the elimination of the profit motive, but over the years the growth of the population has obliged the *gaameyas* to compete with private produce vendors for available supplies. The more the *gaameyas* have to pay farmers for the melons and artichokes and oranges they resell at fixed retail prices, the greater the subsidy. The cooperative stores also sell the soaps, canned goods and cereals produced by Egyptian factories—goods that are cheap because the factories also are subsidized.

Presenting to parliament the proposed state budget for 1977—the budget calling for the subsidy reductions that provoked the riots—Finance Minister Salah Hamed said that the system "represents a waste in the employment of economic resources that should be directed to economic development or basic public services such as health or education." Nobody disagreed with that in theory, but the riots ensured that no comprehensive attempt to dismantle the system would be undertaken.

I had interviewed Sadat about three weeks before the riots, and I asked him if he thought the country's economic problems might lead to unrest. "Not at all," he replied. "It is true that we have difficulties, but it doesn't mean at all that we are in a hopeless case." He said the people understood that the country's difficulties had their roots in the 1960s, when it was assumed that industrialization and growth in agricultural output would be sufficient to finance the services to which the state was committing itself, and before the 1967 war shattered the country.

Perhaps the people understood this, but their patience was wearing thin. After the riots, the desire to avoid a repetition outweighed all other economic considerations. The Jerusalem journey provided a brief diversion, but when that failed to generate overnight prosperity, Sadat felt obliged once again to appease the mob.

In May 1980, more than three years after the riots, Sadat announced a "new economic policy which aims at easing the sufferings of the masses and tackling the problems of inflation" by reducing the prices of basic commodities still further and granting a new round of wage increases to government and public-industry workers. He raised the minimum industrial wage from 15 pounds a month to 20. Just before that, he had ordered customs duties on imported consumer goods to be reduced. The effect of these measures was to buy political relief at enormous cost: imports rose, subsidy costs went up, wages at the state industries went up, and revenues went down. Those measures were taken at the time when hard-currency revenues from oil, tourism and worker remittances were reaching a peak, but their implementation meant that funds once again were diverted from development and capital projects into consumption.

The premise of the "Open Door" policy was that an expanding economy and new jobs would result in a growth in workers' incomes and an increase in industrial output, eventually allowing the state to disengage itself from the subsidy commitment. But there was no way that premise could have been fulfilled under the physical conditions prevailing in Egypt at the time the policy was adopted. The country was not equipped to support an expansion of the economy on the scale that was contemplated. On the contrary, after years of neglect, war and rapid population growth, the country was falling apart.

An expanding economy requires trucks, roads, warehouses, communications, water lines, electric power, facilities for the disposal of industrial waste, and assured supplies of raw materials. An economic program based on foreign investment requires hotel rooms, reliable mail service, housing, office space, parking lots, telephones and stable power supplies for computers. In the mid-1970s, Egypt could not fulfill any of those requirements. Too late, Egyptian officials understood that before the country could

develop new industries and new services, it had to salvage or
replace those that had existed 30 years before. At the time of the
1952 revolution, Saudi Arabia, Libya and Iraq had nothing, while
Egypt had an advanced network of public utilities, transportation
and communications systems, factories and ports. By the time of
infitah, the oil states were ordering the best and most modern of
everything while Egypt was saddled with a decaying physical plant
that required constant rebuilding and patching. The Egyptians
could not simply abandon the capital structure of the past and start
over; they could not just walk away from the telephone system or
the port of Alexandria or the old textile mills or the sewer pipes, but
they also could not build a new economy on that corroded foundation.

Now, the foundation is much more solid. Many of the facilities
that were lacking when Sadat proclaimed *infitah* have been built or
repaired. A foreign businessman who threw up his hands in despair
in the mid-1970s would marvel in the mid-1980s at the availability
of international express mail service, modern office space, industrial
sewage capacity, refrigerated warehouses, reliable electricity supply,
hotel rooms and computer hookups.

Mubarak, in a 1987 speech, ran down the list of accomplishments of his first five years in power: 250 factories renovated;
maximum production of electricity increased from 17 billion kilo-
watts per hour to 45 billion; 3,614 miles of highway paved and 76
bridges built; about 700 miles of railway line renovated, almost
twice as much as in the previous 30 years, and the locomotive fleet
increased from 158 to 485; an increase in telephone lines from
600,000 to 1.4 million. These are impressive achievements. But
meanwhile, the opportunities that had existed a decade earlier have
moved on—only 35 percent of all investment under Law 43
through the end of 1984 came from foreign sources, and little of
that went directly into productive long-term enterprises. It is too
late now for Egypt to acquire the network of business connections,
financial services and regional corporate headquarters driven out of
Beirut by the Lebanese civil war. It is too late for Egypt to become
the service depot and supplier of choice for the oil states. It is too
late to restore the cash-for-expertise arrangement that would have
made Egypt a leading supplier of arms to the Arab nations; the
Saudis pulled the plug on that deal after the peace treaty. It is too
late to redirect the uncounted millions of dollars that flowed

through the black market and into the purchase of trinkets back into the savings system for constructive investment. And it is too late to prevent the births of the 15 million Egyptians who have joined the population since the October war.

The agreement with the International Monetary Fund in the spring of 1987 allowed Egypt to reschedule its debts and reduce its annual debt service payments, which were crippling the treasury. As in any IMF agreement, the very fact of the successful negotiation put an international stamp of approval on the government's economic policies and on the seriousness of its effort, thereby increasing the nation's creditworthiness and investor confidence. As presented to the People's Assembly that summer, economic policy appears responsible and realistic: gradual reduction of the budget deficit by increasing production, dividing the portion of the budget that must be financed beyond state revenues between loans and increased money supply to keep inflation under control; raising prices paid to domestic producers; further deregulating economic activity in general and export sales in particular; continuing to encourage private enterprise to absorb the burden of expansion, not just in industry and commerce but also in agriculture; reducing the cost of imports through long-term trade agreements; encouraging domestic savings and expanding tourism—a program that includes transferring the management of shabby state-owned hotels to foreign operators. As outlined by Prime Minister Sidky, the five-year plan adopted in 1987 calls for increasing overall industrial production by 7 percent; output of caustic soda is to increase 61.8 percent, washing machines by 60.6 percent, reinforced steel by 54.5 percent, cement by 22 percent, and ready-made clothing by 15 percent. At the same time, Mubarak has been emphasizing quality control and pride in national development, with the aim of reducing consumer preference for foreign-made projects.

Aside from the suspicious precision of the production estimates, these are unexceptionable and probably realistic policies. Given the numbers for the years 1981–85, when oil income was soaring, these are probably the only policies that Egypt could pursue. In that period, according to figures compiled by the Export Development Bank, 71 percent of all of Egypt's international trade activity was made up of imports, only 29 percent by exports. Of that 29 percent, two-thirds was oil, a commodity that Egypt possesses only in limited quantities and of which Egypt is using more and more for domestic consumption. With oil prices now half what they were earlier in the decade, Egypt's ratio of exports to imports is not going to improve.

Nothing is heard any longer of Sadat's goal of self-sufficiency, especially in agriculture. Sadat talked of "invading the desert" in a "green revolution" that would match agricultural production to domestic demands. Government policy still promotes expansion through land reclamation, but the "green revolution" was a mirage.

CHAPTER

5

The Dream of Invading the Desert

In the northeast corner of the Sinai peninsula, near the border with Israel, little green plants are struggling up through the hostile sand. This part of Egypt, regained from Israel after the peace treaty, was not well-endowed by nature for farming; it was desert when Moses crossed it and it is still desert. The scrawny fruit trees and bean plants that are being nursed to life here and there are touching evidence of an overcrowded nation's urgent need to increase its agricultural output, and of the dismaying difficulty and cost of doing so.

Egypt would seem to have little choice but to make the investment of money and labor required to convert its deserts into productive land, however marginal. The existing areas of cultivation and habitability cannot sustain the population. Egypt's total area is 386,650 square miles, about the size of Texas and New Mexico combined, but its habitable land is smaller than New Hampshire and Vermont. As P. J. Vatikiotis put it in his definitive history of modern Egypt,

> habitable and historical Egypt—the Nile valley and Delta—
> occupies but a narrow strip of land between vast deserts. . . . To
> speak of the living Egypt, therefore, is to speak of the 15,000
> square miles upon which 98 percent of Egyptians live, work,
> procreate and die—an area slightly less than 5 percent of the
> total surface of geographical Egypt.

South of Cairo, which is upstream on the Nile, the band of habitability is so narrow that the desert is visible from the river. The strips of green along the banks end abruptly, starkly, and the desert begins. Animal life and vegetation end at the demarcation line.

In the Nasser era, ambitious and costly land-reclamation programs yielded only marginal results. By the time Sadat proclaimed *infitah*, Egypt's population had finally outstripped its food production and a new campaign was proclaimed. Sadat's "green revolution" would be a national movement to "invade" the desert, not just to create farmland but to exploit mineral resources. Mansour Hassan, information director of Sadat's New Democratic Party in the 1970s and now a prosperous independent businessman in Cairo, told me that "the green revolution is to us what 'Go west, young man' was to you." The difference is that the American west was as fertile and as rich in minerals as it was empty. The obstacles to productive development of Egypt's deserts are staggering. The government lacks the resources; and the Egyptian people, bound to the Nile since the dawn of history, lack the pioneering spirit for such an undertaking.

On a stroll through the food markets of Egypt's cities, it is hard to comprehend that the country is dangerously dependent on food imports and that many, perhaps most, of its people suffer from dietary deficiencies. In every food shop and on every streetside cart are the brilliant rich fruits of the soil, varying with the seasons but always abundant. Oranges and okra, melons and tomatoes, chickens, eggplant, rabbits, mangoes and lentils, spill over each other in a joyous profusion, at prices that seem shockingly low. Stocking up on these foods and gorging themselves with expensive sweets on every holiday, the Egyptians hardly seem to be going hungry.

As the United States Department of Agriculture representative in Egypt noted in the U.S. embassy's "Annual Agricultural Situation Report" for 1987, "The quantity of food available is adequate and in fact obesity has become a problem. Food is so readily available that it is badly wasted. It is so inexpensive that large quantities are fed to livestock." But the appearance of plenty is deceptive. The food supply situation in precarious, and it is not getting better.

The World Bank team that analyzed Egypt's economy in the late 1970s found a decline in per capita intake of calories from 2,701 per day in 1966 to 2,552 per day in 1973, a period when harvests of wheat, maize and rice were increasing despite the stagnation that settled over the economy as a whole. The decline in caloric intake, the World Bank team said, "reflects food shortages, especially among the poor, and at least in rural areas these shortages become more acute at certain seasons of the year. Similarly, the low income levels, the skewed income distribution, and the high cost of plant and animal protein prevent adequate supplies of protein from reaching the majority of people." A report by the United Nations Food and Agriculture Organization said that "dietary deficiencies in calories are more serious than those in proteins." Egyptians dependent on cash purchases for sustenance are in constant jeopardy; they have enough to eat only so long as the government can sustain them. Most people who live in cities cannot even supplement their cash-purchase diet through garden plots or poultry husbandry because there is no room for such activities in the overcrowded urban communities.

The structure of Egyptian agriculture is profoundly complicated. This is why the old comic question, "Who's in charge here?" cannot be answered. The land is divided into large landholdings that have survived land-reform limits, leased plots, small private farms, reclaimed land owned by private citizens, and state-owned reclaimed land worked by salaried labor. The agricultural economy responds to complex and conflicting demands: to produce staple grains for the basic diet, to produce vegetables and fruits for consumption and export, to produce exportable cotton for the benefit of the state, to produce meat for high profit and to produce clover and other animal feeds for the livestock. Cooperative banks set up by the state control farm credit; irrigation policies are set by the government in Cairo. Mechanization is increasing, but the countryside remains dominated by what John Waterbury calls "animal traction." The small size of most holdings, combined with a surplus of rural labor and a shortage of capital, limits the extent to which mechanization is possible or even desirable. Much of the land produces two or even three crops per year, and the crops are rotated frequently.

Still, however complex the structure of Egyptian agriculture, however controversial or misguided the government's farm policies, the larger picture is easily comprehended. For all its bounty, Egyptian agriculture has long since lost the ability to feed the Egyptian population, and the gap can only grow as the population continues to increase. According to figures compiled by the U.S. embassy, Egypt in 1986 was self-sufficient in rice and beans; the "self-sufficiency ratios" for other essential food crops were: wheat, 22 percent; corn, 66 percent; and chicken, 63 percent. These figures may vary marginally from year to year, but overall they cannot increase because population growth is outstripping agricultural production. The government's long-term plan calls for self-sufficiency in all crops except wheat and corn, but independent analysts agree that there is no way productivity of the traditional land can be increased, or new land reclaimed for cultivation, fast enough to keep the gap from widening. Inevitably, as we have seen, the burden of supporting the nation will fall increasingly on industry and on revenue from non-agricultural sources.

Ideally, Egypt would follow the Japanese development model. Agriculture would be reduced to a tiny fraction of the economy, maintained as a sort of cultural museum, while the nation supported itself on industry and brain power. In an Egypt so structured, the natural breadbasket would be the vast but nearly empty Sudan, just to the south, while Egypt would be the industrial and financial engine of a joint economy. But Egypt cannot develop the industrial or financial power to follow such a course, nor can it dictate policy in the Sudan, which is always fearful of Egyptian hegemony. So Egypt must remain heavily dependent on its own farming sector to provide the basic diet. Nearly half the population still lives on the farms, a ratio unlikely to change much in the coming decades.

Egypt was a net exporter of food until the early 1970s, when the increasing population finally caught up with the farmers. By 1979 the government was importing four million tons of wheat a year to meet the demand for bread; by 1988, the estimated import requirement was 7.5 million tons. The United States is providing more than one million tons of this requirement as part of the aid program, but Egypt is laying out hard currency for the rest, and selling the bread to the public at subsidized prices. As we have seen, the government is and will remain obliged to buy dear and sell cheap, not just for grain but for meat, cooking oil and other essentials. The Egyptian working man's basic lunch of macaroni and hot sauce on coarse bread, or bean sandwich and slice of watermelon, costs him only a few pennies, but the price will remain within his reach only so long as the government goes on laying out the funds to make up their true cost.

Given the magnitude of the country's difficulties in almost every area of endeavor—health, housing, sanitation, communications, transportation, education, agriculture—it is not surprising that Sadat, always more given to grand gestures than to patient, incremental change, resorted to sweeping appeals for unconventional, and unrealistic, ways of dealing with these crises.

After the 1952 revolution and the "Corrective Revolution" and the attack on paperwork that he called the "administrative revolution" came the "green revolution," a grand design for hurdling all those intractable, interrelated shortages and problems and creating a whole new style of national life by "invading the desert."

The "green revolution" would salvage Egypt's hopes for prosperity by a massive redistribution of the population and by development of the deserts to increase production and resources. In the "October Working Paper" of 1974, Sadat clung to the Nasser-era vision of a future built on industrialization, using the income from industry to finance food requirements; but by the time the 1978 five-year plan was issued, the continued growth of the gap between consumption and production led to a new emphasis. Industrialization, while not forsaken, was supplanted as the first priority by "food security."

Sadat envisioned the "green revolution" as a combination of the Oklahoma land rush and the "virgin lands" program in the Soviet Union: opportunity, necessity and incentives would propel millions of Egyptians out of the Nile Valley and out of the cities into the desert, where with government help they would reclaim land, plant new crops, find new minerals, build new towns, live a better life and help the country toward self-sufficiency.

This was enshrined as policy in the 1978 five-year plan:

> By the year 2000, the development of the deserts would be well under way, meaning not only the exploitation of mineral and other resources but also the development of productive communities outside the presently congested Nile valley and Delta, communities where the excess population can be settled and made productive.

That was listed as the nation's first priority, on the first page of the planning document.

But even while Sadat was proclaiming a "food security" campaign and putting his most powerful crony, the contractor Osman Ahmed Osman, in charge of it, it was clear that Egypt was losing

ground in food production for its population. The Americans'
"agricultural situation report" for 1979, for example, said that

> while Egypt's economy in 1978 showed improvement, domes-
> tic problems, such as food production and population growth,
> remained as major obstacles to development. In constant prices,
> food production in 1978 increased less than one percent.
> Population, on the other hand, grew more than two per-
> cent. . . . Because the rate of increase in food production during
> recent years has remained below the rate of growth in popula-
> tion, the country has become more and more dependent on
> outside sources to feed its people—and the food gap is widen-
> ing.

Here is the 1987 assessment, prepared by a different attaché at
the U.S. embassy in Cairo:

> Agriculture is still the major employer in Egypt and one of the
> largest contributors to the gross domestic product. As impor-
> tant, however, is that it is a major supplier of food to a rapidly
> growing urban population. This group is demanding new,
> higher quality products for a more diverse diet. . . . As the
> foreign exchange situation grows tighter, food imports become
> more and more difficult. At the same time, agricultural produc-
> tion faces numerous technical problems which are limiting pro-
> duction potential. . . . Egypt's limited agricultural land base has
> prevented the production of basic and higher value agricultural
> crops in sufficient quantities to feed its population.

What happened to the invasion of the desert?

Sadat talked of "food security," but Egypt's leaders and the
technocrats in the agriculture and planning ministries are not so
unrealistic as to envision a return to self-sufficiency in food. "When
shall we achieve self-sufficiency in grain?" Mubarak said in a dialogue with a group of returned Egyptian expatriate workers as he
was preparing for his second term in office. "I will carry anyone on
my shoulder who could show me how we could achieve self-
sufficiency."

This is realism, not pessimism. Egypt was unprepared, finan-
cially or technologically, to undertake the massive land reclamation
and development of the desert that Sadat envisaged; it has as many
problems as it can handle just to maintain the current productivity
of existing land.

Land in Egypt is measured in *feddans;* one *feddan* equals 1.038 acres. The total land area is 238 million *feddans,* but only 6.5 million are in cultivation, including some 900,000 *feddans* of marginally productive land that have been reclaimed at great cost since the 1952 revolution. (Or, as Richard H. Adams Jr., an American expert on Egyptian agriculture, put it in a gloomy recent study, between the revolution and 1982, "cropped area in rural Egypt increased by less than 20 percent, while the total Egyptian population dependent on that land more than doubled.")

The arable land is generally rich; but its productivity has been limited by administrative, economic and natural misfortunes that have been well documented in extensive analyses, such as those by Adams and Waterbury, and need only be summarized here.

Excessive use of water from the High Dam, which pumped a year-round supply of water onto farms that had always been dependent on the annual flood, and were irrigated accordingly, waterlogged the soil and increased its salinity. That obliged the government to undertake a billion-dollar program to install underground tile drainage beneath most of the croplands.

Prices paid to farmers for key crops have been kept at unrealistically low levels, either to hold down the market price or to increase the state's profit from export crops, chiefly cotton. The low prices are a disincentive to production and encourage cheating. The state seized control of the cotton market, and kept prices paid to farmers so low that returns to producers for this vital crop were lower than for any other. Farmers, naturally, resisted allocations requiring cotton production, and risked arrest to produce other crops that provided more cash to them but less exportable cotton to the state. One of the most popular crops is Berseem clover, which is used for animal feed to satisfy the growing demand for meat. Egypt cannot afford to use its cropland to grow animal feed—the quantity of nutrition for the population that can be produced from a *feddan* of animal feed that becomes meat is far lower than the quantity produced on land used for crops consumed directly by human beings. But the government cannot raise grain and vegetable prices high enough to stop this diversion of the land.

Land-reform rules adopted under Nasser and Muslim inheritance laws, which require the distribution of land to multiple heirs, have made farms so small they cannot be mechanized economically;

94 percent of all farms are less than 5 *feddans;* the average farmed unit is 3.5 *feddans.*

Corruption deprives some farmers of access to seed and fertilizers, distribution of which is controlled by the government, and diverts crops such as rice from the state distribution system into the free market.

Rapid urban development is eating away at the available farmland faster than reclamation can replace it. Factories, roads and apartment buildings are taking over land that was formerly in agricultural production. Even in Cairo, as recently as 1975, there was open farmland between the western outskirts of the city and the Pyramids at the edge of the desert; now most of that land is occupied by housing. The rich land of the Delta is dotted with projects, such as a sprawling new Pepsi-Cola plant on the Cairo-Alexandria road, that have recently been dropped onto what was productive farm acreage. In addition, the making of bricks from topsoil, though illegal, continues unchecked. The price paid to farmers for the right to set up brickworks on prime land near the Nile is said to have reached 50,000 pounds per *feddan,* an irresistible inducement. Overall, according to an aerial survey conducted for the ministry of agriculture in 1985, the loss of arable land is as much as 50,000 *feddans* annually.

The government has been decreasing its control of agricultural decision-making, but basic policies on what should be planted, when and in what quantities are still made in offices in Cairo by deskbound bureaucrats with impressive degrees in agronomy but no field experience. In the field, where technological and engineering help is needed, the farmers are left to their own devices, with predictable results in pesticide application, tractor maintenance and animal husbandry. "One of the tragedies of land reform," according to Adams, "is that while the state has vigorously eliminated the entrepreneurial role played by large landowners, it has singularly failed to assume that role itself."

Much of what does get produced is spoiled because of inadequate storage and transportation facilities. Warehouses, refrigerated trucks and food-processing plants are scarce, so that crop loss, especially in fruits and vegetables, sometimes runs higher than 30 percent between field and market.

As a whole, the system manages to lurch forward year by year. There is no parallel in Egypt to the large-scale catastrophe that hit the American "dust bowl" in the 1930s or Ethiopia in the 1980s. Rather, the system is like a ball team on which one key player or another is always in a slump. The rest play well that season, but the one or two failures seem to keep the whole from making substantive gains.

One time, for example, it was the onion crop. Onions are an important export crop, as well as a dietary staple in Egypt. In the early 1970s, a soil-borne disease known as "white rot" began to attack the fields. Once that disease infested the light, sandy soil where onions were grown, it stayed there for 7 to 10 years, so it became necessary to grow the onions elsewhere, in heavier soils. Yet there it was impossible to pull out the crop without softening the soil by adding water, but the water in turn caused what agronomists called a "post-harvest physiological breakdown"—the onions rotted. Egypt exported 80,000 metric tons of onions in 1978, 10,000 tons in 1986.

One year when I heard there was a problem with the cotton crop, I went up to Alexandria to the offices of the Cotton Marketing Board. That is the state cotton monopoly, which buys cotton from farmers at fixed prices in domestic currency and sells it abroad at world prices in hard currency (a soak-the-peasants policy that has been troublesome for a quarter century). The president of the board at that time, M. S. Zulficar, said there was nothing wrong with the crop in the Nile Delta, which is the source of long-staple, high-quality cotton for export. But in Upper Egypt, he said, which produces short-staple, lower-quality cotton, the crop had been hit hard by an infestation of leaf worms. The cotton from Upper Egypt is used to meet domestic demand for towels, work clothes and uniforms. Rather than divert long-staple cotton from the export markets to meet that domestic demand, he said, the marketing board was negotiating with the United States to import thousands of tons of short-staple American cotton for Egypt's textile mills, at a cost of about $36 million.

The administrative and distributive shortcomings are chronic; the crop failures are episodic. One year tomatoes disappeared from the market. Another time it was oranges that vanished from the markets at the height of the season, not because the crop failed but because the government, trying to take advantage of a scare in Europe about poison in oranges from Israel, overcommitted its export contracts. Sometimes the newspapers report the cause of a

shortage, sometimes not. But always it is clear that the country has
not succeeded in managing its complex mixture of demand, supply,
irrigation, distribution, private land ownership, state control of
prices, prehistoric farming methods and contemporary technology.
The system remains out of balance and out of control, even as the
demands on it are increasing.

The current economic plan calls for an annual growth in farm
output of 3.7 percent. Part of this is likely to come through the fast-
expanding development of greenhouse cultivation, which is new to
Egypt but already producing high-quality fruits and vegetables for
the export market. The bulk of increased output, however, is to be
engineered largely through what Mubarak calls "an ambitious plan
to expand the area of agricultural land in Egypt." In his letter
formally designating Atef Sidki to continue as prime minister in the
cabinet shuffle of October 1987, Mubarak said, "I hereby entrust
the Council of Ministers with the task of increasing the area of land
for reclamation purposes to up to at least 150,000 *feddans* per year,
providing the necessary facilities for citizens and national companies to achieve this target and simplifying all procedures for the
ownership of these arable lands." Prime Minister Sidki told parliament that most of this reclamation is to be undertaken by private
enterprise; the government will designate the areas to be reclaimed
and provide water and start-up loans.

But the land reclamation record since the revolution is not
encouraging. In the Nasser era, large-scale mechanized farms, created with Soviet assistance, were laid out in the western desert. But
the approximately 900,000 *feddans* brought under cultivation in
that period were deemed a failure, not a success, because of vast
overruns in the cost of development and the marginal production
that was achieved. When the United States resumed its aid program
under Sadat, experts from the U.S. Department of Agriculture and
the University of California at Davis who surveyed Egypt's farm
problems concluded that "except for small areas of reclaimed land
from Delta lakes, the new lands have contributed little to domestic
food requirements. Salinity and drainage problems have limited
what can be grown to forage crops, barley and wheat, and small
areas of citrus and grapes. Rice production is not feasible on sandy
soil."

The Americans noted that the five-year plan drafted in 1978
proposed the reclamation of another 2.5 million *feddans* by the end

of the century, but they said that this would cost 1,000 Egyptian pounds per *feddan*. "The Plan," they observed, "gives no indication as to sources of funds, the manner in which these projects would be carried out, or the kinds of crops that could be grown."

With good reason, American experts remain profoundly skeptical about Egypt's land-reclamation efforts. Former ambassador Hermann Eilts, reporting on a 1986 fact-finding trip, said that the American AID mission

> estimates that roughly $10,000 per year would be needed for a period of seven years to bring one acre of marginal land in the Western Desert under cultivation. The Egyptian authorities contend that this figure is inflated. In their view no more than $2,000 per year would be needed, and the reclaimed areas would become productive in from three to five years' time. In either case, such land reclamation would be extraordinarily expensive and would not keep pace with Egypt's rapid population explosion.

A land reclamation analysis issued by the Higher Consultative Committee for Reconstruction in 1986 said that of the total acreage to be reclaimed in the 1986–96 period, about one million *feddans* would be irrigated with Nile water and the remaining 70,000 *feddans* with water from underground reservoirs in the western desert. But it is not at all clear that Egypt has enough water to undertake the irrigation of extensive areas of desert. The great North African drought of the early 1980s so reduced the amount of water stored behind the Aswan High Dam as to raise concerns about Egypt's ability to irrigate even the traditional agricultural areas, let alone additional acreage. The surface of Lake Nasser, as the reservoir behind the dam is called, dropped from 537 feet above sea level in 1977 to about 465 feet 10 years later, reducing the output from the electric generating turbines by 20 percent. A nation that has found the waters of the Nile sufficient for millennia suddenly found itself drilling wells, lining canals to prevent seepage, recycling drainage water and contemplating desalinization projects on the Red Sea and Mediterranean coasts.

Even when the rains are abundant in Ethiopia and Uganda and Lake Nasser is full, there are limits to how much water can be released from the dam without eroding bridges and dikes downstream, and the population of the traditionally settled areas con-

tinues to grow and continues to make new demands on Egypt's
share of the river's water, even before any land reclamation is
undertaken.

At the beginning of this century, the Nile provided an average
of 25 cubic meters of water per day per person in Egypt. By 1977
that figure was down to four cubic meters; now it is three. The
average annual total flow of the Nile is 84 billion cubic meters
(although in some recent years the drought has cut this figure to
about 40 billion). By agreement with the Sudan, Egypt's share of
the average flow is 55.5 billion, and by the mid-1970s Egypt was
already receiving its full allocation. If the Sudanese ever finish the
Jonglei Canal, a massive project that would in effect straighten out
the Nile where it now forms an enormous loop, it is expected to
increase the total flow by saving 4.7 billion cubic meters a year now
lost to evaporation. This means that one of the most ambitious and
expensive development projects ever undertaken in Africa would, if
completed, give Egypt only a marginal additional allocation of
water.

Nor is more water by itself a solution to Egypt's acreage
problems. The Egyptians have discovered that the release of additional water from the High Dam could have destructive effects on
downriver installations, because silt that is in the water when it
flows into Lake Nasser settles to the bottom while it is stored there,
leaving the water clear. Hydrological engineers such as Dr. Ibrahim
Asyouti, head of the Irrigation and Hydrology Department at
Cairo University, say that the clear waters would flow so much
faster than the muddy waters of the annual flood used to do that
they would erode river banks, bridge foundations and smaller dams
downstream. Egypt cannot irrigate more land just by opening the
spillways at Aswan, even if enough rain falls in Ethiopia to re-
plenish the Nile watershed. New channels and canals will have to be
dug, new pipes laid and new pumps installed.

Meanwhile, development of new industries and housing projects and the extension of water lines to additional villages are
increasing the demand for water for non-agricultural uses. Conservation and effective water management have become essential,
but it is difficult to impart this idea to people who have always had
as much water as they need.

It is not necessary to go to a farming village to see the casual
profligacy with which Egyptians use their precious water. At every

house in Cairo, a gardener opens the taps each day and lets the water run for hours to keep orange trees and potted plants from going thirsty. Then he gives the car its daily bath. Meanwhile the ball boys at the sporting clubs are giving the clay tennis courts their second watering of the day, and groundskeepers at the Gezira Club are flooding the golf course. This is the same free and easy use of water that has resulted in the waterlogging of croplands: farmers who for thousands of years irrigated their fields whenever water was available—that is, during the annual flood—continue to irrigate whenever water is available—that is, all the time.

The country is only beginning to undertake modern water conservation methods such as drip irrigation. Prime Minister Sidki told parliament in November 1987 that "the government will leave land reclamation to the private sector," but also "will assist in the expansion of advanced irrigation systems of various types, including the use of sprinklers and the drip method." He acknowledged that "this entails enormous multifaceted tasks during the stages of establishment and preparation. Therefore, departments of the industry ministry and the war production ministry will be assigned the task of attaining national self-sufficiency in the equipment necessary for these tasks, instead of importing them, which involves difficulties." In other words, Egypt is just beginning to plan for an expansion of industrial capacity to produce irrigation equipment that would then be used on land that the government expects to be reclaimed by private enterprise. How many Egyptians will be born while this process goes on?

In Sadat's vision, there was more to the "invasion of the desert" than agriculture and land reclamation. He proposed nothing less than a massive resettlement of millions of people into areas of the country where no one has ever lived. They would inhabit new cities to be built in the middle of nowhere; they would work on new farms, or in new fisheries on the seacoasts, or in new tourist centers on the beaches, or in mines and pits where they would extract the minerals that may be hidden beneath the sands.

Some population transfer has indeed occurred. The development of new cities, such as Tenth of Ramadan, is well under way. Tenth of Ramadan, though, is not a real test of the appeal of desert cities; it is served by Cairo buses and linked to the Cairo telephone system, and as the capital has grown eastward Tenth of Ramadan has become a virtual extension of the Cairo metropolitan area. The lure of the Red Sea has led to a boom in tourism near the coastal town of Hurghada; similar development has taken off along the Mediterranean coast around el-Arish, in the Sinai. But these are modest gains measured against the total situation—the entire population of Tenth of Ramadan, when it is completed at the end of this century, is expected to be 500,000, but more babies than that are born every six months.

One difficulty is that Egyptians don't want to live in the desert. Egyptian society has always existed within walking distance of the Nile's waters, and that link is spiritual as well as physical. Sadat urged the "youth" of his National Democratic Party to go out to the desert settlements to plant fruits and vegetables; he offered to give title to lands in such settlements as the New Valley to anyone with a degree in agriculture or agronomy who would go to work the land there. With agriculture colleges turning out 4,000 graduates a year, that sounded like a promising initiative, but I got the response I expected when I tried it out on a few friends.

"Who wants to live out there?" said a young woman, brushing it aside with a laugh. "There's nothing to do." She was an agriculture graduate, but worked as a secretary at a European embassy. That was a dream job: It gave her money, contacts and pleasant working conditions and allowed her to remain in Cairo, where the action is. Her attitude is similar to that of the armies of agriculture graduates who exercise their option to work for the Ministry of Agriculture, which is in Cairo, rather than out in the field. As Richard Adams told a Cairo magazine after completing his book about Egyptian agriculture, "Egypt has a highly educated class of people, but no one wants to work in the countryside, to get his hands dirty in the field," an assessment that applies to public health and family-planning workers as much as to agronomists. It reflected the same attitude about hands-on work that Don Peretz had described a generation earlier.

I did find one place where the "invasion of the desert" was working much as envisioned by Sadat, though in a project begun long before he became president.

A mile west of the Great Pyramids is the beginning of a road that does not appear on most Egyptian maps. It runs 200 miles in a straight line to the southwest, through desolate brown terrain where the only movement is the swirl of sand blowing across the blacktop. Parallel to the road is a single-track rail line.

At the end of the road and track is the Bahariya oasis. Until recent years, nobody lived there except a few hundred impoverished goatherds and date growers whose squalid village, Bouiti, was linked to the rest of the world only by camel tracks. In 1962, geologists discovered a major deposit of high-grade iron ore nearby. That was the start of a career for Fikry al-Morsi, a Cairo-trained engineer, who was sent out to develop the mines and run the little town occupied by the miners and their families—population 2,781.

He has little in common with the deskbound, business-suited engineers in Cairo who are more bureaucrat than technocrat. I found him at the age of 50, roaming the mines and village in a jeep, wearing a dusty hard hat and saying he was happy with his life. "Of course I like it," he said. "It's better than Cairo."

He said that after the initial discovery of iron ore, it did not take long for him and his team of geologists and engineers to determine that the oasis contained more ore, of better quality, than the small deposits then being worked near Aswan. The problem was getting it out to the steel mill at Helwan, just south of Cairo.

It took eight years, until 1970, to build the road from Cairo; the first load of ore was shipped in 1972, when the railroad opened. Now scrapers and bulldozers dig the ore, which has an iron content of 51 percent, out of an enormous open pit. Soviet-built dump trucks haul the ore to a crushing plant, where it is pulverized for shipment and loaded into hopper cars. According to Morsi, the iron range has known reserves of 236 million tons, not much on the world scale but more than enough to supply the Helwan mill for decades.

Morsi took a few minutes to show me around the mines, then turned to what he was really proud of—the gardens. The mine workers found water 2,000 feet below the surface of the desert, and now their vegetable patches and rose gardens, protected from abrasive winds by new stands of evergreens, are spreading out into land that once was barren. They grow peas, beans, carrots, cabbage, apricots and grapes where nothing lived 25 years ago.

"Production of iron ore is simple," said Morsi, snapping off a string bean and munching it. "This is much more important. Food is our great need, not just here but in the whole country."

Of the 823 miners, about 300 are from Bouiti and nearby settlements. The rest had to be lured out from the Nile Valley, which meant incentives. A miner receives about 50 percent more in monthly salary than a factory hand in Helwan or Alexandria. In addition, he receives housing with electricity and a refrigerator, free water and free schooling for his children—a total benefit package of considerable monetary value, enhanced by the fact that the housing is of better quality and the community cleaner and better organized than any place the miner could live in the cities.

The workers have a swimming pool, cafe, soccer field and community center. The children have a play area and theater deco-rated with big wooden cutouts of Donald Duck's nephews. In the clean air and silence, it is another world from the moldering alleys of the industrial cities where the workers would otherwise live. As for the oasis village of Bouiti, Morsi said, the difference between that and the miners' community is "about 5000 years." Even so, he said, because of the isolation it took several years to get staff turnover down to its present level of about 20 percent annually.

Because the mines were developed with Soviet assistance, it is difficult to put a dollar figure on the cost of the project. Whatever it was, it represented a major investment of the kind that cannot be casually undertaken in so poor a country: building the road and railroad, running in power lines from Aswan, constructing the workers' village, installing the mining equipment, financing the high salaries and adding the fringe benefits—all to provide jobs for 823 men and housing for 2,781 persons.

That is the perspective from which to evaluate the dream of dispersing the population and indeed the entire resettlement strat-egy. Individual projects can probably succeed and benefit the coun-try's overall economic development. If the rewards are sufficient, some Egyptians will go to outposts such as Hurghada to work, just as they migrated to the oil states in the 1970s. But it is doubtful, to say the least, that these outlets will ever absorb more than a small percentage of the population or the labor force.

When Sadat was president, there was a brief flurry of talk about spreading out the population and easing the strain on Cairo by building a new capital city in the desert somewhere, a Brasilia of the Middle East. But this was never a serious proposal; Egypt lacks the resources to do it, and nobody else would pay for it, even if a political constituency for it could be built. Reality dictates that the vast majority of Egyptians are going to remain in the Nile Valley and the Delta. That in turn ensures that the already desperate overcrowding of this small slice of the country will intensify. What is the point at which squalor and deprivation become insupportable? Egypt seems determined to find out.

6

Malthus in the Middle East

More than 35 years have passed since the revolution that ended the monarchy and made the Egyptian people masters of their fate; it is no longer possible to blame the old regime or the British for the country's inability to achieve prosperity. Whatever Nasser, Sadat and Mubarak have accomplished in that period, they must accept responsibility for the one overriding failure that has negated their achievements: They have not halted, have not made any serious effort to halt, the rapid growth of the population.

At the time of the revolution, there were about 20 million Egyptians. In 1986, the population surpassed 50 million. By the end of this century it will be about 70 million. No one imagines that the housing stock, the labor market or the amount of arable land can keep pace.

Before the peace treaty, years of unchecked population growth coincided with a generation of neglect of the whole country's physical plant. As a result, the economic benefits of peace have been eaten up by the need to commit more and more resources merely to maintain the present inadequate level of housing, services, public utilities, health care and nutrition. About 40 percent of the population is less than 15 years old; millions of these young Egyptians will actually live less well than their parents did because of the housing shortage alone.

A popular joke of the 1970s told of Ahmed, who was strolling across one of the Nile bridges in Cairo when he heard a cry for help and saw a man thrashing around in the water.

"Save me!" cries the drowning man.

"What's your name?" Ahmed yells down from the bridge.

"Mustafa," the man gasps. "Help! Help!"

"Where do you live?" shouts Ahmed.

"Sixteen Orabi Street. Now help me, please," says Mustafa, going under again.

But Ahmed gathers up the skirt of his *galabeya* and rushes off to Orabi Street. He grabs the doorman at number 16 and says, "I want Mustafa's flat. He won't be coming back."

"Sorry," replies the doorman. "It's already rented."

Poor Ahmed is hardly alone in his frantic quest for a place to live. At every income level except the very top, Egyptians go through life trying to cope with a housing shortage that is beyond the ability of the government or of private enterprise to deal with. Some individuals may not be affected personally—members of the armed forces, for example, are comparatively well-housed—but their relatives and their children feel the squeeze. The lack of housing shapes their outlook on the future.

World Bank analysts, who conducted an exhaustive study of Egypt's economy and public services in the late 1970s, reached this gloomy conclusion:

> Housing conditions are on the whole better in urban than in rural areas of Egypt, but even in Cairo and Alexandria, which are probably the best served, conditions are very poor. . . . The critical condition of urban housing in Egypt, especially in Greater Cairo, and the relative underdevelopment of secondary cities, have no simple or immediate solution.

In the largest cities, workers and their families often live 8 or 10 to a room in unheated tenements with communal plumbing—or none. The environment is dominated by noise and filth. Even in smaller towns, Egyptians live so packed into squalid apartments that they are ignorant of privacy or silence.

In the villages, two or three generations may live together in a one-room mud brick hut, along with their goats and chickens. Many villages are electrified now, which means lights in the schools and mosques if not in many of the houses—the 1976 census found that 18.6 percent of the households in rural Egypt had electricity— but even the presence of a television set does not alter the basic conditions in most of the dwellings, which are as primitive as ever.

Where a new house has been built, it often means that a man in the family has been working in the Gulf or Iraq and has saved enough cash to build a house—even if, as often happens, its construction violates the law because it takes arable land out of production.

A government report in the early 1970s estimated that 200,000 married Egyptians were living apart from their spouses because they could not find living quarters. The census of 1976 found that nearly a quarter of all Egyptians of marriageable age (18 and over for males, 16 and over for females) had never been married, partly because of the shortage of places to set up house-keeping.

A hundred yards from the house in Cairo, where my family and I lived comfortably alongside the diplomats and engineers and army officers who occupied villas similar to ours, there was a rural village, overtaken but not changed by the expansion of the city around it, where gold-toothed women in long black dresses and plastic sandals carried water from the communal tap in jugs on their heads. In the muddy streets between the houses, goats roamed amid the stagnant puddles, and ragged children scampered through debris. Donkeys brayed and chickens scratched for grain. When we drove through there, the scene reminded us that the streets of central Cairo and the tourist areas of Alexandria, Luxor and Aswan do not reflect the reality confronting most of the population, whose conditions of life are often abject.

This housing shortage is only one manifestation of the intense overcrowding that has become a dominant fact of Egyptian life. Families looking for light and air picnic on the median strip of the road to Cairo Airport, making novel use of the few open patches of greenery. On warm evenings, couples stroll along the elevated freeways over the Nile, where the crowds are less dense and the air is cooler. When automobiles became widely available in the 1970s, whole families would drive into the desert and get out to walk around, just to be free of the urban crush.

Rarely in Egypt's populated areas is one alone. The farms and the canals that irrigate them teem with human life: With the men working in the fields and women washing clothes in the canals and children everywhere, it is rare to be out of sight or hearing range of other people. Public facilities, trains, buses, cafes are all crowded, all the time.

In university lecture halls, hundreds of students gather in space designed for a third their number; many stand because there are not enough chairs. More than 60 percent of the primary schools were on multiple shifts when Mubarak became president. On Fridays, Muslim imams set up microphones and prayer mats to conduct services on city sidewalks because there is not enough room in the mosques to accommodate all the worshipers. (This phenomenon is often cited as evidence of a fundamentalist religious trend in Egypt, but it is mostly a function of numbers.)

In the dingy, noisy offices where overwhelmed clerks shuffle the papers Egyptians need for everything they do, mobs push and shout and elbow each other and shove their documents forward over each other's heads. A young woman I knew, a university graduate, was shattered by her first week of work in the *Mugamma*, Cairo's notorious temple of bureaucracy. The stairways are so crowded that every ascent is a struggle; long lines of shouting men and women clog corridors where the stench from the toilets is overpowering. My young friend, to whose office I went for a re-entry visa and registration of my passport after each trip outside Egypt, responded to her work environment in a predictable way: her assigned shift was 8:30 AM to 3 PM, but she actually worked from 10:15 to 1:45. One of her colleagues, a veteran of that combat, simply locked the door to her office, excluding the citizens she was ostensibly there to serve.

The government has long recognized the urgency of alleviating the housing shortage and of expanding public services to meet the demand, but all gains have been outrun by the growth of the population. In the early 1970s, private industry and government together were developing about 30,000 dwelling units a year in all of Egypt, against an estimated need for 62,000 a year in Cairo alone. U.S. Secretary of State Cyrus Vance's 1978 report to Congress on the American aid program said that "the backlog in housing exceeds 1.5 million units, and another 1.5 million are needed each decade to keep up with current population growth." A national committee formed in 1979 calculated that 3.6 million dwelling units would be required in urban areas alone by the end of the decade—831,000 to clear the backlog that then existed, 589,000 for the replacement of dilapidated housing stock and 2.18 million to meet the anticipated increase in the population. Other reports have given other numbers, but none has suggested that the gap between demand and supply was narrowing.

When Prime Minister Atef Sidki presented to parliament the five-year economic development plan for 1987–1992, he said 812,000 units of housing had been constructed in the preceding five years, more than had been completed in the entire period from 1960 to 1979. Of those units, he said, 58 percent were low-cost housing. The 1987–92 plan proposed a five-year target of one million units, of which about seventy percent are to be "basic," or low-cost, units. Economists and party officials who drafted the plan, however, admitted that this target is unrealistic. One reason is that there isn't any place to put that much new housing. "Location is a vital question," one of those officials told me at the time. "The entire Nile Valley is already too crowded." Another reason is that even though current policy calls for private industry to construct most housing, private entrepreneurs are unlikely to undertake this assignment because they cannot make money at it. Realistically, low-cost housing must be built and maintained at government expense, but it is doubtful that the government can marshal the resources that would be needed for such a vast expansion of the housing stock. The more likely outcome, according to World Bank analysts, is that "a lucky small proportion of low-income families receive such [public] houses while the vast majority continue to expand the squatter areas or increase the density of central city slums."

"Squatter areas" is a reference to illegal, substandard housing, which Egypt has in abundance. The World Bank team found that "an estimated 50 percent of all housing constructed in urban areas is done by private individuals through self-help or by small contractors. This unorganized construction often takes place illegally, without building permits and on land to which the occupant does not have clear title, and often [is done] to expand or rebuild existing structures." In Cairo, this illegal construction often takes the form of additional stories put on top of existing buildings, without regard to whether the foundation can support them.

Furthermore, the type of public housing offered by the government to those lucky enough to be on the list creates a whole new set of problems. These dwellings, built to a standard five-story walk-up design that dates to 1965, result in high concentrations of large, poor families, with inevitable results. A "Joint Housing and Community Upgrading Team" set up by the USAID mission and the Ministry of Housing reported in 1977 that in these concrete jungles, which can be found throughout the country,

The residents of the ground floor units at times build chicken coops and other additions in front of their units. Animals are common in most units, even on upper floors, including chickens, ducks, pigeons, and even goats and occasionally a burro. In some cases, small shops built out of cardboard and other similar materials are attached to the ground level apartments. . . . Due to the inability of local authorities to maintain the units (because of the artificially low rent collected), the clogging of the sanitary drainage system is common, and when the WC of the lower units overflows from the discharges of the upper units, some residents break the exterior drainage pipes, causing raw sewage to discharge into the common ground. . . . The inadequate site planning of public housing plus the lack of site development features such as walks, vegetation, play equipment etc., makes the spaces between buildings quite inhospitable, and they are seldom used by adults for other than the minimal pedestrian circulation and as a common depository of trash. Children's play often occurs here, but the condition of many of the spaces, due to the often present trash and at times raw sewage, creates serious health problems.

This ambience of squalor has been offered to hundreds of thousands of families as an improvement over what they had before.

Egyptians laughed at a newspaper cartoon showing a convict saying to a prison guard, "I've got a friend who can't find a flat. Why don't you let me put him up here?" But especially among the bourgeoisie, whose material aspirations were stimulated by the achievement of peace, the housing crisis can provoke despair and sometimes violence.

In one celebrated incident in 1978, Cairo newspapers reported the story of a landlord who wanted to evict tenants whose rent was controlled by law, so that he could bring in new tenants at the much higher market rate. When the incumbents refused to move, the landlord and four henchmen began throwing their furniture out a third-floor window. When the tenants tried to stop them, the men began throwing the tenants out the window. Two of them were hospitalized with multiple fractures. The landlord and his goons were arrested. The apartment did not change hands.

Another incident led to the severing of diplomatic relations between Egypt and Bulgaria. The Bulgarians bought a building in the fashionable diplomatic quarter of Zamalek, on an island in the Nile. The tenants on the first and third floors moved out, but the Bulgarians were unable to dislodge the family on the second floor. Since their tenancy was protected by law and their rent was controlled at about $24 a month while new flats in uncontrolled buildings cost up to 50 times as much, the Egyptians resisted all efforts by the Bulgarians to get them to leave. The Bulgarian ambassador told reporters he had offered the family 180,000 pounds, then more than a quarter of a million dollars, but the Egyptians spurned it.

When the Egyptian tenant, an official of the ministry of power, went to Saudi Arabia on business, leaving his wife and daughter at home, the Bulgarians resorted to force. They roughed up the women after cutting off the electricity and water. Crowds attracted by screams pelted the Bulgarians with eggs and rocks, and Sadat ordered Egyptian troops to enter the embassy. The next day the two countries severed diplomatic relations. The Egyptian family stayed in the building.

The 1976 census showed that the most densely populated quarter of the capital was Rod el Farag, not far from downtown. In that neighborhood, there were then 261,348 residents per square mile—10 times the population density of New York. I found one of them, Khalil Ibrahim, a toothless illiterate of 70, in the cubbyhole on a crowded street where he scratched out a living ironing other people's clothes. He said he lived upstairs with his wife and two children in a single room.

They had no kitchen and all the families in the building, perhaps 50 people, shared a toilet. But, he said, he was actually better off than in the past because four other children who used to live with the family had married and moved away. That left their place less crowded than it had been, and the rent was still only two pounds a month.

As he talked, the deafening, chaotic street life of Cairo swirled around his storefront ironing stand: children, pushcart vendors, goats, donkeys, buses and trucks, bouncing off one another in incredible profusion. But Ibrahim hardly seemed to notice the unending tumult; he had lived with it as long as he had lived with his one room. What really bothered him, he said, was the rising price of food, which meant that "children today cannot grow up as strong as I did" because their diet is poor.

John Waterbury, who lived in Cairo during some of the leanest years, noted in a 1973 study for the American University's Field Service that the housing crisis does not affect only the "urban proletariat." It is equally serious for "the educated Cairenes who consider themselves part of the middle class but are unable to obtain shelter commensurate with their image." All of us who lived in Egypt as foreigners, sending the bills to our employers, knew Egyptians caught in the squeeze Waterbury described.

A teacher at a school for foreign children, a woman who spoke English, had traveled abroad and was even being paid in hard currency, was unmarried in her mid-thirties and living in a small apartment with her two sisters. When she heard that our teenaged housemaid, an illiterate girl from a Cairo slum, was about to get married, her response was, "Where are they going to get a flat to live in? That's what I want to know."

The answer was that the girl was marrying a man who had worked in one of the oil countries and had saved enough to pay for a modest apartment in Cairo. After the wedding, it turned out that the bride's new home was less attractive than she expected. It was small, noisy and dirty, and the water ran only in the middle of the night, but she did not live there long. Less than a year after they were married, her husband went abroad again on a new job, leaving her pregnant, and she moved back in with her mother, accepting the arrangement because it held out the promise of something better when her husband returned. As for the school teacher, she was able to acquire an apartment only after 10 years of saving her hard-currency earnings. From an army officer, she bought a permanent leasehold on a comfortable two-bedroom apartment. The officer's income, of course, was much less than hers, but Egyptian officers have privileges that ordinary citizens do not; the right to acquire a good apartment built at state expense is one of them.

A fashionable tailor who caters to ambassadors and cabinet officials at his shop downtown lives handsomely in a five-bedroom apartment in Garden City, one of Cairo's choicest neighborhoods. He has been there nearly 30 years, and his rent is controlled at 16 Egyptian pounds a month. When the identical flat upstairs changed hands in 1979 and was no longer subject to rent control, the rent went to 900 pounds.

One afternoon in his shop, the tailor stared morosely into his cup of Turkish coffee and worried about the future. "It's all right for me," he said, "but what is my son going to do? Where is he going to live?" The answer was that his son shortly thereafter emigrated to the United States. Ironically, had he remained in Egypt, he would now find no shortage of places to live if his father came up with enough money. Throughout the first half of the 1980s, private developers rushed to construct apartment buildings in Cairo and Alexandria in an effort to cash in on the wealth that flowed into the country from economic liberalization and the oil boom. But thousands of these apartments stand empty, largely because the builders want to sell them as condominiums at prices well beyond the reach of most Egyptians, rather than rent them and subject themselves to controls on rents and occupancy rights.

Estimates of the number of vacant new flats in the mid-1980s ran as high as 14,000 in the Cairo area alone. Mubarak was asked in a 1987 magazine interview about reports that the nationwide total was 1.8 million. "The figure surprised me just as it did everyone else," he said, but whatever the correct number it was certainly high. He said he had asked the Council of Ministers for a detailed report on the reasons so many desirable apartments stand vacant. What he would not do, he said, was order vacant apartments seized by the state, as some politicians were urging. That would have constituted an assault on private property reminiscent of sequestration.

Mustafa Amin once wrote a column about an advertisement that offered 704 apartments for sale. He said he was shocked to read that "a five room flat was offered for a total of 26,000 Egyptian pounds, with 5,000 pounds to be paid in advance and 3,500 in installments every six months. . . . Well, this is hardly the solution for a 30-year-old engineer with a monthly salary of about 60 pounds."

Throughout the late 1970s, while Sadat was defending the peace treaty as a step on the long march to prosperity, the newspapers were carrying reports each week of this or that recommendation, this or that ministerial directive, about the housing situation. One new law, for example, required public sector corporations to set aside 15 percent of their profits for the provision of services, including housing, to their workers. This was almost meaningless: most of the public sector enterprises don't make enough profit for such a fund to be meaningful.

In fact, the country seemed to be losing almost as much ground as it was gaining in the effort to increase the housing stock. Some new buildings designed as apartments were being converted to hotels in mid-construction because hotels were more profitable. Meanwhile, old residential buildings began to give way and collapse with increasing frequency.

In the first six months of 1978, six buildings fell down in Cairo alone, killing at least 50 people and leaving hundreds more homeless. In one of them, a 100-year-old block of one-room cubicles, the residents had been warned that they should move out, but they had nowhere to go. Estimates by various officials and committees put the number of buildings in Cairo that are unsound and should be condemned at anywhere from 30,000 to half a million. The report on "Housing and Community Upgrading" prepared by the joint American-Egyptian study team estimated the annual national loss of housing to structural failure at 12,000 units.

Nor is it only old buildings that fall down. For years there was a vacant lot opposite the Soviet Cultural Center on a busy boulevard in the Dokki neighborhood. It had been the site of a modern apartment house that collapsed in 1974. It turned out that the builder, Hassan Bayumi, whose name became a generic term for the new "fat cat" class, had ignored the specifications of the building permit issued by the authorities. He built higher than was allowed, used cheap materials and cut back on steel reinforcing rods. His was just the most extreme case of a phenomenon that erupted all over the city, as builders rushed to cash in on the demand for housing.

Few people are actually without shelter altogether; hardly anyone is homeless the way many Americans are homeless. What happens is that families double up, cramming more and more people into the same space, with a forbearance that strains the credulity of foreigners. Shopkeepers rent space in their back rooms. Villas are cut up into apartments. Buildings are expanded by the addition of stories on top.

Every tourist hears about the City of the Dead, a six-mile-long string of cemeteries on the eastern edge of Cairo where several hundred thousand people live as squatters. Winking at the illegality of their presence, the government long ago capitulated to reality and put in water and electricity lines, opened schools and provided bus service. This was easier and cheaper than trying to move the squatters elsewhere.

In a speech in May 1979, Sadat said he had given orders to "do something about the people living in the cemeteries." They are, of course, still there.

The same forces that created the housing shortage have overwhelmed other public services in similar fashion. The conditions in Cairo's apartment buildings are reflected in the classrooms, on the buses and in the hospitals. The nationwide percentage of illiterates, for example, declined from 70.5 in 1960 to 56.5 in 1976; but the total number of illiterates remained about the same because of the growth of the population. A century after Egypt developed a school system that was the envy of the Arab world, there are still rows of little tables outside any post office or bureau that deals with the public. At those tables sit scribes who fill in forms and write letters for the millions who cannot do it themselves. In 1981, the USAID mission agreed to provide $19 million to construct 1,300 schools over a ten year period. At the time, Egypt's primary school enrollment ratio was about 80 percent, lower than that of Bolivia, Mozambique or Mongolia. It has since increased to 94 percent, according to suspect government statistics, but half the children who enroll in primary school drop out before the seventh year because their families need them to go to work.

In 1970, the year of Nasser's death, life expectancy was 46.7 years; by 1986, it was 58.3 years. This is a spectacular gain, attributable to the expansion of health care facilities begun under Nasser, to the greater availability of treated drinking water and to advances in treating endemic diseases. The infant mortality rate was 116 per 1,000 births in the mid-1970s; now it is down to 102, an improvement that still leaves Egypt behind such nations as El Salvador, Vietnam and Papua-New Guinea. A traveler who knew Egypt before the revolution and returned now would notice immediately that the endemic widespead blindness caused by trachoma has been brought under control. According to government figures, blindness afflicted an appalling 2.6 percent of the population at the time of the revolution; the figure now is less than 1 percent.

Nevertheless, the Egyptians are not a healthy people. They suffer from chronic intestinal diseases, rotting teeth, poor eyesight and uncorrected deformities. Preventive medicine and dentistry seem to be almost unknown outside a few hospitals in Cairo and Alexandria; the values of hygiene and proper nutrition are only dimly perceived.

The National Charter of 1962 proclaimed that the "first right of all citizens is health care—not bare treatment and drugs like goods bought and sold but rather the unconditional guarantee of this care to every citizen in every corner of the country under conditions of comfort and service." This was a pledge that could not be met.

Nasser's government spent heavily to set up a network of

community and village health centers. In theory almost every Egyptian lives within three miles of one of these units. New medical schools were created; in 1960 Egypt had one doctor for every 2,600 residents; by 1986, there was one for every 798, one of the best ratios in the developing world.

But those doctors are like doctors everywhere; they want to be in the big cities where the major hospitals and the money are, not in the villages or the rural health clinics. Even young doctors, who are obliged to take rural assignments because the government gave them a free medical education, spend as much of their time as they can in the cities (and in the best neighborhoods of the cities). Because Egyptian law limits the types of medical procedures that can be performed by auxiliary personnel, little medical service is actually available at the clinics. Doctors assigned to public health facilities have discovered, like the schoolteachers, that they can make more money by selling their services privately than by delivering them through the state system.

Even in the cities, there is only so much the doctors can do with antiquated equipment in outdated, dirty hospitals where technicians are poorly trained and underpaid, laboratory work is unreliable and secondary care is left to families of patients.

When my wife, Sidney, broke a finger, we went to the office of Dr. Mohammed Diab, an orthopedist whose name appeared on lists of recommended doctors circulated by the American embassy and the American University.

Dr. Diab, a friendly man with a certificate of graduate training in England on his office wall and an impressive collection of current medical literature on his shelves, splinted the finger and told us to meet him the following morning at 7:00 at Dar al-Shifa hospital for X-rays. The reason for the early hour was that he, like many doctors, made his hospital rounds early in the morning and ran his private clinic in the evening, the hours between being committed to some government job—teaching in a medical school, serving in a military hospital, working at the ministry of health. (Our pediatrician often came to the house in his colonel's uniform, which he wore during the day when he was on duty at Maadi Military Hospital.)

At Dar al-Shifa, we picked our way through the dingy, crowded corridors to the X-ray lab, where we found an X-ray machine that belonged in a museum and two technicians ready to operate it. My wife was pregnant and not eager to be X-rayed. She rejected the technicians' instructions to climb onto a table, where they would have X-rayed her torso along with her hand, and she refused to permit any X-rays to be taken until the technicians produced a protective shielding apron.

Dr. Diab was sympathetic, but there was little he could do about conditions at the hospital. It wasn't up to him to train the support staff or purchase the equipment.

He said he understood that patients were unhappy, but he said, "We, the doctors, we're the ones who pay the price. Patients only come here for a few days. We have to put up with these conditions every day of our lives." He was particularly bitter because he had just visited King Faisal Medical Center in Riyadh, Saudi Arabia, which of course was equipped with all the latest and most sophisticated medical gear. Patients there lived in luxury.

"The Saudis don't even have anybody who knows how to use that equipment." Dr. Diab said. "All the doctors are British. We Egyptians know how to use it, but there hasn't been a new general hospital built in this country in 30 years." Construction work began in 1979 on a replacement for Cairo's medieval Kasr al-Aini Hospital, the main teaching hospital for Cairo University; it and 13 others, with a total of 4,030 beds, are scheduled for completion by 1990. While urgently needed, these are replacement facilities; they do little to increase the availability of health care for much of the population.

For those who have money, any serious illness or potentially risky medical procedure, such as surgery, automatically means going outside the country. Anecdotal information about the health care system was never reassuring. The 14-month-old son of an American banker died when nobody at the main military hospital knew how to turn on an oxygen tent. The minister of justice died in the operating room during routine surgery. At the inoculation center in a downtown hotel where health workers give immunizations for international travel, they reuse the hypodermic needles. (We brought our own.) The government responded to a cholera scare by forcing incoming travelers at Cairo Airport to consume four—four!—tetracycline tablets on the spot.

One foreign journalist burned his hand on the cord of an electric appliance. (Considering the condition of the electric lines and fuse boxes, it's remarkable that more people aren't electrocuted.) He went to a doctor who treated and bandaged his burn, but it did not heal.

A few days later, he was a dinner guest at the apartment of another doctor, a well-known man who is popular with the foreign community, is charming at parties, and works at the U.S. Navy's tropical medicine research unit in Cairo. Those credentials inspired some confidence in his ability.

Inquiring about the journalist's bandage and hearing that he was still having some pain, the doctor invited him to step into another room so he could unwrap the dressing and inspect the burn. Sure enough, the doctor discovered that the wound was infected—so he threw the used bandage out the window.

Partly as a result of this casual attitude about hygiene, Egyptians are plagued by chronic intestinal and diarrheal illnesses. The USAID mission, in its presentation to Congress for the 1988 fiscal year, reported that "half of all deaths in Egypt occur among children under the age of five, and half of these are due to diarrheal diseases." In nonurban communities, where more than half the population lives, those who survive childhood continue to suffer from a disease that has afflicted Egypt since the beginning of time: schistosomiasis, or bilharzia.

Napoleon is said to have called Egypt "the land of menstruating men" because they pass so much blood in their urine. The reason is that their intestines have been penetrated and eroded by parasitical worms that their environment inflicts on them. As long as Egypt remains dependent on its system of slow-flowing canals for irrigation, drinking water and even recreation, there seems little hope that this plague can be eradicated. Doctors know how to treat this disease, how to cure it. What they do not know is how to keep people from reinfecting themselves.

Schistosomiasis is a debilitating parasitical ailment that attacks the kidney, bladder, liver and other internal organs. Untreated, it causes lassitude, pain, bladder cancer, brain damage and early death. The disease is commonly known as bilharzia, after Theodor Bilharz, a nineteenth-century German scientist who identified the tiny threadlike worms, called schistosomes, that cause it.

The worms live in fresh water. Upon contact with humans, they penetrate the skin and take up residence in the intestines and urinary tract. They burrow and penetrate tissues, erode vital organs and lay eggs, some of which are excreted, beginning the cycle anew.

They breed in waterborne snails that thrive in the warm, slow-moving waters of the canals. That means they are part of the environment of every one of the millions who bathe and wash and play in the same water used for drinking and irrigation.

According to specialists such as Dr. Ahmed Garem, professor of tropical medicine at Cairo University and first director of the German-financed Theodor Bilharz Institute in Cairo, and Dr. Samir Bassily, a researcher at the U.S. Navy's medical research unit in Cairo, schistosomiasis is more a social and environmental problem than a medical one. There is no vaccine, but drugs such as praziquantil can keep the affliction under control.

As Dr. Garem said when I talked to him about the Bilharz Institute's mission, it is one thing to pipe safe water into the villages, another to get the villagers to line up at the tap instead of dipping their buckets into the canal as they have always done. When the temperature hits 110 degrees, no cautionary lectures in school will keep little boys from leaping into the canal for a swim. No amount of research in Cairo will prevent an infested villager from defecating into the canal, spreading the worms. And the annual Nile flood, which used to cleanse the river and some of the canals and wash the snails downstream, was ended by construction of the High Dam.

Dr. Bassily says new data reported at a bilharzia conference in 1987 show that the disease has declined in prevalence and intensity because drug therapy is now widely available. But there are still villages where up to 90 percent of the boys suffer from the disease. Government estimates of the annual loss to the country in direct cost and lost productivity have run as high as $400 million a year. Even the police are alarmed. They say that bilharzia is partly responsible for the widespread use of hashish and other drugs by men seeking antidotes for the lassitude and loss of sexual potency associated with the disease.

Schistosomiasis is by no means unique to Egypt. It is just another of the endemic problems that made expectations of prosperity after peace unrealistic from the start. The government has made heroic efforts to recover the ground lost to war and penury under Nasser. But even as Egypt has struggled against illiteracy, ill health, inadequate housing, agricultural stagnation and the collapse of its physical plant, it has lost ground to the rising population. Ten years after the "Green Revolution" was proclaimed, more Egyptians do live outside the traditional areas than ever in history; but more Egyptians are born each year than the total number who have been resettled in that decade. Even as the 1978 plan proclaiming the invasion of the desert was being published, the population was increasing by one million people per month. No resettlement and redevelopment program, however ambitious and well financed, could make headway against that human tide.

Napoleon's team of scholars counted 2.4 million people in Egypt in 1800. Since Egypt has no natural area of population dispersal, no Great Plains, no Amazon basin, no Siberia, the 70 million people who will be living there at the end of this century will occupy little more space than those 2.4 million encountered by the French. This would seem to dictate the necessity for strong, immediate measures to bring the population growth under control. But Mubarak, like Sadat, has failed utterly to address this issue in any realistic or forceful way.

Here is the government's view of the population issue, as given to parliament by Prime Minister Sidki in his message accompanying the five-year plan adopted in 1987:

> The population problem in Egypt, with all its inherent aspects, which impede comprehensive development, is a very important socioeconomic topic affecting our lives and national economic standards. The dimensions of this problem are notable in the high rate of population growth, the disproportionate geographic distribution, the low ratio of productive manpower in relation to the total population, and the high rates of illiteracy and disability. All this is reflected in the low productivity of the Egyptian worker and the rapid increase in the rate of consumption for goods and services.
>
> Overcoming these aspects or curbing their sharp effects could transform the population into a source of national wealth through proper utilization. Therefore the government acts to enhance social aspects in development programs through national plans which seek to change the social behavior connected with the concept of reproduction. This can be accomplished by reducing population growth rates, intensifying efforts to gradually eliminate illiteracy, linking education policy with future manpower requirements, expanding technical education, expanding education qualitatively and linking it with development, introducing suitable advanced education technology, promoting training efficiency and preparing teachers well. This should be coupled with economic and social development in the

rural areas, raising health standards and subsequently increasing productivity.

The government is aware that solving the population problem requires full coordination with the popular efforts sponsored by [private] associations. The political parties can also play a positive role in tackling this problem, which is a national issue. Mass media and cultural services have a very important role to play, as do men of religion, who bear a major responsibility in solving this problem.

In other words, the government will not take the lead in curbing population growth, especially because it is a religiously sensitive issue—the Muslim Brotherhood has publicly opposed birth control, arguing that God is able to provide food for all. And when everyone is responsible for dealing with the population question, no one is responsible. Sidki's five-year plan in fact presumes that population growth will continue unchecked, at nearly 2.8 percent per year, the same as it has been through most of this decade. But a government report issued in December 1987 put the actual rate for that year at 3.1 percent.

This is not to say that nothing has been done. From 1977 through 1988, the aid program from the United States contributed $170 million in family planning assistance, through such organizations as the State Information Service and the ministry of health. The World Bank and other foreign governments have also contributed aid for this purpose. Contraceptives are widely and cheaply available; an estimated 30 percent of married couples use them, compared to 17 percent in 1975.

That sounds like progress, but many of these couples already have three or more children. And the government organizations responsible for implementing family planning programs are so inefficient and so crippled by bureaucratic infighting that Egypt has actually been forced to return millions of dollars donated by foreign governments and organizations for population control. The country has made only minimal progress in changing the social and religious environment that encourages large families.

Under Sadat, the man who bore official responsibility for the family planning program was Aziz Bindari, a laconic physician who readily admitted that he was making little progress in a "catastrophic situation."

The traditional patterns of family and village life, he said, are not favorable to birth control. Though the percentage of couples using contraception was rising, Bindari said women in the villages often had to sneak into the clinics to acquire their pills because their husbands disapproved. Egyptian women are not independent—only 8.2 percent of adult females are in the labor force—therefore, Bindari said, "any attempt to replicate Western patterns is irrelevant" in persuading them to have fewer babies.

He said Egyptians will respond to exhortations about family planning only if they have some concrete incentive to do so. They aren't interested, he said, in reducing the size of their families to help the government reach some abstract statistical goal. They have to be persuaded to stop viewing children as assets, as field hands or shop assistants or old-age insurance.

Unfortunately, Bindari said, "the whole pattern of village life is based on supporting traditional virtues, which include fertility. The male's personal pride and ambition can be expressed only by having children. That's why you will see a man of 50 take a new young bride and have another family."

Because the economic and political systems provide little opportunity for the village male to improve his station in life, Bindari said, the government's responsibility is to provide economic incentives to limit family size and to ensure a reliable supply of contraceptives to those who respond. Where that combination has been achieved, favorable results have been observed, showing that a demand for family planning exists or can be created.

Under Mubarak, the man who has assumed Bindari's role as chief family planning officer is Dr. Maher Mahran, a prominent obstetrician on the faculty of Ain Shams University medical school in Cairo. He believes that most Egyptians now want to limit the size of their families—they cannot afford six children and don't have room in their houses for them. The problem today, Mahran says, is the failure of the government to deliver the family planning services the people want.

"The majority of Egyptians are convinced of the need for family planning," he said in a 1987 interview. The evidence, he said, lies not just in the increased use of contraceptives but in "the huge number of abortions, even though it's illegal." The problem, he said, is not to create the demand for family planning services but to meet it, and in that, he said, the government has failed and will continue to fail.

Ten years elapsed between my conversation with Bindari and my conversation with Mahran, but in crucial respects they were identical. The doctors agreed that the need for population control is understood and the demand exists; they also agreed that sheer incompetence and lack of will on the part of the government health network, attributable to a failure of political leadership, have torpedoed every family planning program.

In *Where Is My Freedom?*, a provocative feminist documentary film that caused a political stir in the 1970s, director Layla Abu Seif captured in one scene some of the most critical failings of the family planning programs. It showed a young woman, a family planning counselor from the ministry of health, wearing a sweater, skirt and city shoes as she lurched and stumbled through a plowed field to make contact with squatting, black-robed, illiterate village women. Everyone knew the scene was accurate; field workers are usually the kind of people who qualify for government jobs—educated, urban Egyptians in city clothes, conscious of their status, ill-equipped to sell new ideas to clannish farm women who are totally dependent on their husbands.

But even if women are persuaded to accept the idea of limiting their families, the government agencies responsible for supplying information, contraceptives and clinical assistance are likely to fail in their mission. The system keeps breaking down.

The American aid mission supplied condoms in bright colors, much as the Americans had done in Vietnam, apparently on the assumption that red or yellow or green condoms would be more attractive to use than ordinary white ones. But many were never distributed because they were stolen off the docks in Alexandria and sent into the black market in countries where they are illegal. The same fate overtook several shipments of birth control pills.

When pills are available, their effective use is impeded by administrative failures in their distribution. Women depend on the staff of government clinics and their field workers to tell them how to use the pills and to ensure a reliable supply. But the distribution centers were for some time handing out as many as five different brands, not compatible with each other, substituting one for another as supplies varied. The effect of this, according to Bindari, was to disrupt menstrual cycles, leading many women who were taking the pill to abandon it and to talk their friends out of using it.

A system of incentive payments to workers in the clinics, in which everyone from doctor to janitor shared in proceeds from the sale of pills and bonuses for the insertion of intrauterine devices, was abandoned when it quickly became a new source of corruption—phony figures, coercion of women into buying pills when they sought other clinic services, multiple insertions of the same IUD into the same woman—but abolition of the incentive payments had such a depressing effect on staff morale that field work came to a virtual halt.

Bindari said the criticisms leveled against the government's performance on this vital matter were "100 percent true." But he said the family planning program should not be singled out for criticism because "it functions at the same level of efficiency as the rest of the government's services."

In January 1985, Mubarak created a National Population Council, the latest in a 30-year series of councils, boards, organizations and conferences charged with addressing the population problem. The National Population Council was to be an umbrella organization that would coordinate all the family planning activities of the ministries of health, planning, education, information, social welfare and local government. Dr. Mahran was appointed secretary general of this organization. More than a year elapsed before the Council even met.

"It was a giant turf fight," Mahran said. None of the cabinet departments wanted to give up any of its responsibilities or to permit the Council to run parallel programs more efficiently.

"Many people are allergic to anybody monitoring them or watching their activity," he said. "The sketchy, patchy arrangements that existed were useful for some people."

Mahran said Mubarak was "keen to correct things" and approved a four-part program in which the Council would work separately from the existing government organizations. The four parts were to be family planning; expanded work opportunities for women; an attack on illiteracy, to expand job qualifications and knowledge on family planning; and child health and immunization to keep more babies alive. If fewer infants died, mothers would nurse longer and stretch out their postpartum amenorrhea, and there would be less incentive to replace children who died, especially boys.

A decree was issued to this effect, Mahran said, and was presented to the first meeting of the Council, attended by the ministers of all the appropriate cabinet departments. "They all objected," he said. "They said the only power of implementation of any program lay with the government departments, not with a parallel agency." The result, he said, was that nothing came of the four-part program and the Council was reduced to research and reporting functions.

"Now, freeze the video here," he said. "The president could tell them all, 'Do this or you are out,' but that's not how things are done here. When was anybody ever kicked out in this country for failure to do the job?"

This was not much different from what was going on in Bindari's time, when the ministry of health and the ministry of social welfare were fighting over who was going to control family planning programs—a struggle that led to such absurdities as the establishment of rival clinics within 100 yards of each other. But Mahran put his finger on the overriding reason why such things are allowed to happen: Egypt has not made a serious effort at population control because the country's leaders have not been committed to it. The wholly unfounded belief that industrialization, technology and land reclamation could increase production enough to keep everybody fed and housed has allowed all three post-revolution leaders to dance around an issue that is politically and religiously volatile.

Under Nasser, the National Charter of 1962 stated explicitly that family planning was a priority issue, and the ministry of health began setting up the network of more than 3,000 family planning centers that exists today. But the government adopted few disincentives to childbearing. Mubarak has occasionally spoken strongly but has done little. Sadat and his prime ministers hardly even gave lip service to birth control, despite all their speeches about the demands posed by the rising population. They did not hide their embarrassment at the dogged, outspoken support for family planning by the only nationally prominent figure to make that commitment—Sadat's wife, Jehan.

When Dr. Mamdouh Gabr, then minister of health, arranged a conference on this subject in 1979, it was Mrs. Sadat who spoke, not the president. The newspapers duly recorded her observation that "previous efforts have proved to be futile" and that "we no longer have any time to waste. The problems have accumulated in such a way as to urge all of us into immediate action, avoiding the mistakes of the past." When the conference ended, no more was heard of it, and of course what little influence Mrs. Sadat had died with her husband. Mubarak's wife, a much more conventional woman that Mrs. Sadat, does not take public positions on controversial matters.

With about 40 percent of the population aged less than 15, the proliferation of children is threatening to overtake the gains made since the revolution even on so emotionally clear-cut an issue as child labor. In theory, it is regulated by law and preempted by compulsory education, but in fact, the more children who have been born to the poor, the more the poor have had to put those children to work to supplement family incomes. And the more money those children have brought in, the more their parents have found it desirable to have more children to earn more money.

Cairo is a city of working children. Little boys and girls collect the garbage, rummaging through it for anything useful or saleable. Boys on bicycles with trays of bread on their heads weave through the traffic. Little boys start early to learn the auto-repair trade, and they can be seen at any hour, black with grease, crawling around under transmissions or banging out dented fenders. When a ring at our doorbell was followed by the cry of "laundry," the person at the door was 10 years old. Nobody really knows how many children work on the farms, but every rural road and field is thronged with children at work—planting, picking, hauling, herding animals.

Naturally, editorialists and sociologists and government officials deplore child labor, just as they deplore illiteracy and malnutrition. Speeches and planning documents and food supply studies and political platforms all recognize that the country cannot go on as it is. But except for Mrs. Sadat and people such as Mahran and Bindari, who are directly involved in family planning work, I have never met anyone, in the government or not, who urged unequivocally that the problem be attacked directly, at its source, through a comprehensive and well-organized program to reduce the number of births—a program that would include tough disincentives for large families and direct economic rewards for those who had fewer babies.

Mahran has said that even if everyone who is already married were to stop having babies, the population would continue to increase for 60 years. And what will this unending human tide mean for the future of Egypt? Perhaps it was best expressed to me by Boutros Boutros-Ghali, the veteran minister of state for foreign affairs: "Egypt with 20 million people could have been a Mediterranean country, a Greece or Portugal. Egypt with 70 million people will be Bangladesh."

7

Cairo

Cairo is at its best in the twilight.

From the edge of the western desert just before dusk, when the sun drops behind the Pyramids into the trackless sand sea of North Africa, Cairo twinkles like a storybook city in the Nile Valley below.

In the cool tranquility of the dusty plateau where the Pyramids stand, it is possible to hear the call to prayer rising from the minarets of a thousand mosques. The chant of the *muezzin*, even though nowadays it is tape recorded and amplified, evokes the golden city of history, the exotic, sensual center of Muslim civilization.

From terraces on the upper floors of the apartment buildings and new hotels along the Nile, the pastel colors of sky and water and the majestic silhouettes of the *feluccas* with their sails full in the breeze stir memories of the colonial paradise where European royalty and British functionaries played out their fantasies.

To the tourists on well-regulated itineraries who see Cairo from air-conditioned buses, the city emits the magical charm that once lured Greeks and Armenians, White Russians and Turks, Italians and Lebanese, Britons and Frenchmen, to settle there and give Cairo the overlay of their cultures that made it the most cosmopolitan city of the Middle East or Africa.

But Cairo viewed from above or from the inside of a tour bus is like a belly dancer seen through the smoky haze of an Egyptian nightclub: alluring and desirable at a distance, but much less appealing up close. The truth is that Cairo is a creaking wreck, acutely afflicted with every urban ailment: overcrowding, filth, decay, disorganization, noise, pollution. The city is utterly unequipped to bear the burdens of Egypt's quest for prosperity and development. The Mubarak government, with substantial American assistance, has expended vast amounts of money and energy on improving conditions in the Cairo metropolitan area, with some success in transportation, water and sewer service and housing. Private and public construction projects have transformed the city in the past 15 years: apartment buildings, hotels, hospitals, sewage treatment plants and a new ministry of foreign affairs have all appeared, along with elevated freeways, parking garages, and a new passenger terminal at the airport to facilitate transportation. Combined with the flashy boutiques and restaurants that opened during the days of *infitah* and the oil boom, these improvements give Cairo a veneer of livability, at least for those with money. But the veneer is thin.

It is an exaggeration to say, as some writers have, that Cairo is the Calcutta of Africa. Nobody is starving in the streets; there are no emaciated bodies floating in the Nile. And hardly anyone is truly homeless in the sense of having to sleep on the sidewalks or under the bridges. But no government concerned with improving the living standards of Egypt's people, or with ensuring political stability, can overlook the fact that Cairo is an urban time bomb that will have to be defused if those goals are to be reached.

The significance of Cairo to Egypt's overall political and economic prospects can hardly be overstated. With a metropolitan area population of about 14.5 million, Cairo is home to more than a quarter of all Egyptians. It is the largest Arab city and the largest city in Africa. It is not only the seat of government but also the country's industrial, artistic, intellectual and economic center, and thus is a powerful magnet drawing ever more people from the countryside.

Tourists find it thrilling, but businessmen and potential investors tend to recall the noise, dirt and confusion more than they recall the sunsets on the Nile. It is easy now for a potential investor to find a good hotel room or comfortable apartment and to make international telephone calls, but whether employees of his enterprise will be able to get to work on time is another question. Cairo is at once Egypt's greatest asset and its greatest liability.

It takes only a short while for a newcomer to feel the impact of this charming, maddening metropolis. The first ride through the city gives a sense of the vibrancy and intensity of its life: dense crowds milling about on the rutted streets, boys hustling with their battered tin tea trays to serve the men playing backgammon and puffing on water pipes in dim cafes, drivers shouting and horns blaring in the tangled traffic, neon lights flashing at the nightclubs and clip joints, commuters jamming the water taxis on the Nile, lines forming at the movies and the juice bars, lovers whispering beneath the banyan trees along the river, worshipers praying, shoppers haggling with vendors at outdoor markets, their voices rising over the confusion of peddlers, goatherds, children, beggars, soldiers, students and windowshoppers who form the Cairo parade.

The very names of the streets evoke Cairo's flamboyant, violent history: Ramses, the greatest Pharaoh; Champollion, the Frenchman who deciphered the Rosetta stone; Huda Shaarawi, the daring feminist who took off the veil; Oum Kalthoum, the singer who mesmerized the Arab world; 26th of July, the day King Farouk sailed into exile; Saad Zaghloul, the nationalist patriot sent into exile by the British; Shagarat ad-Dur (String of Pearls), the Turkish slave girl who ruled as queen for 80 days in the thirteenth century until outraged Mamelukes had her beaten to death and her body, clad only in underwear, thrown from the Citadel of Saladin—the same citadel that still dominates Cairo's skyline.

From the Pyramids to the mosque of Muhammad Ali, Cairo is studded with rich relics of its Pharaonic, Roman, Coptic, Mameluke and Ottoman eras that would take a lifetime to explore. Many of them are shabby and neglected, even though tourism is a bulwark of the economy, but they still symbolize the city's brilliant and diverse history. A day spent wandering the covered bazaar of Khan el-Khalili and the thousand-year-old mosque and university of al-Azhar nearby is a day spent immersed in another era and another culture.

In the Nasser era, these monuments of culture fell into disuse because there were more important demands on Egypt's resources and few tourists visited Cairo anyway. With the onset of the "Open Door" policy and the collapse of Beirut as the premier Arab business center, Cairo had an opportunity to become an international commercial capital. But Egypt in the 1970s paid a heavy price for the decades of neglect. The city simply could not accommodate the financiers fleeing Lebanon or the investors lured by *infitah*. They didn't want history or colorful bazaars, they wanted international telephone and telex lines, modern office space, reliable supplies of water and electricity, comfortable apartments, adequate roads, temperature-controlled warehouses and a tolerable airport, none of which the city could then provide.

The result, a decade later, is that the facilities have improved but the opportunities have mostly moved on. Cairo's essential underpinnings are much less shaky than they were when Sadat invited the world to move in, but the true boom that the city could have enjoyed if it had been ready evolved for most residents into a superficial redecoration.

New facades went up on refurbished shops selling the prized imported goods that had been unavailable in the era of economic restraint. Expensive restaurants proliferated—the 1987 Dining Guide published by *Cairo Today* magazine had 36 pages of restaurant listings. Trendy boutiques with pseudo-chic names like "Baby Jean" and "Playboy" took over neighborhoods where a decade earlier there were still signs in Russian. Colonel Sanders beams out at Cairenes from Kentucky Fried Chicken stores (which are owned by Kuwaitis, not Egyptians). Virtually every major international hotel chain opened a big new establishment—each, of course, complete with expensive night club.

It is easy for a visitor to spend days in Cairo, moving among the new hotels, seeing friends in handsome villas in Heliopolis and Maadi and meeting urbane Egyptians in their eight-room apartments in Zamalek, and be only dimly aware of the rot that afflicts most of the city and its population.

From the Nile Hilton Hotel, a ten-minute walk into the back streets of the Bulaq quarter or a ten-minute ride into the alleys of medieval Cairo is a journey into another world, a world of such squalor that it would overwhelm the senses of the comfortable classes tooling along on the new elevated freeways. The contrast is comparable to that between chic Manhattan and the slums of Brooklyn, except that the occupants of Cairo's downtrodden neighborhoods are not ethnic newcomers or outcasts from the fringe of society; they are civil servants and factory workers and merchants, the backbone of the society.

One of the first Israeli journalists to visit Cairo said it was not a city but an overgrown African village. He had a point. Many of the metropolitan area's people are not really urbanized at all but live in communities of family, alley and neighborhood that function independently of other parts of the city. Naguib Mahfouz's famous novel, *Midaq Alley,* recounts tales of violence, love, greed, lust, generosity and village-like intimacy that all unfold among the residents of a single block-long alley. But the modern city is actually much more complex than that in its patterns of housing, transportation, employment and communication—so much so that the Egyptians worry about the breakdown of family tradition and the diminution of traditions caused by the sheer size of the city and the time required to move from home to school or work. Families whose members have always lived near each other are increasingly being driven apart by the lack of housing in their own neighborhoods and the spread of jobs into the distant suburbs. Grandmothers and uncles who watched over children and taught by example are out of reach.

As the Pyramids and Roman ruins and early Christian churches attest, there have been urban settlements where Cairo now stands for millennia. The history of the modern city, however, is conventionally dated from 969 AD. In that year, a former slave named Gawhar marched an army of Fatimid warriors into what was already an established Arab settlement called Fustat. Rather than camp among those he had subdued, he set up his own headquarters nearby and named it *al-Qahira,* the Victorious, which in Arabic is the name the city still bears.

The Fatimids took their name from Fatima, daughter of the prophet Muhammad, and they claimed descent from her and her husband, Ali—that is, they were Shiite Muslims, adherents of the same branch of the faith practiced today in Iran. Their reign over Egypt lasted only 200 years, until the Seljuk Turks installed the famous Saladin as vizier in 1169 and restored the Sunni form of Islam, but the Fatimids' royal enclosure formed the core of the city and remained its center until the development of the "European" city in the nineteenth century. The outlines and monuments of Fatimid Cairo are still there and still define the center of life in the old city. The three great gates of Bab al-Futuh, Bab al-Nasr and Bab al-Zuweila (gate of succor, gate of victory, gate of the tribe of Zuweila) and the mosque and university of al-Azhar are now the core of a teeming, decaying neighborhood where the squalor has not entirely erased the charm and artistry of the past.

Today it might be said that there are acutally four Cairos. The old Fatimid city is part of one of them, the one that is the festering agglomeration that is home to most Cairenes. It includes working-class quasi-slums such as Bulaq, Shubra and Sayeda Zeinab. These neighborhoods are home to millions of people, and they cannot be described as comfortable. The atmosphere is a heady blend of spices, tea, dung, soot, tobacco, coffee, exhaust fumes, hashish, frying fava beans and a relentless din raised by shouting women, enthusiastic vendors, braying and barking animals, children kicking soccer balls and radios playing at full volume.

A second Cairo is the new middle-class city: villas, high-rise apartment buildings and up-to-date shops. With its gardens and garages and wide streets, this Cairo, made up of patches that skip all the way from the airport at the eastern end of the metropolitan area to the Pyramids on the west, takes up a lot of the community's total space, and because it is so spread out consumes a disproportionate share of the bus service and water and sewer lines. Even though many of the villas are being converted into multifamily flats through the addition of new stories on top, this part of Cairo is still relatively uncrowded. This, of course, enhances its desirability, and its inaccessibility to the mass of Cairenes who come there mostly to clean the kitchens and repair the appliances and work in the shops. Paradoxically, despite its relatively up-to-date appearance, this Cairo in its expansion has surrounded and incorporated pockets of rural Egypt where nothing seems to have changed for centuries. At the western end of the city, hidden among new apartment buildings and behind sleek new shops is an open area the size of two football fields where camels, goats and donkeys are traded. Here, crafty semiliterate traders from upper Egypt gather at dawn several mornings a week to haggle over the price of their animals; the camels are sold for food. Hundreds of camels, donkeys and goats are tethered, to be examined from tooth to hoof by prospective buyers; it's hard to say which is more powerful, the noise or the stench. The camel market is a popular stop on the tourist itinerary.

A third city is "European Cairo," the central city of continental appearance and continental pretensions that began to develop in the nineteenth century, after the Napoleonic invasion, and flourished during the British occupation. This includes what is now downtown Cairo, where the banks, movie theaters, airline offices and department stores are, and the residential communities of Garden City (site of the American and British embassies) and the

Zamalek quarter, on the island of Gezira in the Nile, where prominent Egyptians such as former Prime Minister Mustafa Khalil,
former Foreign Minister Ismail Fahmy and Sadat's confidant Sayed
Marei have their apartments. If it were cleaned up and the sidewalks
repaved, this Cairo would again resemble the European cities that
were its model; it would look like Genoa.

The fourth Cairo is hardly visible from the street at all. It is
rooftop Cairo, a clandestine city that has sprung up on the roofs of
the other three. This community, probably home to at least half a
million people, consists of huts, shanties, lean-tos, chicken coops
and even little gardens that have defied periodic attempts by the
government to clear them out because their occupants have nowhere to go. This is another manifestation of the acute overcrowding that populated the City of the Dead; its effect, residents of
Cairo say, is that from the ground Cairo looks like a big modern
city but from the air parts of it look like a string of Delta villages.

European Cairo, once the opulent playground of the prerevolutionary continental set who kept the natives at a distance, is
still the most important in terms of Egypt's international image, if
not in domestic political terms. It was European Cairo that was
found inadequate by the bankers and corporate executives looking
for a new Middle East base after the collapse of Beirut. Modern
office space is plentiful now, mostly in sprawling new neighborhoods west of the Nile, but the shortage of it that was the
inevitable consequence of the Nasser era cost Egypt dearly in lost
opportunity when Beirut blew up.

Athens, London, and Nicosia are home to dozens of banks and
corporate offices that probably would have gone to Cairo when
Egypt's "Open Door" concided with the civil war in Lebanon, if
the city had been prepared to accommodate them. The dimly
lighted trash-filled lobbies, filthy stairways and rickety elevators of
once grand buildings sent businessmen fleeing, even before they
heard the bad news about telephone service. This shabby disarray
was Nasser's legacy to Egypt's capital, and no optimistic pronouncements from his sucessor could sweep it away. Only now,
nearly two decades after Nasser's death, has Mubarak's government
begun to make Cairo functional again.

The savants of the Napoleonic expedition found Cairo, in Alan
Moorehead's account, "a warren of narrow unpaved streets and
nondescript Turkish houses covering about three square miles.

Rubbish lay about on every side, the haunt of scavenging dogs and cats, and in the worst slums it was hard to say which were the ruins of the fallen buildings and which the hovels of the present generation."

But by the middle of the nineteenth century, Cairo had been transformed by an invasion of Europeans, who were drawn by the plans for the Suez Canal, by British interests in India, and by the demand for Egyptian cotton in European textile mills. The population was about 15 percent non-Egyptian by the turn of the twentieth century; eventually the European population exceeded 100,000.

For more than a century, European Cairo was the preserve of foreigners who ran their own shops, set up their own entertainments and lived the life of colonial comfort, sheltered from the reality of the rest of the city. Their role in the development of the modern city was summarized in the "Housing and Community Upgrading for Low-Income Egyptians" report that the government and the USAID mission published jointly in 1977:

> Their political power reinforced by legal and fiscal privileges under the capitulations [granted by the Egyptian government], they soon dominated every field of urban economic activity. The emergence of a colonial structure with increasingly sharper differences between Egyptians and foreigners was paralleled by the growth of modern districts adjacent to the older quarters. . . . Businesses, offices, hotels, theaters, department stores, clubs, restaurants, and amusement places, including the first movie theater, stretched westward from Azbakia [the center of the old city] constituting the nucleus of the modern Central Business District. Foreign franchises took over transport and the provision of utilities: water and gas in 1865, electricity and tramways in 1893, street lighting in 1898. Municipal services were confined to street paving and maintenance, and work on a sewage disposal system only started in 1909. These public utilities were directed to serve the new developments, while the majority of the city's population continued to live under medieval conditions.

That era ended with the Suez war of 1956, when France and Britain joined Israel in attacking Egypt. Nasser was determined to rid the city of foreign domination as he had the government and the canal. But Egypt is still wrestling with the unhappy legacy of that era of foreign domination; the city constructed by prosperous foreigners to serve themselves was ill equipped to be the teeming capital of a Third-World country.

James Aldridge, in his affectionate history of the city, has described what happened as the foreigners were driven out:

> After 1956, the shops employed mostly Egyptian girls behind the counters. European barbers became Egyptian barbers, European restaurants became Egyptian restaurants. The streets themselves began perceptibly to lose their European pedestrians, and already one noticed large numbers of poor Egyptian men in galabayas and Egyptian peasant women in black meliyas (shapeless gowns) walking the streets of European Cairo, not trying to tell you something but simply being there as part and parcel of their own city. At first they were a sort of a lower middle class overflow from their own old territory across the Ezbekiya, but by 1960 they were established in the western part of the old city for good.
>
> Inevitably too, as these poorer and lower middle class Egyptians began to fill up the European places, the modern city deteriorated a little. The Europeans had insisted on European standards, but the poorer Egyptians had poorer standards. Pavements began to get bumpy, paint began to peel, trams began to rattle, porches went unswept, metros got dusty and the back streets filthy.

The decline of Cairo had begun. The question was not only one of standards; it also involved money and politics.

In the post-revolution environment, it was not only desirable but essential that the Egyptian people become at last the masters of their own capital city. But they were poor and unsophisticated. Their control of the streets, added to the lack of public funds and the concealment of private wealth for fear of sequestration, made it inevitable that Cairo would deteriorate. The result, which Sadat's advisers failed to foresee, was that when representatives of foreign businesses arrived to look for office space and apartments and qualified staff, the city had little to offer that did not require substantial capital investment for renovation, and those accommodations that were available quickly shot up in price. This was a crucial defect in a country that had tied its economic revival to an anticipated influx of foreign investment.

Our own first apartment in Cairo was emblematic of what had happened to the European city since the revolution. It was on the fifth floor of a fortress-like building behind Shepheard's Hotel, between the American embassy and the Nile. The elevator, at the rear of the dingy lobby, was unreliable and many of the light sockets on the stairwells were empty.

The apartment itself had once been splendid: big rooms, high ceilings, French windows, gilt cornices, two full bathrooms, servants' entrance, a view of the Nile from the terrace. It was typical of that part of the city.

But it had long needed the kind of work that nobody was prepared to pay for. The plumbing was so erratic that at certain hours of the day there was no water, at others only cold water and at others only scalding hot water, even in the toilets. The fuse box was a jumble of exposed wires. The appliances were worn out and the furnishings were as decrepit as they were ugly. The Nile view had been cut to a sliver by construction of the new Shepheard's some years before and now the river was visible only at the end of a rubbish-filled alley behind the hotel kitchen.

There are thousands of apartments like that in Cairo. They are an indispensable part of the housing stock and until the early 1980s they were also the chief source of office space. It was thus common for a new enterprise in Cairo to lay out $100,000 to find one apartment for its director to live in and one to be the office (both with telephones in place, of course, since new telephone service was impossible to obtain), pay the *simsaar* or agent his fee, shell out key money and put the two places into habitable condition. And all that had to be done amid the noise and the paralysis on the streets and in an utterly unresponsive bureaucratic environment. Newcomers were frustrated and exhausted even before they tried to accomplish any work, and it soon became apparent that Egypt's economic opening had been undertaken backwards: the infrastructure should have been repaired first, but of course there was no money to do that. Nasser had left Cairo as broke as it was dilapidated.

The deterioration of the city is attributable to many of the same causes that crippled the national economy. Sequestration took some of the best buildings out of private hands and consigned them to public ownership, with a corresponding decline in care. Fear of sequestration reduced the incentive of other owners to invest in maintenance. Rent controls restricted income. Shortages of foreign currency cut off the supply of building materials and replacement equipment. Skilled plumbers and carpenters emigrated. The constant threat of war overrode the need for maintenance. And the ever growing population kept increasing the burden on an ever creakier structure. (In Cairo, the population increase is caused not only by birth but by migration. Amin Abdel Hafez, then governor of Cairo, told me in 1976, when every train from the south bore a cargo of men on the roofs of the cars, that 2,000 peasants were arriving each day from Upper Egypt alone. I asked him if the government could not stop this; he said no. "This is a free country," he said. "People can go where they want. This isn't China.")

The virtual abandonment of maintenance that eroded the country is said to have been the result not only of the lack of money but of an aversion to maintenance in principle on the part of Nasser. Mustafa Amin says that he once came upon Nasser, who was notorious for keeping all details of government in his own hands, going over the proposed national budget and striking out with bold red strokes an entire section. When Amin asked him what he was deleting, he replied, "Maintenance. In the army I was in the maintenance branch, and that's where all the thieves were."

This is not to say that prosperous Egyptians, or those fortunate enough to have secured apartments years ago when flats were plentiful and rents cheap, are living in slum conditions. On the contrary, within those shabby buildings are tenants who have often been able to keep their own apartments comfortable. Those un-prepossessing lobbies are often the gateways to luxurious living upstairs.

But the water and electricity can fail even in the best buildings. And the high-rises that have sprung up in the past decade in fashionable neighborhoods along the Nile and near the Pyramids are not immune. The 1986 edition of *Cairo: A Practical Guide,* published by the American University in Cairo, contains this advice to house hunters: "Be wary of living very high up, despite the attractions of the view; there are occasionally difficulties with 'out of order' elevators, water pressure is weaker the higher you are in a building, and firemen say that anything above the third floor is not safe." But to live on the lower floors, of course, is to live closer to the deafening noise of the streets.

Nor was it only the housing stock that deteriorated under the assault of war, socialism, overpopulation and indifference. Side-walks cracked. The few parks were strewn with litter. Movie the-aters that once were palaces became grimy and smelly. Government offices open to the public surrendered their dignity to the crowds, the noise and the dirt. And virtually every public service, from transportation to sewage treatment, began to break down. While Sadat was exchanging banter with Barbara Walters, Cairo's sewer lines were giving way and the city's ordinary citizens were climbing into buses through the windows because there was no way to get through the mobs at the doors.

Outside European Cairo conditions were, and remain, correspondingly worse. Millions of Cairenes live in small, dark, dirty buildings that date back hundreds of years and are reached through narrow alleys piled high with dung and garbage. Thirty percent of Cairo's dwelling units have no water supply, according to the 1976 census, and at that time only 58.3 percent were connected to a sewerage system—but even so, the sewers frequently overflowed. Only now is a sewerage network being installed in the sprawling new neighborhoods on the west side of the Nile.

"So the city hasn't actually sunk yet," a newspaper editorialist wrote in 1978,

> or suffocated from lack of oxygen. Or collapsed all at once in a heap. The ever thickening knot of cars and people which strangles the city center for a good part of every day still manages to disentangle itself at dusk. But housing space is divided and redivided into increasingly uninhabitable accommodation resembling containers more than living quarters. The appalling state of public transport, of the city power supply, of the sewerage network, the telephone system and other basic utilities and services are already topics of international comment, since they concern potential investors. By slow adjustment we are narrowing our mental and physical horizons to what must be humanly unacceptable levels. We get up at dawn to get to work on time, lock ourselves inside our container homes at dusk to escape the dirt in the street, eat more tack and less fresh food to survive rising prices, do dreadful things to our fellow passengers to secure a place on the bus, we bribe and cajole to jump waiting lists and seek out crooks to do us a favor. . . . A quarter of the country's population is decaying in one decadent city. Cairo has had a thousand rich and fruitful years. It deserves a more dignified retirement. The desert cities may be the country's top priority now. Whatever they have to offer must be better than this.

By 1978, the year of Camp David, while Sadat was inviting the world to Cairo, the city had become so rickety and disorganized that it was vulnerable to paralysis even from minor incidents. For example, a water main break beneath a downtown street put thousands of telephone and telex lines out of commission for a week because the water soaked through old paper-insulated cables at a main relay point.

The difficulty of repairs in such incidents is compounded by the incoherence in the pipes, electric wires, water lines and other utility connections beneath the streets. The lines and pipes were installed by different suppliers from different countries in different decades and nobody knows which pipe or wire connects to what. Consultants from the Continental Telephone Company who were brought in to analyze the phone system reported in 1977 that there was no map of the existing phone lines; the wires just ran here and there beneath the streets. Several years later, French engineers building Cairo's first subway line encountered the same problem— they hit unmapped telephone, sewer and electricity lines that brought the excavations to a halt every few yards.

The entire structure of the city was so fragile that a single mistake could paralyze entire systems for hours. One afternoon a truck came to Cairo from Alexandria, hauling crates of Soviet-made equipment for the steel mill at Helwan, just south of the capital. Because there was then no bypass road, the truck had to go directly through the city and down the Nile corniche. The cargo was stacked so high that it ripped down overhead wires carrying electric power to the battered old trolley coaches that provided the only public transportation along that heavily traveled route.

There were no police or fire units around to shut off the current or splice the wires or move the truck, and even if the bystanders had known whom to call they would not have been able to get through because of the condition of the telephone system.

So the truck just sat there, blocking the only road linking downtown Cairo and the southern suburbs. The driver exchanged shouts with motorists trying to go around him while all the trolley coaches back up the line, filled to overflowing as usual, came to a halt because the power line had been severed. At every coach stop, of course, a mob of would-be riders waited, with no way of knowing that service had been interrupted, no way of finding out how long they would have to wait and no alternative means of transportation.

In fact, Cairo's transportation system veered between chaos and paralysis throughout Sadat's presidency. Like the housing supply, the water and sewer network, the electric system and the telephones, the transportation facilities were terminally inadequate for the burdens being placed on them by the "Open Door" economic policy. Foreign representatives of service organizations could work in makeshift quarters, but it was nearly impossible to find sites for industrial operations where all the necessary facilities were adequate. This was true not just in the Cairo area but throughout Egypt, and explains the necessity for the vast expenditures on new cities such as Tenth of Ramadan.

American officials correctly saw the need for transit improvement as an opportunity to make a quick impression on the Egyptians, whom they were trying to convince of the benefits of the country's new relationship with Washington. The AID program arranged for the Egyptians to purchase 1600 American buses on concessionary terms, and these were rushed into service on the streets of Cairo, each bearing the familiar "Hands Across the Sea" emblem of USAID. (These vehicles, though welcome, emitted so much noise, even amid the customary din of Cairo, that the Egyptians complained. They referred to the blast of sound as the "Voice of America" and demanded muffler modifications, which they got.)

Of course, the traffic congestion was already such that the addition of more buses only compounded it. Mahmoud Abdel Hafez, then governor of Cairo, told me in 1976 that he had received two sets of studies about the city's transportation problems. One showed how many more buses would have to be put on the streets to carry all the riders and the other showed that if that many buses were added to existing traffic the congestion would harden into a complete halt.

The city's transportation crisis was not caused by the sheer number of motor vehicles, which was negligible by European or American standards. At the end of 1977, there were approximately 225,000 motor vehicles registered in the greater Cairo area. That was fewer than in Washington, D.C., a city with less than a tenth of Cairo's population, and only about 10 percent of the number in New York. And traffic analyses showed that Cairo's population travels relatively little as measured against European cities, because the women generally stay at home and so many of the residents of the capital are children.

But the city still puts a heavy strain on its transportation facilities because it is so decentralized. Some government ministries are downtown, others are in Nasr City, on the road to the airport. Banks, insurance companies, the newspapers, embassies, shops and hotels are clustered in the central city, drawing workers and clients into the heart of town. But the three huge universities—Cairo, Ain Shams and al-Azhar—are in three widely separated parts of the city. The big industries are in Helwan, south of Cairo, and Shubra al-Kheima, to the north. Major military facilities are scattered throughout the area. The result is heavy traffic in all directions night and day, with surly and ill-trained drivers bulling their way along inadequate roads through crowds of pedestrians, delivery boys on bicycles, donkey carts, and horse-drawn vehicles.

Mubarak's government can take credit for improvements in the Cairo transport network that hardly seemed possible a decade ago. A subway line that linked the central city with main employment centers opened in 1987, financed mostly by France. The metropolitan area now is crisscrossed by "flyovers," or elevated highways, that have taken through traffic off the congested streets (though at a high price in aesthetics; the flyovers are irretrievably ugly). The government has encouraged merchants and vendors to acquire small pickup trucks to replace the slow-moving donkey carts that blocked traffic. A fleet of mini-buses has supplemented the city's public transportation network. (But there is a very high price for these improvements, too: The rapid growth in the number of motor vehicles, which is now estimated to be more than one million, has so polluted the air over Cairo that physicians have been advising pregnant women to leave town. Egyptian gasoline is refined only to low levels and many vehicles are poorly tuned, compounding the emissions problem.) A direct highway link from the airport to the southern suburbs has diverted heavy traffic away from the central city. And a police campaign that began under Sadat has cut down on the chronic indiscipline for which the city's drivers were notorious. Cairenes now are much less likely than they used to be to drive on the sidewalks, ignore traffic signals or park wherever they please.

Nor is transportation the only area of conspicuous improvement. The United States has contributed $1.04 billion to expand the water supply and sewage treatment network. Sewers are at last being installed on the west side of the Nile, cutting off an immediate threat to public health. The government took advantage of the construction of a wastewater treatment line in the Abbasiyya quarter to raze several blocks of slums and convert the site into a park; that and the landscaping of the grounds around the Citadel have added patches of greenery and a touch of civility to a city sorely lacking in both. (Cairo in 1970 had 1.6 square meters of recreational open space per capita; comparable cities in the developing world have at least 16.) New branches of the state-owned grocery store network have been established throughout the city, eliminating the long lines that used to form before dawn. Construction of a 1260 megawatt power plant, with $263 million in AID funds, has stabilized the electricity supply—and helped to end the power surges that blew out computers. After an expenditure of nearly $2 billion, the telephone system, which was one of Cairo's greatest liabilities in the attempt to attract foreign investment, is now almost adequate. In fact, Cairenes credit the improved telephone service with some of the improvement in traffic flow: The work of all those messengers and drivers who used to have to travel around the city to make appointments and deliver notes for their bosses can now be done by telephone, which takes their vehicles off the streets.

In short, the deterioration of the city has been arrested, basic services have improved and conditions have stabilized. In combination with the new hotels, office buildings, shops and restaurants developed by private investors, these improvements have enabled Cairo to throw off a generation of lethargy and rot. The city is again the most dynamic in the Middle East. The stodgy grimness of the Nasser era is gone, along with the piled-up sandbags at the entrances of buildings that characterized the era of war.

But in the meantime, of course, the city's unchecked growth continues to make expensive new demands on these services. The vast blocks of apartments rising around the perimeter of the city require ever more electricity, water and sewer lines, bus service and telephones, to say nothing of schools and roads. And because the sprawl of residential neighborhoods has not been coordinated with industrial and commercial growth, more and more people are required to travel greater and greater distances to get to work.

During the bread riots of January 1977, some of the demonstrators turned on motorists and hurled rocks at the cars; after all, ownership of a car was a sure indicator of a person who was prospering amid the general misery. That was at a time when the first criticisms were being heard about the "fat cats" and new millionaires who were benefiting from Sadat's policies while nothing was being done for the masses. In that atmosphere, it seemed politically risky for the government to commit its limited resources to improving the roads and the telephone system instead of building housing and hospitals. Only the rich, the argument went, owned motor vehicles and telephones, so only they would benefit from such improvements.

The counter-argument prevailed. Egypt was dependent on foreign investment for its future, and roads and telephones had to be brought up to date if any foreign investment was to be attracted. The upper classes were going to drive whether traffic conditions improved or not, and in any case the industrial and commercial life of the city demanded improvements in the flow of traffic. Buses and trucks use the flyovers too.

In a way, this was Egypt's version of the "trickle down" theory, and on some levels it seems to work. The highway improvements have made it easier for Cairenes who own cars or can afford taxis to get to work, and on their way they can see at last the first hospitals and schools that they expected to be built when peace came. More money is in circulation and there is more to spend it on.

But the gap between Egypt's haves and have-nots continues to grow, and it is especially visible in Cairo. Here, for example, is how *Business Monthly,* the magazine of the American Chamber of Commerce in Egypt, described the "World Trade Center" under construction in 1987 on "33,000 square meters of prime river-front property" just north of downtown:

> The World Trade Center will be housed in an expansive six-level structure linked by passenger elevators and escalators, and complete with exclusive shops and restaurants, cinemas, exhibition halls, conference facilities, tennis courts and sports facilities, underground garage space, communications links to international networks of on-line information service and data banks, access to satellite broadcasting computer terminals, business services, and simultaneous translation services which will use the most modern microchip radio transmission. The trade center facilities will overlook an open-air courtyard where terrace restaurants will adjoin a series of internationally known department stores and fashion salons. . . . On the south side of the complex, two 31-story, luxury residential towers will accommodate 208 spacious apartments with central air conditioning, garbage disposals, separate maid's quarters, swim-

ming pool, health club, private gardens, children's play areas
and a supermarket. From the imported Spanish tiles to the
streamlined Japanese elevators, every component of the trade
center project will emphasize quality.

Garbage disposals? Spanish tiles? Internationally known fashion salons? And all this an enormous black marble complex that
towers over the city, a visible symbol of exclusivity and unap-
proachable wealth? It may be that Cairo needs this kind of project
to attract the international business to which it aspires, but it is
politically volatile by definition. Every up-to-date person in Cairo
seems to know that this project is being financed by the Arab
International Bank, which is headed by Mustafa Khalil, who was
prime minister at the time of the peace treaty; where did he get this
kind of money? This is not to say that Khalil, a man of known
rectitude, has done anything unethical, but the very fact that he is
associated with such a project, in partnership with foreigners, provides ammunition to the economically disenfranchised and the
xenophobic religious extremists, to whom the era of foreign-domi-
nated opulence is anathema. In the 1977 bread riots and the 1986
riot by police conscripts, the targets of destruction included such
visible symbols of wealth and foreign influence as the exclusive
hotels and night clubs on the Pyramids road. Egypt cannot afford a
repetition of such incidents because they shut down the tourist
trade.

There is no doubt that Cairo today is much more hospitable to
anyone with money, Egyptian or foreign, than it was at the time of
Nasser's death. But there are still millions of residents trapped in
squalor for whom those new high-rise buildings serve only to cut
off the view of Cairo's glorious twilights. As the political center
of Egypt, Cairo lives in a state of fragile balance between the need
to encourage private investment and the free market, and the need
to channel resources into development that aids ordinary people.
To allow that balance to tip on the side of conspicuous consumption and ostentatious displays of new wealth is to invite political
reaction, especially from the religious extremists, who pose the
most intractable challenge to the regime.

CHAPTER

8

The President-Patriarch and the Limits of Democracy

Sadat, ignoring the evidence, always insisted that the other Arabs would follow him on his one-man stampede toward peace with Israel. He ridiculed the notion that a separate peace would leave Egypt "isolated" from its cultural family. Egypt's population is greater than that of all other Arab nations combined; this fact alone, Sadat said, meant that Egypt could never be "isolated." Arab leaders who declined to follow him—leaders whom he ridiculed as "dwarfs" and "shoeless goatherds," as "mice or monkeys" manipulated by the Soviet Union—could cut themselves off from Egypt, but the isolation would be theirs, not Egypt's.

Egypt needed peace and had earned peace. In the Arab struggle against Israel, it was Egyptians who died while other Arab states postured and orated. (Syria's participation on the eastern front was rarely mentioned in Egypt after Syria rejected the peace initiative and joined the "Steadfastness Front" of Sadat's opponents.) Had Sadat been less impetuous and less arrogant—had he, for example, consulted the leaders of Saudi Arabia in advance of his journey to Israel and refrained from public denunciations of them afterward— he might have gained at least sullen tolerance of his peace initiative. But Sadat was less than statesmanlike in defending his policies. He responded to Arab criticism with shrill and contemptuous denunciations. He made a great televised show of turning his back on the rest of the Arab world and embracing Western leaders such as "my friend Giscard," President Valéry Giscard d'Estaing of France.

In substance and in form, this was Sadat's most serious mis-calculation, his most dangerous political blunder. The other Arabs expelled Egypt from the League of Arab States and moved the headquarters of the organization, symbolic center of Arab unity, from Cairo to Tunis. They cut off financial assistance to Egypt, closed their embassies, pulled out their national airlines and aban-doned joint development ventures. These were not empty gestures: They cost Egypt whatever chance it had to be the business center of an oil-rich Arab world, they cut off incalculable amounts of de-velopment capital that might have been invested in Egypt, and they contributed to the religious and cultural unrest that culminated in Sadat's assassination.

With the abandonment of Arabism, the repudiation of Nasser was complete. In Heikal's words, "Egypt's opting out had a cen-trifugal effect on all other Arab countries, diverting their attention from what had for long been the dream of unity—however imper-fectly understood or pursued, yet a noble and stimulating dream—into barren territorial rivalries, religious conflicts and social strife. The Arab world had become well and truly balkanized." Arab unity in the political sense has never existed; the pretense of it vanished with Egypt's acceptance of a peace agreement that brought only promises to the Palestinians.

The "Arab Nation" had always been more illusion than reality. Egyptians knew this; they joked about it. Khalid Kishtainy includes in his anthology of Arab humor a story about a young man sitting outside the Cairo headquarters of the Arab League with a trumpet in his lap. A friend, passing by, asks what he is doing.

"This is my new job," says the young man, "to wait for Arab unity and then blow the trumpet to declare it to the world when it is achieved. I get 50 pounds a month."

"That's a miserable salary," says his friend.

"Yes, but it's a lifetime job."

Egypt's commitment to the Arab nationalist movement, its involvement in "Arabism," has never been total. Unlike Jordan and the sheikhdoms of the Arabian peninsula, Egypt has a complex cultural heritage rich in non-Arab influences. Even Nasser, who found it politically expedient to claim, and exert, leadership of all the Arabs, dwelled on Egypt's African heritage as well. Sadat, courageous and foolhardy in equal measure, acknowledged that pan-Arabism as a political movement had outlived its usefulness. In his view, which was of course widely resented by his erstwhile allies, the Arabs were nothing without Egypt, but Egypt was strong and self-confident without the Arabs, and it was time for Egypt to act in its own interests. He was often said to be leading Egypt back into a "pharaonic" nationalism—telling the Arabs, in effect, "You can't fire us, we quit."

This isolation from Egypt's Arab brethren created an intractable domestic political irritant that Mubarak inherited. Egyptians no longer wanted to fight on behalf of ingrates, but neither did they want to forfeit their cultural and political leadership of the Arab world. Mubarak began almost immediately to try to heal the breach. He adopted a far more conciliatory tone toward the other Arab states; he refrained from insulting them, and he instructed the Egyptian media to abandon their campaign of invective. But the Arab question was not one that Mubarak could resolve on his own, short of abandoning the peace treaty with Israel, which he could not afford to do. In 1982, when Israel invaded Lebanon, drove all the way to Beirut and expelled the Palestinian armed forces from their bases—a humiliation for all Arabs that was televised around the world—there was deep anguish in Egypt, but Mubarak could offer nothing more than token gestures, such as withdrawing Egypt's ambassador from Tel Aviv. To abandon the treaty and take up arms once again in a cause that is not Egypt's would be to assume a burden that Egypt can no longer carry. Egypt does not have the planes and tanks to do battle with Israel, nor the money, nor the will, however intense the feelings of those Egyptians who regard the peace with Israel as shameful.

But Mubarak has been lucky as well as resolute. Events that had nothing directly to do with Egypt or Israel forced the Arabs to turn back toward Egypt and end their painful breach. At a summit conference in Jordan in November 1987, 10 years almost to the day after Sadat's journey to Jerusalem, the members of the Arab League authorized the reopening of diplomatic relations with Egypt on a bilateral basis, and several of the most important countries, including Saudi Arabia, Iraq and Morocco, acted within a week to restore full relations. This was not a vindication of Sadat. Their motivation was fear of revolutionary Iran, which overcame their aversion to Egypt's arrangement with Israel. What had begun as a war between Iran and Iraq had evolved into a new phase of the centuries-old struggle between the Shiite Persians and the Sunni Arabs; Iraq and the rich but weak states on the Arab side of the Persian Gulf now needed the support of Egypt.

This was a political boon to Mubarak. The end of the long breach with the other Arabs removed what had been one of the most effective arrows in the Egyptian opposition's quiver. Though the ruling National Democratic Party, which Sadat founded and Mubarak heads, easily retained its dominant position in parliamentary elections in the spring of 1987 and the new parliament duly endorsed Mubarak for a second term as president, he faces an increasingly vigorous and outspoken opposition. Egypt is now a country where the president can be made to feel political heat, and Mubarak has been feeling it. Egypt was placed in an uncomfortable position in December 1987, when Israeli troops opened fire on Palestinians to suppress unrest in the occupied territories; the discomfort would have been considerably greater had Saudi Arabia and Iraq still been in a posture of hostility to Egypt, pointing fingers at the country that had abandoned the Palestinians.

The scope of democracy and the limits of freedom in Egypt have been the subject of endless debate and analysis. It is clear that now, as in 3000 BC, political power is centralized in the leader and he sets the rules; the "consent of the governed" has never been the operative principle. A nineteenth-century British diplomat wrote that any ruler of Egypt can play upon only two motivations, hope and fear, "and as he can hold out hope only to a few, but fear to all, fear is his principal instrument." This is less true than it once was. Egypt's rulers since the revolution have played upon hope and fear alternately; Mubarak has so far emphasized hope. He has chosen to tolerate and confront the opposition, not to suppress it. He has insisted on "stability" above all, and the definition of stability resides with him, but he has demonstrated that his insistence on stability does not require the quashing of dissent. In any case, many Egyptians believe that it is no longer possible to suppress domestic opposition as Nasser did, and as Sadat tried to do with the notorious roundup of political enemies that preceded his assassination.

It is still inconceivable that a mass opposition movement could organize itself, disseminate its message, challenge the leadership and actually rise to power through any legal channel. But Sadat opened the door to opposition and political dialogue, and he died when he attempted to reclose it. Through legal political parties, open debate in the parliament, the sermons of dissident preachers and an energetic press, the opposition makes itself heard, and, if it can't take power, at least it has sufficient weight to oblige the leader to respond to it.

A good example of the interaction between a vigorous opposition and a reasonable leadership was the national debate about Egypt's foreign debt that took place during the economic slump of 1986 and 1987. In that period, foreign debt rose to $44.1 billion, by American embassy calculations, and hard currency repayment obligations equaled nearly half the Gross Domestic Product. The opposition naturally raised an outcry about the debt burden, accusing the government of jeopardizing Egypt's sovereignty and evoking the nineteenth-century reign of the profligate Khedive Ismail, when Egypt's bankruptcy allowed Britain and France to take over the country. During debt-rescheduling negotiations with the International Monetary Fund, for example, commentator Adil Hussein wrote in the xenophobic opposition newspaper *al-Shaab* that Israel was responsible for international pressure on Egypt over the debt issue. He said that "The enemies [the IMF, the United States and Israel] are trying to strike a deal with our government. They would make it easier for us to repay debts by reducing interest and spreading repayment over a longer period in return for the ceding to them of whatever is left of our sovereignty in the political, military and economic fields." This debate revived the xenophobia that is always lurking just below Egypt's sophisticated surface: whatever the prolems, they can be traced to international conspirators—Zionists, communists, the CIA, the British, whoever is the whipping boy of the moment.

Mubarak's response, delivered in a May Day speech to the nation in 1987, is worth quoting at length.

> I would like to take a little moment here to explain how foreign loans have been used in the past few years. We laid down narrow limits for ourselves, and established controls, after introducing, for the first time, the principle that loans were only to be sought in the case of utmost need. The state and government borrowed only $10 billion between the beginning of 1982 and the end of 1986. Where [else] would I obtain money for you?

Pointing out that the state budget was mostly consumed by salaries and subsidies, he said, in the end only 193 million pounds are left, and there is nothing left over for the construction of schools, hospitals and so on. The budget funds are all earmarked for wages and salaries. Our construction is paid for by foreign and domestic loans. If we need to build a hospital, we have to get a loan, either at home or abroad. So where did the $10 billion go?

You know that at the beginning of the five-year plan [of 1982] there was no infrastructure. Had we not started this plan and decided what our needs and priorities were, I do not believe we would have been able to reach the level of implementation we attained by the end of this plan. So the infrastructure was zero. In Cairo—where people do not go to the polls [a reference to a low Cairo turnout in the 1987 elections]—had we left the sewerage system unattended to, all of you today would have to wear boots to walk around, like firemen, as the streets would be full of sewage. We have spent about seven billion pounds, not in Cairo alone, on water and sewerage systems, telephones, electricity, tunnels, railroads and other utilities—seven billion pounds. We have no choice but to rely on loans. We have spent 1.8 billion on production requirements, renovations and other related matters, and 1.2 billion on wheat, so that you may eat and throw half of it in the garbage [a reference to widespread reports of waste of subsidized bread]. This is how the 10 billion pounds borrowed by the state have been spent. Now you know where the money has gone.

Let me tell you that a loan can be obtained only through an agreement, and this agreement specifies how the loan is to be used. For example, if a certain country gives Egypt a loan for its railroads, I cannot demand that this loan be spent on tomatoes, motorcycles or something else. No. The fact is that I need locomotives, equipment, workshops, and a certain country is giving me a loan to keep the railroads, which are in a slump, operating. I need the railway and he wants to make an investment. This is the deal. I cannot tell him that I want to use the loan to buy Coca-Cola, for instance. Of course he would say no, because he wants to keep some of his factories running. Each country grants loans for a specific purpose, and the loans can never be diverted to something else unless another agreement is signed.

This is a reasonable response to the criticism, delivered as if in a conversation among equals. In allowing the critics to express themselves and in responding calmly, Mubarak shows a common touch that Sadat claimed to have but lacked. The differences are substantive, but also stylistic. Mubarak, though often criticized for his plodding style, for his very ordinariness, cannot be accused of pharaonic pretension, as Sadat was. Sadat lifted the heavy hand of repression that gripped Egypt in the Nasser era. He broke down the monolithic single-party structure that he inherited. He was not cruel. But neither was he merely first among equals. Sadat's democracy was not a democracy of the masses; it was a democracy of the family, and he was the father. When his children were unruly, he was quick to discipline them.

Sadat's rule was undoubtedly one in which individual Egyptians enjoyed vastly greater personal freedom than they did under Nasser. But the "state of institutions" he claimed to be developing was a slogan, not a fact. Sadat's rule was a personal one, and became more personal as time went on. In all his poses, he came to think of himself as the embodiment of Egypt. The country and the man were one. The flattering attention of the world fed Sadat's grandiose vision of himself. The adulation that was heaped upon him after his bold venture to Jerusalem went straight to his head.

In December 1977, a month after Jerusalem, about two dozen members of the press were invited to meet with Sadat at his official residence on the Nile in Giza. At the time there were hundreds of foreign journalists in Cairo, because Sadat was at the center of world attention and the first direct negotiations between Egypt and Israel were under way. But Sadat was not interested in reporters from Italy or Australia or Brazil. He was trying to influence public opinion in the United States and Israel, and it was the representatives from the major media organizations in those countries, along with a handful of Egyptian reporters, who were admitted to talk to the president.

We sat on gilt-trimmed chairs in a pale blue parlor decorated in the quasi-continental style favored by the Egyptian bourgeoisie; fake medieval tapestries adorned the walls, and chubby cherubs on the cornices bracketed paintings depicting stout lovers in arboreal settings. As we waited we could see Sadat, all business, looking presidential in a dark suit, conferring with Vice President Mubarak in the next room.

Sadat was an expert at flattering the press. Just the invitation to be there inclined us to be well-disposed toward him, because in those days everything he did or said was sure to make the front page or the top of the network news and all our editors were demanding that we gain access to him. By granting that access, he made us look good with our home offices and gave us a privileged status among our less-favored colleagues. If there was dissent in the working class cafes and provincial mosques, we were in no position to hear it.

Sadat strode in with a cheery "good morning," greeting many of us by name—another ego-booster. He welcomed the correspondent of Israeli television and installed him in a front-row seat—this at a time when Sadat's courtship of the Israelis was inspiring outrage among all the Arabs. Then he took out a pipe, one of his favorite props, to signal that he was ready to talk.

This was Anwar Sadat the master of the media, at home in the television lights, never off balance, equally at ease in banter or in policy discussion, always ready with joke or bromide to fend off questions he did not want to answer. He understood that his personality was as noteworthy as his policies and that his credibility as a peacemaker was essential to the process. He was using the press to convince the Americans and the Israelis that he was a serious statesman committed to peace, not the erratic lightweight or belligerent ideologue with whom they had previously dealt. He knew that the brow-mopping, lectern-pounding style of his three hour speeches to Egyptian audiences would alienate the foreign press, so he maintained an informal tone and kept the meeting low-key, more a chat among friends than a press conference.

After some discussion of the peace talks and intra-Arab politics, a television correspondent took advantage of the light atmosphere to ask a surprise question. Mr. President, he said, a group in Italy had just named you on its list of the world's ten best-dressed men. How do you feel about that?

Sadat puffed his pipe for a minute, then answered seriously. "Well, really," he said, "it is an honor, because I am a farmer. For a simple farmer to be one of the best dressed, it is an honor. I am not embarrassed, it's really a pleasure."

Farmer? This man in the custom-tailored suit and polished boots, chatting easily with the press in excellent English? This statesman of the Jerusalem trip, this man who was comfortable at the lunch table with Henry Kissinger or the president of France?

We laughed, but he was not joking. He really believed that his boyhood in an agricultural village of the Nile delta left an indelible mark on his social and cultural development and on his political ideas. He believed it gave him a rapport with the *fellahin* that only one who had shared their experiences could have. It set Sadat apart from Nasser, who was born in Alexandria, and also from the traditional politicians with their university educations and well-developed sense of status. Sadat played on his rural background, embellished it, but this was not altogether a pose. His confidence in his role as village headman and father of an extended family encouraged him to ignore or suppress the dissenting voices he did not want to hear.

In the opening line of his highly selective autobiography, Sadat speaks as "I, Anwar Sadat, a peasant born and brought up on the banks of the Nile." Actually Sadat was "brought up" in Cairo and he never had to make a living tilling the soil or herding cows. He did pull up carrots and tend cattle as a little boy, as he recounted, but he was never just a village yokel. His grandfather was literate, which was rare in rural Egypt at the time; his father, who went to a secular school and spoke English, and was not a farmer but a clerk in the army, of enough status to be known to the other villagers by the honorific *effendi*. Sadat, after an early religious education that centered on memorization of the Koran, was sent by his grandmother to a Christian school outside the village to broaden his learning. He read widely from his early years.

His sister Sekina told an American journalist that young Anwar read about Mahatma Gandhi, which introduced him to the idea that the British were alien despots in India as well as in Egypt. He began roaming the village dressed in a white sheet, leading a goat on a string, imitating the attire and manner of the Indian nationalist hero.

Sadat said in his memoirs that he left the village of Mit abu el-Kom when his father was transferred to Cairo in 1925. Since Sadat was born on December 25, 1918, that would make him less than seven years old when he went to the city and was enrolled in a school with children of the middle class. If so, he was a prodigy of political awareness and remembered more of the first six years of his life than do most people. But even if, as seems likely, his happy memories of his boyhood village were mingled in later life with influences that came to him in adolescence, his political ideas, as well as his style, were always linked in his mind with what he believed he assimilated in his village: Islam, of course; hatred of the British; understanding of the *fellahin;* a love of reading; and a sense of theatrics and costume that would serve him well in public life. The village, he said, instilled in him a "feeling of inner superiority" that he always retained.

As in his Gandhi role, costume became substance. As president, Sadat always dressed the part—whatever part he happened to be playing. Praying at a village mosque in a display of piety, he wore a turtlenecked shirt with his sport jacket. Speaking before parliament or receiving dignitaries, he wore the tailored suits and ankle-high boots and spread-collar white shirts that earned him his accolade from the Italians. At military events, he wore an absurd field marshal's uniform, complete with knee boots and spurs. Touring land reclamation projects, he wore a leisure suit. At Mit abu al-Kom he was seen in a *galabeya*. Once he was photographed wearing shorts for his daily walk.

His theatrical sense of timing and costume helped him develop his image as a statesman. He spent many hours watching news film of Israel's leaders, trying to understand them and decipher their personalities. In the same way he studied the foreign press, using his knowledge of the correspondents and their organizations to gain their good will.

That went beyond his well-known habit of calling Walter Cronkite by his first name or allowing Barbara Walters to fly on his plane. A year before the Jerusalem trip turned him into "Anwar Sadat Superstar," I was talking to him at his residence north of Cairo and he showed me how carefully he tracked the American press.

Referring to "the Watergate problem" he said, "you have started it in the *Washington Post,* I think." He mentioned an interview he had given years before to Arnaud de Borchgrave of *Newsweek* and said, "that is your magazine." (*Newsweek* is owned by the Washington Post Company.) As I was leaving he asked me to convey his greetings to "Madame Graham"—Katharine Graham, then publisher of the *Post*.

Sadat had a Reaganesque indifference to the details of domestic government, but he knew which journalists and which organizations were influential and he knew that correspondents like to be recognized by heads of state and engage in banter with them. The weekend after the Jerusalem trip, I was a member of the panel that interviewed him for the CBS television program "Face the Nation." He carried a brass-knobbed cane, and when I asked him if he needed it to support himself, he said he would have me "put in a concentration camp." He knew Americans responded well to his proud claim to have put an end to political "concentration camps" in Egypt. When a director dusted powder on his face, he joked that "in my village, this is for the women."

For the interview we sat in wicker chairs on the terrace of his house at Ismailia, overlooking lake Timsah. It was disarming, charming, and effective. Jimmy Carter's observation in 1979 that Sadat was "the most popular politician in America" was the result of Sadat's ability to present himself favorably to the press.

Sadat's image building was more than gratification of his own ego. It was essential to his rule. He came to the presidency with a reputation as a lightweight, wholly unsuited to fill the shoes of the giant Nasser, and seemed always to struggle to be taken seriously. He often recalled that at his accession in 1970, both British intelligence and the CIA predicted that his tenure would not last six weeks.

Nasser is said to have remarked that Sadat was interested only in two things: a big American car and gasoline paid for by the government. True or not, that kind of story reflected the low opinion of Sadat that was widely held when he became president and resurfaced in cruel jokes throughout his presidency. His opponents were contemptuous of him as no one had been of Nasser. Political wits called him "the black donkey" because of his dark complexion. Students made fun of the rough patch of skin on his forehead; they said it was not the result of years of prayer with head pressed to mosque floor, as on most Muslim men, but of Nasser reaching across the conference table to slap Sadat on the forehead and say, "You, shut up!"

In countering such unflattering assessments, Sadat was never content to let his undeniable achievements speak for themselves. He devoted a great deal of his energy to the public relations aspects of rule, choosing settings, costumes, words and audiences that would reinforce what he was trying to do. The most spectacular public relations gesture of all, of course, was the trip to Jerusalem. It was not the words of his speech that impressed the Israelis—the words were tough, and provoked some anger in Jerusalem—but the presence in their country of an Arab leader who was urbane, sophisticated and flexible. He forced the Israelis to take him seriously and respond to his initiative. And it was only his act of traveling into the enemy camp that convinced the Americans of his sincerity. His public appearances at home were similar exercises in stagecraft, some more effective than others.

His Volkswagen Rabbit, for example, fooled nobody. After the food-price riots of January 1977, he announced an austerity-at-the-top campaign in which the Volkswagen was to replace the Mercedes as the car for high-ranking officials. Sadat took to showing up for public appearances in a Rabbit, occasionally driving it himself. This was ludicrous; everyone knew that Sadat did not live austerely. His sumptuous style of living was a favorite target of criticism.

Nasser had lived modestly, in military quarters; he disdained the palaces left behind by King Farouk and he was on nobody's best-dressed list. Mubarak is similarly circumspect; at a White House state dinner in his honor in 1988, he wore a conservative business suit, not a tuxedo, knowing his photograph would be in the Cairo newspapers. Sadat, however, revelled in elegant living. He rose late, napped often and quit early. He had luxurious residences all across Egypt and moved frequently among them. He claimed his boyhood village as his true home but as president he lived everywhere and nowhere: in Alexandria, in Aswan, in Ismailia, in Giza, and on the Nile north of Cairo. He and Jehan, his half-English second wife, arranged to marry their children into the nation's richest families. The heads of those families were among Sadat's political cronies. Men such as Sayed Marei, the agronomist, and Osman Ahmed Osman, the contractor, were known to all Egyptians as millionaires and wheeler-dealers. There was always some new coffee-house rumor about some alleged corrupt transaction or other involving the president's wife, his children or his friends.

After Sadat's death his brother, Esmat, who had parlayed his relationship with the president into vast commercial and real-estate holdings, was convicted of corruption and imprisoned; Mubarak kept his hands off the proceedings. But it was more than the specific actions of individuals that tarnished Sadat's reputation with his countrymen; it was the let-them-eat-cake atmosphere of lavish social events and high living that could not be countered by speeches about improved conditions. One Egyptian friend, for example, told me seriously, and with genuine disgust, that thousands of pounds had been spent on medical treatment of a pet ape that lived in a cage on the grounds of Sadat's house at Alexandria. I had seen the creature a short time before and it appeared healthy, so I asked my friend how he knew about the medical bills. He said everybody knew it. It did not matter whether the story was actually true, it was perceived to be credible because of the way Sadat was known to live.

Sadat always claimed to be creating a "state of institutions" under the "rule of law," rather than a state of autocratic power and arbitrary actions. But as he had noted many years earlier in *Revolt on the Nile*, his memoir of the 1952 revolution, "In Egypt personalities have always been more important than political programs." Believing that, he found it essential to project a personality: father of the Egyptian family, foe of the British and stalwart of the revolution, hero of the crossing, peacemaker. This was not, of course, a complete picture of the man, but throughout his presidency, however much he liberalized the political climate, he drew the line at words or actions that challenged the public image he worked so hard to present.

He appealed to "family values" and "love" as the foundations of a state dedicated to "science and faith." But incidents from his life before he became president reveal a man for whom the end always justified the means.

In *Revolt on the Nile*, he denounced terrorism:

> Acts of this sort—spectacular gestures designed to capture the imagination of the masses—were contrary to our principles. We did not believe in the isolated gesture, the action of a lone man, and we were determined to avoid the excesses of political fanaticism which we ourselves had witnessed. The glorification of violence is fatal to the hot-blooded people of the East because it unleashes their most animal instincts; the result is a series of hideous crimes committed in the name of an ideal.

That was consistent with what he said as president about the need to settle disputes "in a civilized way," but not with his own record.

In 1945, when he was between jail terms under the British and already conspiring with Nasser, he was outraged by the refusal of the British ambassador, Lord Killearn, to discuss Egyptian claims to the Sudan with the Egyptian prime minister. Sadat "went to see Gamal Abdel Nasser and put up a plan for revenge. My idea was to blow up the British embassy and everybody in it." Nasser rejected the idea, not because it was abhorrent but because it would have invited reprisals from the British.

Later Sadat participated in an unsuccessful attempt to assassi-

nate Prime Minister Mustafa Nahas by hurling a grenade through
the window of his car. Sadat was on shaky ground when in 1978 he
sought to discredit Israeli Prime Minister Menachem Begin as a
terrorist.

Similarly, in his later memoirs, cataloguing the virtues he
prized, Sadat said, "I hold friendship to be sacred." And he did
establish a record of rewarding loyal companions. Mohammed
Ibrahim Kamel, an obscure diplomat then serving as ambassador to
West Germany, was appointed foreign minister at a crucial time in
1977, after Ismail Fahmy quit in protest over the Jerusalem venture. Kamel had been arrested with Sadat in 1946 in a conspiracy to
assassinate the finance minister, and he had refused to confess or
implicate others. When Kamel resigned in turn less than a year after
his appointment because he could not accept the Camp David
agreements, Sadat let him go without a word of criticism—unlike
other high-ranking defectors, such as Mohammed Heikal, who
were harassed and excoriated after breaking with Sadat.

In the same way, Sadat gave the premiership to Mamdouh
Salem, a career police officer with little political experience. He was
chief of police in Alexandria at the time of the "corrective revolution" and stood with Sadat against the conspirators. Sadat's insistence on welcoming and sheltering the deposed Shah of Iran
when no other country would take him in was required, he said,
because the Shah had helped Egypt with emergency oil shipments
after the 1973 war.

But Sadat was not above trading on a friendship or duping a
friend in the interests of expediency. One victim was Dr. Yusuf
Rashad, a friend of the Sadat family who was King Farouk's
personal physician. He had used his influence with the king to
arrange Sadat's reinstatement in the army in 1950, when Sadat was
broke and struggling to support his family, but that did not deter
Sadat from victimizing him at the time of the revolution. Sadat
went to him to plant false information about conditions in the
army, used him to relay misleading details to the king, and prevailed
on their old friendship to allay suspicion about the very conspiracy
that the authorities were trying to uncover. "The issue at stake was
greater than friendship," Sadat wrote later.

And Sadat as president, talking of Egypt as "one big family," of
which he was the patriarch, never mentioned his first wife, a country girl whom he married young and simply put aside when he no
longer wanted her.

Sadat was trying to develop a political system that would look like participatory democracy but would really be one-man rule. That one man, himself, had to be above reproach if he was to be accepted as the president-patriarch. In fairness to Sadat, it must be said that his political vision was necessarily colored by his observation of events during his life. Before the revolution of 1952, the country's political parties were indeed self-serving, opportunistic organizations that were unable to free the country from British rule. After the revolution, for all the high ideals, Egypt became an authoritarian police state. Sadat wanted neither system. But because of his deep conviction—supported by considerable evidence—that unrestrained political and press freedom would result in turmoil and make the country a playing field for extremists of the left and the right, he imposed restrictions that were founded solely on his own judgment, not on any self-perpetuating independent system. Serious opponents of the regime, communists, Muslim activists, pan-Arabists, Nasserites, liberal pluralists and even the prerevolutionary party known as the Wafd were driven to operate ouside authorized political channels because they could not be embraced by Sadat's "family" of "responsibility" and "social peace."

"I have always mistrusted theories and purely rational systems," Sadat wrote in *Revolt on the Nile*.

> I believe in the power of concrete facts and the realities of history and experience. My political ideas grew out of my personal experience of repression, not out of abstract notions. I am a soldier, not a theoretician, and it was by an empirical process that I came to realize my country needed a political system which responded to its essential needs and reflected its true spirit.

Given that aversion to ideology, it was hardly surprising that he seemed to run Egypt on an ad hoc basis, ruling by intuition and springing new notions upon unsuspecting cabinet ministers. There was no theoretical framework. There were, however, two basic documents that recorded his overall objectives and how he intended to achieve them.

The first was the "October Working Paper," issued in April 1974. (The October of the title refers to the war of the previous autumn.) This document was more than 100 pages long. Much of it was vague and tedious. But political science is an underdeveloped discipline among all Arab leaderships, and Sadat's political blueprint was more reasonable and practical than most. By comparison with the Baathist screeds of the Iraqis or the primitive rantings of Muammar Qaddafi's "Green Book," Sadat's "October Working Paper" is a model of clarity and vision.

Egypt's era of suffering, Sadat declared, had ended. First, the "corrective measures" of 1971

> did not end with the liquidation of the centers of power but rather went on to attain their more important objectives, namely assertion of the sovereignty of law, respect for the judiciary, the establishment of the State of Institutions and the laying down of safeguards through which a citizen can know his rights and duties clearly and easily and practice them fearlessly.

The October war, he said, ended a quarter century of defeat, despair, self-deception and treachery. As a result of it, he said,

> we see those on whose doors we knocked, receiving no answer, coming to knock at our door, and those who shrugged when-ever we spoke of our problems trying hard to understand us. . . . The October war was the first war which we started on our own initiative, away from the fear of Israel's domination, the inclinations of foreign countries and considerations of inter-national balance of power. We have succeeded in breaking those shackles and have proved that we can choose freely and impose our will as far as issues of our country are concerned. The opportunity which the Arab world has been seeking since its renaissance in the modern age is now at hand, and it has only to grasp its significance, to hold on to and rise to the level of its exigencies.

With that corner turned, he said, it was time for "a new phase of national action with which we can push forward to progress along the same line and with the same rates we achieved in the magnifi-cent battle."

Next, he introduced the idea of *infitah*, and turned to "social development," without which, he said, mere material gain would have no enduring value.

> It is our duty toward the Egyptian citizen, who is our principal asset, and by whom and for whom we work, to prevent his falling prey to illiteracy, disease or backwardness. . . . The time has come to begin seriously this difficult task we have postponed for so long, namely, the task of revolutionizing the

systems and concepts of general education and culture of all
sorts and standards, from the eradication of illiteracy to general
technical education to scientific and technological research.

Reform in education, Sadat said, should be matched by a
commitment to technology, comprehensive health care, land reclamation, dispersal of the population out of the overcrowded cities
and the introduction of systematic long-range planning. Then, he
said, with democracy in place, economic development and technological advancement under way and society shaped by its own
traditions and the precepts of Islam, the "new Egyptian man"
would find a brighter future in a community of "science and faith."

Few Egyptians quarreled with these lofty pronouncements;
but at that early stage of Sadat's presidency they did not understand
the difficulties, both political and economic, of translating them
into action.

It took five years to achieve peace, and even then it was peace
on terms that would have been unthinkable when the process
began; the domestic political and economic reforms lurched ahead
just as slowly. When the peace treaty was finally signed in March
1979, Sadat turned his emphasis to internal affairs. He dissolved
parliament and ordered the election of a new one that would take
office at the beginning of an era of peace.

The ostensible reason for the dissolution of the People's Assembly when only halfway through its term was that signature of
the peace treaty marked the beginning of a new era, which required
the installation of a new parliament to grapple with the new issues
of peacetime. The real reason was that the parliament elected in
1976 contained several annoying, if ineffectual, opponents of the
government, vociferous pests who said embarrasing things in open
session. Sadat was determined to get rid of them. He and his
interior minister, Nabawy Ismail, did so through heavy-handed
manipulation of the 1979 elections.

Sadat's address to the opening session of that new parliament,
on June 23, 1979, may be seen as the second comprehensive
statement of what he was trying to achieve.

The previous People's Assembly, Sadat said to the new one,

> had accomplished its constitutional message in the best manner,
> despite all the maneuvers that took place in this arena [i.e., in
> the previous parliament] including the exploitation of democ-

racy to defame the essence of democracy, the return to the
obsolete methods of slander—the pre-revolution methods—and
the slippage into ethical excesses, which we did not expect from
them.

Mopping his brow with a white handkerchief and pushing his
heavy black-rimmed spectacles up his nose as he perspired in the
television lights, Sadat was in full rhetorical cry. He called upon the
compliant new parliament to establish

> a flexible socialism which would solve the contradiction be-
> tween the freedom of the individual and the freedom of society,
> whereby the society would not dominate the individual and
> usurp his freedom and the individual's right would not domi-
> nate the society to usurp the freedom of others. We want a
> balanced freedom for the individual and the society, as well, to
> boost and consolidate the political and social freedom and serve
> as a fence for them. Our idea of socialism will not be the same as
> that which prevailed during the phase that ended in May 1971
> [with the "corrective revolution"]. We do not want the so-
> cialism that distributed poverty and imposed the centers of
> power. We want a socialism that defends the political and social
> freedom of man.

This new socialism, he said, would be built upon new ideas
and new methods adapted to the new situation: decentralization of
the government, to end the paralyzing system "whereby Cairo
alone was the source of decisions"; political stability based on
"ethics" and knowledge of Egyptian history; tax reform, to impose
a greater burden on those able to pay; "the establishment of
woman's rights as a wife and mother," protected by social insurance
from the traditional forms of subjugation and mistreatment; a
reformed press that "adheres to the principles of freedom, sincerity
and ethics"; "a social peace and national unity" that would "show
no leniency toward him who challenges the rule of law or who
attempts to harm social peace or threaten national unity"; and hard
work.

As a program for political and governmental action that shared
the virtues and the defects of the "October Working Paper," it was
admirable, indeed unexceptionable in its declared objectives, but it
was entirely the product of the man who handed it down, and that
man remained the arbiter of it. He alone decided whether groups or

individuals were acting in accordance with it. Who was to determine whether the press was behaving ethically or the parliament was fulfilling its duty or any group was attempting to harm social peace? Who defined ethics or sincerity? Who interpreted tradition? The answer, of course, was Anwar Sadat, and his interpretations became more and more restrictive and less and less tolerant as his presidency stumbled toward its bloody end. But always, until the pointless temper tantrum that precipitated the mass arrests of September 1981, Sadat gave all his actions a veneer of legality and popular approval. The usual technique was a referendum in which his policies were put before the voters, with an invariable result: approval, by announced margins of at least 96 percent and usually 99 percent.

Miles Copeland said of Nasser that his objective was "not to move from a military dictatorship to parliamentary government but to bypass parliamentary government except for a pretense of it, and go on to Bonapartism—i.e., rule with a 'mandate from the people' expressed through plebiscites and the like." Sadat, while repudiating Nasser and tearing down much of the political edifice he built, nevertheless adopted the same technique. The referenda that he called when dissatisfied with parliament, vexed by critics or impelled by public relations considerations to show that the masses were behind him, were the despair of his admirers precisely because they were devoid of credibility. If ever a support figure of, say, 80 percent had been announced, it would have had the virtue of being an overwhelming endorsement while showing that the regime was unafraid of legitimate opposition. But it never happened; 99 percent was the rule.

We in the press usually paid scant heed to these exercises in popular will because the outcomes were so numbingly predictable. On one occasion when things were dull elsewhere in the region, we looked around as a referendum was being held and we found what we expected. Correspondents from several news organizations visited polling places in crowded areas of Cairo where no voters were in sight and voter traffic was light throughout the day, but participation figures approaching 100 percent were of course announced. (Voting is technically compulsory for males, though voluntary for females. In practice the nominal fine for nonparticipation is rarely levied.) During that same referendum, a camera crew from NBC, visiting a polling place after voting hours, found poll workers frantically marking the remaining unused ballots and stuffing them into the box.

These matters would be of interest only to Egyptians except that Sadat used his claim to have restored "democracy" in Egypt as a tool to gain international legitimacy; in presenting himself to the Americans, and in slashing back at Arab leaders who denounced him, he stressed that Egypt was the only democratic society in an Arab world dominated by corrupt monarchs and tinhorn dictators, and that the Egyptian people showed by their massive mandates that they supported him fully. The real situation was proclaimed by Sadat himself in an interview with *October* magazine on September 23, 1979: "Either I rule or I go home. . . . Under the constitution, I am responsible for Egypt. On the basis of this responsibility, I will not permit anyone, whatever his position, to exceed his limits."

Sadat never seemed to understand that the exercises in mass approbation embarrassed his allies and supporters rather than persuading them. The Americans especially would have accepted the argument Sadat often advanced in private that Egypt could not support unfettered democracy and absolute freedom of party and press. But beginning in 1977, with the bread riots and the assassination of a prominent Muslim sheikh by religious fanatics, Sadat became increasingly intolerant of opposition even as he became more insistent that there was none.

This is not to say that he merely put a more benevolent face on the despotic system he inherited. On the contrary, he planted the seeds of political pluralism and free expression that gave rise to the vigorous opposition Mubarak faces today. The overall effect of Sadat's policies was to make life more flexible and less coercive than it was at the beginning of his rule. Egyptians who grumbled about the restrictions he imposed after 1977, who complained that Sadat was reneging on his promises of democracy, appeared to have forgotten the paralysis of political action and the sterility of debate under Sadat's predecessor. The mass arrests of 1981 were doubly shocking because they came after a decade in which Egyptians had been encouraged by their relative political freedom.

Through a ban on activities that would disrupt "social peace"—a ban endorsed, of course, in a referendum—Sadat kept in place some longstanding and clear-cut restrictions. Strikes were not permitted on the grounds that Egypt was a socialist state. Students were not free to demonstrate on campus, because that would disrupt education, which the state was paying for. ("Education is an investment, and I want the proceeds," Sadat once said.) Military personnel were not allowed to engage in politics. When Sadat permitted the formation of political parties, the Communist Party remained illegal. No political organization could be based on religious, ethnic or regional affiliation, nor could any party maintain a paramilitary auxiliary. (The lessons of Lebanon were understood by everyone in the Middle East, except the Lebanese.) No political party could be a branch of any party based outside Egypt—that is, no communists or Baathists—and no political organization was permitted to espouse principles that conflicted with Islamic law.

Under Nasser, Egypt had been a typical Third-World one-party state. The only legal political organization was the Arab Socialist Union, which was not a party at all in the sense that a party is formed at the grass roots by like-minded individuals. It was an organization of control, created by the leadership to serve the interests of the leadership.

Nasser abolished all political parties by decree on January 16, 1953, just six months after the revolution. He experimented with various formats for organizing political activity and in 1962 announced the establishment of the ASU. It was to be a monolithic, broad-based political machine, with branches and cadres all over the country. As was inevitable in a country so closely tied to the Soviet Union, it served in some departments as a channel of Soviet influence. At the time of the "Corrective Revolution," the power struggle of May 1971, the ASU was a center of leftist opposition to Sadat, organized by Ali Sabry. After the purge of Ali Sabry and of the ASU's cadres, the organization became a docile appendage of Sadat's new order.

Egyptians joked that the answer to Cairo's hotel shortage was to convert the ASU's massive headquarters building on the Nile into rooms for tourists. (In fact, in a transformation even more revealing, it has been converted into offices for a foreign bank.) It was clear the organization had outlived its usefulness, but what was to replace it?

On the one hand Sadat was proclaiming the establishment of democracy and social freedom, incompatible with a one-party state. On the other, Egypt had had multiple political parties before the revolution and they were discredited as self-serving tools of the monarchy and the "feudalists," which the revolution was sweeping away. Unrestricted political parties meant factionalism, a narrow-minded and selfish approach to issues, political irresponsibility, and religious involvement in public affairs. Even Sadat's critics acknowledged that there would be chaos if he simply allowed parties to form and operate at will. Some change, however, was required; some formula had to be devised that would permit the useful expenditure of political energy without undermining stability. Egypt's political history since the October war consists largely of a search for that formula.

Accepting the recommendations of a committee that reported to him after a long debate in 1975, Sadat stuck a toe into the waters of political pluralism by announcing early in 1976 the creation of three "platforms" or "pulpits" within the ASU to present different political points of view. These groupings were popularly known as the "left," the "center" and the "right." While they were neither independent nor representative, they did offer new, legal outlets for expression, and they were permitted to run candidates against each other in the parliamentary election of 1976. That was the first of four contested parliamentary elections that have been held under Sadat and Mubarak, in 1976, 1979, 1984 and 1987. Each, in a different way, was a watershed of Egypt's post-Nasser political development.

When the "platforms" were created, the "center," naturally, was by far the largest group. Sadat, as head of the ASU, had the power to select the chairmen of the three groups. By installing his prime minister, Mamdouh Salem, as head of the center group, he in effect made it the official voice of the regime and ensured that it would dominate parliamentary and ministerial affairs.

The "right," headed by a well-known but colorless orthodox politician, Mustafa Kamal Murad, differed from the center mostly by asking for still more liberalization of the economy than Sadat was offering; on international issues, it was an echo of the center.

More interesting, because it represented the only real source of legal dissent, was the "left" grouping, headed by the "red colonel," Khaled Mohieddin. Mohieddin was Sadat's contemporary and, like him, one of the "Free Officers" who carried out the revolution with Nasser. He and Sadat had little else in common, as Mohieddin is a forthright Marxist. When I went to his office in the ASU building, I found a burly man in a leisure suit, working behind a metal desk under fluorescent lights that cast a grayish glare upon the institutional green of the walls. Mohieddin seemed indifferent to aesthetics—he wanted to talk politics.

Because the prime minister was organizing the center grouping and because imams in mosques all over Egypt (who were employees of the state) were urging their faithful to avoid the left, Mohieddin said, creation of the forums was hardly true democracy, but "It's a start. It's not bad. I have the right to come down into the street and present my program, which I didn't have before."

That program, he said, emphasized the value of Egypt's links to the "socialist" countries—links that Sadat was rapidly cutting—and opposed the government's new economic policies. *Infitah*, he said, benefited ony the "parasite classes and land speculators." Ordinary Egyptians, he said, "thought they were going to eat better when the American money flowed in, but now they see that it's not happening." Those were prescient words, uttered well before the Jerusalem journey and the false expectations of prosperity that it aroused.

Mohieddin said his group had 30,000 members, of whom only 600 were Marxists. Most of the others, he said, were "Nasserites," whom he defined as those who "believe that the laws of 1961 were the proper starting point for Egypt." Those were the nationalization laws under whch the state took over the industries and banks.

He said he knew his group had no hope of winning a majority of the 342 parliamentary seats that were contested in that October of 1976. As it turned out, the leftists were able to field only 65 candidates and only two, including Mohieddin, were elected.

That election campaign was the liveliest and freest Egypt had experienced in a generation. There were 1,660 candidates, of whom nearly 900 were independents, not members of any of the three ASU forums. Among the independents were supporters of the Muslim Brotherhood, which Nasser had suppressed, and of the prerevolutionary nationalist party known as the Wafd, which Nasser had abolished. As expected, the center group, officially known as Egypt's Arab Socialist Forum, dominated the results, winning 280 seats. But independents won 48 seats and Murad's right forum won 12; combined with two won by Mohieddin's National Progressive Unionist Forum—the left—this gave the opposition 62 seats, ensuring at least that there would be vigorous parliamentary debate on some issues.

At parliament's first session, on November 11, 1976, Sadat

took the next step: He announced that the Egyptians and their revolution were sufficiently "mature" to permit the return of multiple parties. The three forums were to be permitted to go outside the ASU structure and become independent organizations, allowed even to publish their own newspapers. Later, new parties that were not associated with those three were also to be authorized.

That announcement appeared to be another long step on the exhilarating march toward democracy. But two months later, the food riots slowed the pace of political experimentation. Sadat went ahead with a law that authorized the formation of independent parties, provided they had principles clearly different from those of the existing parties but not in conflict with the constitution or the "October Working Paper," and provided they could meet certain technical requirements, such as enlisting 20 members of parliament to join. But his determination not to permit either a recurrence of the riots or, by the next year, serious criticism of his peace initiative, led Sadat to impose restrictions that stifled debate, paralyzed the party press and muzzled prominent individuals. One of the first to test the limits of the new rules was Kamal Eddin Hussein, and he found them tight indeed.

He too was a "Free Officer" and had been a prominent political figure for a generation. He had worked with Nasser since the 1930s, serving in his cabinet and as vice president. Later he fell out with Nasser and was under house arrest for several years, until freed by Sadat. In 1976 he was elected to parliament as an independent from his home town of Benha, 30 miles north of Cairo. His political stature was as high as that of any other person in the country, and if anyone's opinion was worthy of dissemination, it was his. But his opinion quickly ran into conflict with Sadat's authority.

After the riots, Sadat rammed tough new restrictions through parliament aimed at preventing a recurrence—"a police response to an economic problem," as one of my friends put it. Activities such as strikes and demonstrations were made punishable by life imprisonment at hard labor; predictably, these measures were approved in a referendum. The only prominent person to take a forthright stand against them was Kamal Eddin Hussein.

In an open letter to Sadat that was published in a newspaper just before the referendum, he said the "anti-riot" measures were "an insult to the intelligence of the Egyptian people." The riots, he said, had been caused by "your government's shortsightedness and the foolish policy of former governments." He accused Sadat of planning to "forge" the outcome of the voting, "as was the case in all previous referenda."

Hussein's stature was sufficient to get the letter published but not to protect him from the consequences. By a vote of 281 to 28, parliament expelled him. When a special election was held to fill his seat, he sought to run in it, making it in effect a real referendum on his comments and his ouster. A court upheld his right to run, but two days later parliament passed a law prohibiting anyone expelled from parliament from being elected to the same session. Hussein was the only person in that category. The rejoicing in the streets of Benha that followed the court decision turned to surliness, then to indifference as the special election approached, matching political nobodies against each other. I went to Benha on election day and found truckloads of baton-wielding riot police on duty, but the atmosphere was desultory and the turnout small.

Members of parliament who voted for Hussein's ouster said he had been rude and insulting, and had used vulgar language. That was true, but he was the people's choice in Benha, and his expulsion left them unrepresented. When Sadat dissolved parliament in 1979 and called new elections, Hussein tried again, and I went to see him.

I found him surrounded by his father and a group of supporters, drinking tea and talking about the "terrorist" campaign against him. "All the authority of the government is being used against me personally," he said. "In the election of 1976, I got more than 90 percent of the vote here in the town of Benha, so this time they have deliberately cooked the rolls to exclude my voters." In districts where he was popular, he said, the government had suddenly announced a requirement that women would be required to produce identity cards in order to vote. "They know that most of the women are included on their husband's identity cards and don't have their own," Hussein said. A few days before the voting the interior ministry, which is responsible for conducting elections, moved 14 polling places without announcing it.

Hussein had criticized the terms of the peace treaty with Israel, signed the month before. The provincial governor, he said, had been telling Benha's voters not to elect "those who are against peace. Nobody is against peace, he would be a fool, but everyone has the right to say what he wants about the treaty."

If the election was such a sham, I asked, why did he lend it credibility by participating? "Good question," he said. "It's so the people don't give up all hope. Even under the pharaohs, there were priests and princes with their own followers who had to be listened to. Pharaoh didn't rule all by himself. We have to keep trying."

His opponent was Hussein Mahdi, a colorless lawyer and organization politician, who operated out of a shabby office above a candy store in downtown Benha. When I got there in the late morning of a working day just before the election, there was no one in the office except his brother. The atmosphere was lethargic, but Mahdi had the advantage of being the candidate of the National Democratic Party—Sadat's party—and when the votes were tabulated he was announced as the winner.

When the law creating political parties went into effect in 1977, the three "platforms" or forums of the ASU transformed themselves into parties, a metamorphosis that implied no substantive change in what they were or whom they represented. The Arab Socialist Party of Egypt under Prime Minister Salem—later transformed by a stroke of the pen into the National Democratic Party, headed by the president—dominated the system. The response from the public was the same as that accorded to any Third-World political organization dreamed up by an unchallenged ruler and presented to the voters with its program already written and its leadership in place: indifference. Having watched Nguyen Van Thieu use the machinery of the South Vietnamese government to superimpose his party on the truculent peasants and opportunistic clerks there in 1973, and having seen the impact on Iran of the Shah's Rastakhiz Party, I was familiar with this script. Signs go up and proclamations are issued, but nothing happens.

Khaled Mohieddin's leftist party, the National Progressive Unionists, was like a wasp buzzing around the head of a giant. Its weekly newspaper, *al-Ahali*, sold out as soon as it hit the newsstands, but it soon ceased to appear. The police routinely seized it before it was distributed; its editors reduced it to a mimeographed sheet and then gave up. Sadat accused the party of harboring "agents of the Soviet Union."

On such a short tether, the leftists had little opportunity to spread their ideas. In 1978, after another restrictive referendum, they announced their withdrawal from participation in the political process. In the parliamentary elections of 1979, all candidates of the leftist party, including Mohieddin, were defeated.

The predictable dominance of Sadat's party, and the impotence of the other two spinoffs from the ASU, accounted for the intense interest and excitement that ran through Egypt like an electric charge at the formation of a genuinely independent, popularly based party with strong links to heroes of the past. In the spring of 1978, the Wafd was reborn.

There is no analogy in American politics to the place of the Wafd in Egyptian history and in the country's political consciousness. At the time of the 1952 revolution, the Wafd was undoubtedly corrupt, its leaders detested for their personal opportunism and for their collaboration with the British. The British, in fact, had restored the Wafd to power at gunpoint, in a famous incident in 1942. The British ambassador to nominally independent Egypt, Sir Miles Lampson, delivered an ultimatum to King Farouk, and by accepting power under its terms the Wafd blackened its reputation and undercut the nationalist basis of its appeal. But when the Wafd surfaced in 1978, what was remembered was the Wafd's unique and honorable history as the party of Egyptian nationalism and patriotism.

Wafd is the Arabic word for delegation. At the end of World War I, three prominent Egyptian politicians, led by Prime Minister Saad Zaghloul, asked permission of the British occupation authorities to send a delegation to present the case for Egyptian independence at the Versailles peace conference. They were rebuffed, and sent into exile on Malta, which touched off the anti-British insurrection of 1919, the Egyptian equivalent of Lexington and Concord. When the three returned to Egypt, they formed the nucleus of the Wafd Party. For 30 years, until the revolution, Egyptian politics was a game with three players: the king, the British and the Wafd.

The Wafd was among the parties abolished by Nasser in 1953. Those of its leaders still alive spent years in prison. Released by Sadat, they stayed out of public life until the political parties law allowed them to resume their activities legally. Prerevolutionary parties were still banned, so they could not call their party the Wafd; they called it the New Wafd, a distinction without a difference.

Sadat denounced the Wafdists as "mummies" coming back from the grave to promote outdated ideas. (The Wafdists' depictions of themselves and their predecessors wearing the fez, which were still appearing on walls all over Egypt as late as the 1987 elections, did nothing to disassociate them from the past; they claimed the past as their patrimony, as their mantle of legitimacy.) Sadat said the party's revival would not be tolerated because it would "turn back the hands of the clock" to the unmourned days before the revolution. But the appeal of the Wafd name was such that the party was able to meet the stiff requirements of the political party law, including the enrollment of at least 20 members of the People's Assembly. The government had no choice but to legalize it.

Going to interview the leader of the Wafd, Fuad Serageddin, I asked my driver to take me to the house of "Fuad Pasha," as many Egyptians still called him. "We don't have pashas any more," my driver said, but he knew who I meant and where the house was. A man who lived in such a house was the embodiment of the word pasha.

Seraggedin's house in the Cairo neighborhood known as Garden City is the kind of marble palace that once represented the epitome of the Europeanized tastes and luxurious ambitions of Egypt's rich bourgeoisie. Like its owner and his politics, it is a crumbling relic of a bygone era.

When I visited, the sockets on the ornate crystal chandeliers were empty; a few bare bulbs hooked up to exposed wires on the marble walls created little circles of brightness in the gloom. Thick dust coated rococo statuary and frayed gilt-edged furniture. The decor was all bronze goddesses, gargoyled vases, dancing nymphs and stained glass. The place looked as if some baronial family had abandoned it intact in some historical cataclysm; but the baron was still there.

Seraggedin was then in his seventies, a lawyer of ample girth and failing health. He was wearing an expensive suit of soft gray flannel and an off-white silk shirt; he brandished the long cigar that is always in his hand. The cigar was his trademark, featured even in the drawing of him on the cover of his pamphlet, "Why the New Party?"—an illustration that also featured portraits of a fez-topped Saad Zaghloul and his Wafdist successor as prime minister, Mustafa Nahas.

Serageddin's link with them was genuine. He had been a cabinet minister in several Wafdist governments, including the last one under Farouk, and he was secretary-general of the Wafd before it was suppressed. A quarter century later he was again, and still, the embodiment of the Wafd, deliberately evoking the bygone days when rich lawyers and fez-wearing pashas dominated political life.

"Our party fills a vacuum that has existed in Egyptian life for 25 years," he said. "This can be seen from how many people have asked to join, even among the youth—especially among the youth." It was questionable whether any great number of young Egyptians were asking to sign on, but Serageddin was at least getting a hearing. A speech he had given at the party's first meeting, rejecting everything that had happened since 1952 and scorning the revolution as a mere military coup, was being talked about all over the country, even though the newspapers had not published it. Politicians from the Marxist left to Islamic fundamentalists were aligning themselves with the Wafd.

Serageddin's program was hardly radical. In foreign affairs, he said, the Wafd fully supported Sadat. At home, the Wafd wanted a change to parliamentary-style democracy on the British model, with cabinet ministers, including the prime minister, selected from the ranks of elected members. The Wafd wanted an end to government ownership of all but a few heavy industries, an end to the policy of guaranteeing jobs for university graduates and a completely unrestricted press, which would allow the Wafd to publish its own newspaper.

"I am an optimist," Serageddin said. "You see defects all around you in our society, but a cure can be found for them. They are the result of autocratic rule, and the evils will be eliminated through democracy."

It seemed incredible that Sadat would regard this old man and his resurrected organization as a threat, however wide its appeal, but the president never let the Wafd's legal status hinder his repression of it. The party, he said, represented "a return to the feudalist and corrupt political life before 1952." It was based on "the very corruption and feudalism the revolution was made to get rid of."

In that brief spring of the Wafd's appearance, I saw middle-aged Egyptian friends who had stayed out of politics for 20 years rush off to attend meetings, applaud party officials and plan publication of a newspaper. Twenty-four members of parliament joined the Wafd. Arab journalists in other countries wrote about the Wafd and what it portended for Egypt. But the flurry of excitement did not add up to political power. When Sadat moved to cut down the Wafd, the party offered little resistance and there was no popular movement in its defense.

A referendum in May 1978, the announced purpose of which was to "organize the political process," got rid of the Wafd by excluding from political activity those who had held ministerial posts under the monarchy—namely, Fuad Serageddin. The party issued a statement saying that the new restrictions revealed Sadat's "true intentions, that is to say, democracy is to be a mere empty slogan, a facade for the benefit of local and international public opinion." Because the New Wafd was "unable to practice its functions under these measures," it dissolved itself, little more than three months after it had been legalized.

The restrictions approved in the referendum also proscribed political activity by "atheists" and "corrupters," so Khaled Mohieddin's leftists also opposed them, knowing who was meant by "atheists." Their newspaper, *al-Ahali,* called for a negative vote, but the paper was seized by the police just as it came off the presses and few copies made it out to the streets. Mohieddin called a press conference to defend the editorial. "To hold a referendum means that its outcome is not a foregone conclusion," he said. "It is the right of every citizen to say yes or no to what it presents. In its statement, our party exercises its legitimate right to explain to the people why they should say no." His statement received more coverage in the foreign press than it did in the tame semi-official newspapers of Cairo. With *al-Ahali* operating under tight restrictions and finally driven underground—its license revoked on the grounds that it failed to appear regularly—Mohieddin's party, though technically still legal, became as impotent as the dissolved Wafd and announced its "withdrawal" from a process in which it could not fully participate.

In the spring of 1979, while Egyptians were still reeling from the events of the previous two years—the food riots, the Jerusalem journey, legalization and suppression of independent political parties, an outburst of religious fanaticism, Camp David and the peace treaty—Sadat dissolved parliament three years early and called new elections. His motivation for doing so was not clearly stated, but it was not hard to conclude that, even though the parliament elected in 1976 was firmly under his control, he wanted to get rid of the few powerless but vociferous opponents who used parliament as a protected forum from which to say unpleasant things.

The 1979 elections achieved the purge Sadat wanted. When the results were announced, Khaled Mohieddin, Kamal Eddin Hussein and a handful of other opponents ranging from Marxists to Islamic activists were reported to have been defeated. Ahmed Taha, a prominent leftist, was arrested before the election on charges of spying for Bulgaria. Ismail Fahmy, the foreign minister who had resigned in protest over the Jerusalem trip, was denied permission to challenge Prime Minister Mustafa Khalil in their Cairo district on the grounds that he was not a registered voter—even though he had voted there in the 1976 election and the 1978 referendum. But the most flagrantly improbable outcome, the one that stripped the entire process of credibility, was the defeat of Ahmed Abu Ismail.

Ismail, then 62, could not be lumped in with the atheists, corrupters or feudalists. He was a banker and a professor of economics who had been minister of finance under Sadat and a member of parliament from the town of Samannud, in the Nile Delta. He generally supported the government's policies, including the peace treaty with Israel. But when Sadat announced the transformation of the center party into the National Democratic Party, with himself as its head, Ismail refused to join. He sought to retain his seat in the 1979 election by running as an independent. The candidate of Sadat's party was Mustafa Hefnawy, the minister of housing, who had not previously stood for election and who could not match Ismail's record of service to the voters of Samannud.

Word began to circulate in Cairo that the government was using particularly heavy-handed and conspicuous tactics against Ismail, so a few days before the voting I went to Samannud unannounced to see him. He did not know I was coming, so what I saw could not have been set up for my benefit.

At the scruffy canalside villa that was serving as Ismail's campaign headquarters, I found agitated and angry young men firing each other up with stories about the government's tactics. Twenty-six civil servants who supported Ismail had been transferred out of the district. According to Ismail's supporters, Hefnawy, the NDP candidate, had used his position as minister of housing to trade building materials for electoral support—a charge Hefnawy never refuted. The governor of the province, a presidential appointee, was supporting Hefnawy. But the greatest anger was centered on a police raid a few nights ealier in which 45 men who supported Ismail had been arrested in their homes at 4 AM. "We were in bed with our wives and they came in and took us," one man said. "They came right in and took us away from our beds with the women watching!"

They said they had been arrested because they helped organize a big rally for Ismail; the police said the rally had become a brawl and the men responsible were those arrested. Whatever the truth, the raid appeared to have galvanized sentiment in Samannud in favor of Ismail and against the government, the NDP and Hefnawy. Ismail took me out in his car to show me what was happening.

It was already mid-afternoon, which is siesta time, and it was raining, so few people were on the streets and few shops were open. But men sitting at a cafe recognized Ismail's car and they rose as we passed. "Abu Ismail, Abu Ismail has come!" they shouted. "God is with you, Abu Ismail!"

Within minutes, the car was surrounded by chanting, waving, singing, applauding admirers, throwing themselves at him. People poured out of buildings like bees from a hive. The car was immobilized in a surging mass of people, pounding on the hood, grabbing at Abu Ismail through the window, kissing his hand, weeping and shouting. Small boys ran through knee-deep puddles to approach the car. A blind crone waving a cane was boosted onto the hood and capered there in a grotesque dervish-like dance, applauded by the mob.

They were six-deep around the car, then twelve. Ismail's driver nudged the car forward a few feet at a time while the candidate, in the rear seat, smiled and waved, greeting people by name as they pressed against the doors.

"If it's a fair election, I'll win," he said dryly. "If you hear that I didn't win, you'll know it wasn't a fair election. You should see what it's like when they know I am coming."

He said he had appealed to Prime Minister Khalil for the release of the 45 men who had been arrested, and that the incident had reinforced support for him. "I built my position on the people here, before there were any parties," he said.

Only one small village in this district still lacks electricity. We got a clothing factory—there are 1,200 people working there, mostly girls, earning good money. Now these people are all being told that the government wants certain candidates to win. Then why bother with the election? Why not just appoint them and be done with it?

Why not, indeed? When the returns were announced, Hefnawy was declared the winner over Abu Ismail by about 250 votes of more than 40,000 cast. Abu Ismail was out of the People's Assembly, along with Kamal Eddin Hussein, Khaled Mohieddin and almost every other dissenter or critic who had any personal following or credible voice. Of the 362 candidates fielded by the National Democratic Party, 330 were declared elected. Of the 1,192 independent candidates, only 10 were elected. The parliament was saved from total pliability and impotence only by the determination of a few of those 10 independents and by the unexpected spunk of the official government-sponsored opposition party, the Socialist Labor Party, headed by Ibrahim Shukri. That party was established with Sadat's encouragement after the demise of the Wafd to represent a showcase opposition and prevent the de facto return of the one-party state Sadat claimed to have abolished. By attracting into its ranks some critics of Sadat who had a particular affinity for Shukri but nowhere else to go, the party became more of a nuisance than Sadat had intended. Its newspaper, *al-Shaab* (*The People*) printed occasional stories that irritated the regime (such as the news of the government's campaign to defeat Abu Ismail). But with only 28 seats in the parliament, the party was able to do little more than fire verbal broadsides.

The 1979 elections and a referendum the following May that amended the constitution to allow Sadat to seek additional terms as president completed the establishment—always by ostensibly legal methods—of Sadat's personal control over the national political system, the government and all key institutions. This one-man rule was disguised as a manifestation of popular will, but even as this charade was being acted out, dissent was increasing. Unhappiness over economic conditions, the separate peace with Israel and Sadat's increasingly regal style and heavy-handed political methods, combined with religious agitation stimulated by the revolution in Iran, began to fragment the "family" over which Sadat was presiding. With legal channels of opposition closed off, dissenters began resorting to extralegal channels, such as public demonstrations. Sadat, who appeared increasingly detached from reality, responded with yet another law limiting the opposition. This was the measure, promulgated in May 1980, known as the "Law of Shame."

It became illegal to allow children or young people to "go astray" by advocating "the repudiation of popular religious, moral or national values or by setting a bad example" in public. Anything that would "undermine the dignity of the state" was prohibited. It became illegal to form or join any organization not authorized by the state. Broadcasting "false or misleading news" was prohibited. Alleged offenses were to be tried before a special court; verdicts could not be appealed. Penalties could include house arrest and suspension of political and economic rights.

Enactment of that breathtaking law brought Sadat's brief flirtation with democracy to an end. Just over three years had elapsed since the food riots, two and a half years since the journey to Jerusalem. His ever loftier pronouncements about "sincerity and faith," his appeals to "cleanse your hearts of the epidemic of hatred," were a transparent veneer over one-man rule.

Individuals who were loyal to Sadat and owed him their jobs were running every important governmental, economic and cultural institution: the People's Assembly, the universities, the ruling party, the Suez Canal, the armed forces, the economic institutions, the "food security" program, al-Azhar mosque and the press. The impotence of the opposition was shown to the nation one night when Sadat was delivering a televised address to the People's Assembly. An independent member from some remote district stood up to heckle the president. He shouted and waved his arms, but Sadat was patient. "*Ya ibni*," he said again and again, "*ya ibni*"—my son, my son. After a few minutes the heckler sat down, frustrated, and the speech resumed.

The press, except for *al-Shaab* and the magazine of the Muslim Brotherhood, was thoroughly under control. Sadat had proclaimed freedom of the press and eliminated censorship; his prime minister, Mustafa Khalil, had announced the abolition of the ministry of information to end, symbolically, government control over the press. But freedom of the press is relative in a country where newspapers are required to have licenses, where the state controls the importation and distribution of newsprint and ink and owns the print shops. The government also appoints the editors of the major journals and public-sector corporations keep the opposition newspapers afloat with advertisements that can be withdrawn at any time. The three big national newspapers caused occasional difficulties with impertinent reporting on domestic affairs, such as the scandalous arrangement that would have permitted foreign developers to take over the land around the Pyramids for an exclusive residential community. However, they were slavishly docile on matters of foreign policy, national security and economics, taking their orders directly from the president. Yet as early as 1976 Sadat was assailing the press for what he called a "campaign of doubt" that undermined the credibility of his administration. As a result, by the late 1970s Cairo was overpopulated with writers and editors, such as Heikal and the prominent leftist Loutfi al-Kholy, who had been silenced. While they remained on the payrolls of their organizations, they were exiled to the "sunshine club," a mythical institution of journalists who had nothing to do but sit in the sunshine and draw their salaries. They were not exiled from Egypt, arrested, put under house arrest or deprived of their passports—that was not Sadat's style, at least not until the very end. He was less the dictator crushing his opponents than the stern father sending unruly children to bed without supper.

When Hermann F. Eilts, the American ambassador, was preparing to retire in 1979, Ismail Fahmy gave a farewell party for him in his elegant apartment, the kind of spacious upper-floor apartment with balconies over the Nile that a man of Fahmy's stature could be expected to have. Having quit in protest as foreign minister and having been barred from running for parliament, Fahmy had joined the ranks of the dissidents and his party for Eilts was a gathering of once-powerful figures who had been cast aside. Mohammed Ibrahim Kamel, the friend of Sadat's youth who had succeeded Fahmy and had quit over Camp David, was there; so was Gen. Mohammed Abdel Ghani al-Gamassi, former commander of the armed forces and war minister, who had been unceremoniously let go in a shakeup of the military hierarchy. Also present was Heikal, once the editor of *al-Ahram* and the voice of Egypt, long since silenced after falling out with Sadat. He was still published abroad but not at home, and was the subject of a sporadic campaign of defamation in the government-controlled journals; Sadat said he was "blackening the name of Egypt" in the columns he wrote for Arab newspapers outside Egypt. I asked him if his latest book, *Sphinx and Commissar,* would be in Cairo bookstores any time soon. "Are you a newcomer here?" he replied. "Of course you're not, so you know the answer."

The fact that these men and other malcontents felt free to

gather openly and talk forthrightly at a party attended by foreign journalists illustrated the relative benevolence of Sadat's system. No such event was conceivable in Iraq or Libya. In Egypt, so long as they refrained from violence, they—and Khaled Mohieddin and Fuad Seraggedin and Kamal Eddin Hussein—remained at liberty. They could travel, give interviews to foreign journalists, meet and grumble. And most of them lived well too—especially Heikal, the "socialist millionaire," who at the end of Fahmy's party was driven away in an immense silver-gray Mercedes to his apartment, which was even more spacious than Fahmy's.

But these party guests could not be likened to Democrats in Washington during a Republican administration. They were not only out, they were silenced. There was no channel by which they could be heard, no organization by which they could oblige the regime to take their views into account, and no way they could rally their fellow citizens to support them. Nobody was going to interview them on the domestic radio, or in *al-Ahram*, the mainstay of the establishment press. No political opponent of Sadat, except in the underground of religious extremism, had any mass following that could put pressure on the regime to respond to its demands. Sadat's pluralism was a pluralism among the educated urban elite; the degree of mass participation in conventional politics was, and remains, negligible. Only those organizations that arise from the grass roots and are independent of the elite—that is, the religious organizations—command any mass following. The situation of Sadat's critics was as Morroe Berger had described it in his analysis of the Egyptian system published 20 years earlier: "Unlike the West, where private economic power and the political system have built up competing power groups, in the Near East men have had relatively little leverage against government except revolt, indifference or flight into the desert." Only a handful of religious zealots were prepared for revolt, or for flight into the desert.

Enactment of the "Law of Shame" in the spring of 1980 put an end to the pretense of democracy. "We have been tolerant and will continue to be tolerant," Sadat said at the time, "but let no one provoke me."

But by then it seemed as if everyone provoked him. He tolerated the existence of an opposition but refused to concede anything to it or allow it to participate in national decision making. The result was disillusionment and frustration among groups all across the political spectrum who had believed his promises of political pluralism; they responded by intensifying their criticism. The legitimacy Sadat had earned in 1973 was being eroded by his pharaonic posturing, an erosion that encouraged activism among the malcontents. Throughout the rest of 1980 and most of 1981, Sadat appeared to be provoked all the time—by domestic critics, by religious agitators among Muslims and Christians alike, by the foreign press, and by commentators who likened him to the Shah. The Israelis bombed a nuclear reactor in Iraq and thus encouraged critics of the peace treaty, who had argued that it neutralized Egypt and gave Israel a free hand to the east. Sadat's response was a return to the tactics of his predecessor: arrests.

The knocks on the doors began in the early hours of September 3, 1981. Within two days, 1,536 people were arrested. Most of them were members of Muslim activist groups, little known to the public, but about 250 were among the most prominent political, intellectual and religious figures in Egypt: Heikal, Fuad Serageddin, the veteran politician Hilmi Murad, former Planning Minister Ismail Sabri Abdallah, the communist intellectual Fuad Morsi, Omar Tilmassani, head of the Muslim Brotherhood. There were, in John Waterbury's words, "leftists, Nasserists, rightists, Wafdists, extremists, and gadflies. Anyone, it seemed, who had ever seriously crossed swords with Sadat was picked up." At the same time, seven publications were suppressed and the leader of the Coptic Christian Church, Pope Shenouda III, was stripped of his temporal powers.

Sadat railed at the "plotters," and unveiled laughable evidence against them. He excoriated foreign critics. He staged elaborate shows of support for what he was doing. But this sad episode, which embarrassed all Egypt and Sadat's erstwhile admirers abroad, was Sadat's last hurrah. While he was ordering the arrests of these respectable and prominent citizens, a genuine threat was developing among obscure conspirators in Cairo's back alleys. On October 6, 1981, during the annual parade that commemorated the crossing of the Suez Canal in the 1973 war, Sadat was assassinated by religious fanatics who burst from an army truck and opened fire into the reviewing stand.

Egypt was shocked by the audacious and successful attack, which took place in broad daylight before a crowd of thousands and showed that extremists had penetrated the military. But Egypt did not mourn for Sadat. Everyone who was in Cairo at the time

remarked upon the contrast between Sadat's funeral and that of
Nasser 11 years before. The foreign leaders whom Sadat had
courted turned out in impressive numbers, but the Egyptian masses
stayed home. Grief had rent their souls when Nasser died; Sadat's
death brought apathy. Egyptians did not want to return to war
with Israel, but they were fed up with Sadat's poses and promises.
In this ultimate referendum, they showed their true feelings about
the "father" who had stood above them.

Mubarak's succession to the presidency, unlike Sadat's, was
uncontested. He had been vice president under Sadat since 1975
and had never publicly put an inch of distance between himself and
Sadat's policies, but he had managed to remain untainted by Sadat's
excesses. Mubarak, a career air force officer trained in the Soviet
Union, was the direct heir of Sadat and yet represented an important generational change. Nine years younger than Sadat, he was
only 24 at the time of the revolution. He had no link to the "Free
Officers" and had never participated in the struggle against the
British. His distinction was his outstanding performance in the
1973 war—the war that gave rise to the "October generation" of
leadership.

As vice president, Mubarak was widely understood to be
strong where Sadat was weak. He is unpretentious, he works hard,
he is apparently incorruptible, he keeps his family out of public
view and he has a very thick skin. "He's just an Egyptian, like
everybody else," says a senior diplomat who has worked closely
with Mubarak and Sadat.

If there were doubts about Mubarak's qualifications for the
presidency, they centered on his intellectual capacity, not his integrity or dedication. Students called him "La Vache Qui Rit," the
Laughing Cow, because of his supposed resemblance to the trademark animal on the French cheese.

One joke gives the tenor of the intelligentsia's view of Mubarak. Preparing for his first address to parliament as president,
Mubarak told his speechwriters he wanted something short and
snappy, "not one of those rambling three-hour harangues that
Sadat gave." When the text was delivered, he picked it up and went
directly to the People's Assembly to read it—and it took three
hours. Furious, Mubarak raged at the chief speechwriter: "I told
you to keep it short." "But Mr. President," stammered the speechwriter, "You read the original and all ten copies."

Mubarak's first term as president, 1981–87, was a series of balancing acts. He clung resolutely, against vigorous opposition, to the letter of the peace agreement with Israel, even when repudiation of it would have been politically popular. He also clung to *infitah,* even as disenchantment with the economy pervaded the country, and to Sadat, whom he honored frequently and in public even as he pulled back from his predecessor's excesses.

Egypt's basic form of government has remained intact. The president, with the support of the armed forces, is unchallenged as its head. The sophisticated but impotent political elites of left and right operate within a framework controlled by him, and the masses are politically inert. But world events and Mubarak's sound instincts have combined to effect significant changes in Egypt's domestic and international policies. Mubarak promptly released the prisoners rounded up in the September 1981 dragnet, sending a conciliatory signal to the opposition and calming the tense atmosphere that enveloped the country after Sadat's death. Israel's invasion of Lebanon in 1982 and the forced downing by American warplanes of an Egyptian civilian airliner in the *Achille Lauro* hijacking affair put some distance between Egypt and the United States; Mubarak has since restored diplomatic and commercial relations with the Soviet Union and other communist countries. He has also cultivated with considerable success the Arab leaders whom Sadat spurned, making it possible for them to restore ties to Egypt when they were ready. He has tolerated the return of an opposition press unrivaled in the Arab world for the venom and intemperance of its attacks on the government.

Mubarak is essentially a technician, not a systematic thinker or a visionary. His idea of political theater is to put on a leisure suit and make a surprise visit to a state-owned department store to check the quality of the merchandise and urge customers to buy Egyptian-made products. His political philosophy can be summarized in an address he gave at a conference in Cairo shortly before the end of his first term:

> Democracy is not a mold from which copies and samples can be made to be applied everywhere in the world. Democracy is a means and a goal. . . . You know that democracy takes many forms, which differ from one country to another. Democratic practices that are good in one country—which has achieved a

high degree of economic growth, social stability and the ability to confront the basic challenges facing it—might not necessarily be appropriate for another country that has different circumstances and values. . . . The democracy in which we live is the result of practices, experiences and changing circumstances. It is the natural line that constitutes a balance between various ideas, trends and beliefs to ensure that no minority can impose an intellectual terrorism and that the majority does not turn into a naked dictatorship. . . . We did not want democracy to be merely for adornment. We did not want it to be a democracy for settling accounts and venting grudges. We did not want it to be a fragile democracy that could be exploited and manipulated for personal ambitions. We did not desire a democracy too weak to defend itself against its enemies. We also did not want it to be a democracy of slogans that soon wither and die. . . . Democracy is a system that respects duties, as there can be no freedom without responsibility.

That last phrase, "no freedom without responsibility," has become the basic operating principle of Mubarak's government. He tolerates vociferous, engaged dissent, but he does not tolerate extralegal activities, mob coercion or violence that he regards as threatening to stability. He can rightly claim to have demonstrated respect for the independence of the judiciary, from which he has accepted unfavorable rulings on critical issues. At the same time, there is abundant evidence that some persons regarded as political extremists have been arrested without charge and tortured while in custody. One well-publicized case in 1985 illustrated both of these points. A Cairo court acquitted 10 people accused of membership in an illegal communist organization on the grounds that their confessions had been made in "an atmosphere of torture and coercion." The Amnesty International organization has documented several cases of political prisoners who were tortured in police custody.

While proclaiming democracy, the government has left in force a "state of emergency" declared after Sadat's assassination, giving the police a cloak of legality for arbitrary arrests. Alleged extremists of the communist left and the Islamic far right are rounded up periodically. The opposition has rightly denounced the state of emergency as incompatible with the constitution—Fuad Serageddin, for example, calls it "a flagrant violation of freedoms and sanctities and a sword held by the ruler above the heads of the people." The regime's answer to this has been delivered by Zaki Badr, who as minister of interior is responsible for domestic security: "You ask why the emergency law while security in Egypt is stable," he told the magazine *al-Mussawar,* a favored organ for government policy pronouncements, in December 1987. "I say the stable security situation in Egypt at present is at least partially a result of the existence of the emergency law, which gives the police greater freedom to take necessary and urgent security measures." To the charge that the law is applied selectively, he said, "Yes, the emergency law is enforced only against specific strata of the population. These are the extremists, terrorists, drug traffickers, criminals and currency smugglers who undermine the national economy." It is the police, of course, who make the determination of which individuals fall into those categories.

Mubarak inherited the docile parliament that Sadat had installed in the rigged elections of 1979, but Sadat's death brought Egypt's politicians back to life. A new party, the Ummah, or Party of the Nation, was legalized in 1983 even though it is a sectarian organization, espousing Islam as its platform. Then the Wafd, which had dissolved itself in response to Sadat's repression, reentered the lists, saying it had only suspended its activities, not disbanded. When the parliamentary commission on parties said the Wafd would have to reapply for legalization, the party went to court, and won. The government accepted a court ruling that the Wafd had remained a legal entity and could resume its activities, which it did with vigor. The Wafd and the other legal parties, Socialist Labor under Ibrahim Shukri, the Liberal Socialists under Mustafa Kamal Murad and the leftist National Progressive Unionists under Khaled Mohieddin, began negotiating with each other, and with the Muslim Brotherhood, over slates of candidates for the 1984 election.

These opposition leaders were, of course, the same respectable, domesticated politicians who have been familiar to Egyptians for a generation. They could not be said to represent any new ideas, and their party leaderships did not include any charismatic new figures who might develop into rivals to Mubarak. Nevertheless, the 1984 elections began a process, which the 1987 elections were to accelerate, of generational change in Egyptian politics.

In 1984, the elections were held under a law that strongly favored the ruling party, at the expense of the legal opposition and the independent candidates. Each party would receive a number of seats in the People's Assembly proportional to its total vote, but any party that failed to get eight percent of the total would be excluded from parliament and its votes distributed pro-rata to parties that surpassed that threshold. Independent candidates, who in the parliamentary elections under Sadat had outnumbered the party-affiliated candidates and had fared relatively well, were banned. These restrictions had the effect of pitting the smaller parties against each other in a bid for allies such as the Muslim Brothers who could would help them pass the eight percent minimum.

More than 5 million votes were cast in that 1984 election. Mubarak's National Democratic Party naturally dominated the outcome, capturing 73 percent. The New Wafd, which had several Muslim Brothers on its ticket, received 15.1 percent. The other three legal parties received a total of 11.9 percent but none of them by itself surpassed the 8 percent barrier, so their votes were distributed between the NDP and the Wafd according to the 73–15 ratio established in the balloting. Abdel Monem Said Aly, an Egyptian political scientist, pointed out in an analysis of this election that the redistribution formula meant that "although the opposition parties obtained about 27 percent of the valid votes, which should allow them to obtain 120 seats [of the 448 total to be filled], they only obtained the 58 of the NWP [the New Wafd Party], which represented 13 percent of the People's Assembly elected seats, in spite of the fact that even the Wafd Party [by itself] obtained more than 15 percent of the valid votes."

Active political participation remained the province of a relative handful of Egyptians, but among those who were involved, the 1984 elections began a period of wide-open politicking such as Egypt had not seen since before the revolution. The opposition press was in full cry, and the major state-owned dailies fired back, denouncing the Wafd as feudalist and Khaled Mohieddin's leftists as tools of Moscow. A group of self-described "Nasserites" surfaced, attempting to form a political party. Opposition politicians attacked the election law, the deterioration of the economy, the government's handling of the *Achille Lauro* hijacking affair and the trial and suspicious death in prison of a policeman who murdered seven Israeli tourists in the Sinai.

There was a brief truce in February 1986, when some 17,000 low-paid conscripts in the central security forces mutinied and rioted, apparently in response to a report that their tours of duty were to be extended. Opposition leaders supported Mubarak when he called out the army to suppress the mutiny. But in the meantime, a constitutional challenge to the validity of the election law was working its way through the courts.

In the winter of 1986–87, events moved swiftly. Facing the likelihood that the Supreme Constitutional Court would invalidate the election law as a violation of the rights of individual citizens, the People's Assembly amended the law to allow independents to run and to end the distribution of the votes of the parties that failed to reach the eight percent threshold, but the threshold itself was retained.

Leaders of all the opposition parties scheduled a conference for February 5, 1987, to call for amending the constitution to have the president elected by direct popular vote, instead of by the People's Assembly. They also asked for abolition of special security courts, a ban on party activities by a sitting president, and extension to the People's Assembly of the right to bring down a cabinet by a vote of no confidence. Mubarak pre-empted this movement the day before the conference by calling for a referendum to dissolve the People's Assembly and hold a new election three years ahead of schedule. The opposition front dissolved into bickering and negotiations over who would have the support of the Muslim Brotherhood.

The elections were held in April. Experienced foreign analysts who observed the campaign and the balloting said that the authorities, under the heavy hand of Interior Minister Zaki Badr, imposed unreasonable restrictions on opposition candidates and resorted to arrest to intimidate voters. But within a few weeks, the campaign and the outcome were nonetheless being talked about as a watershed in the evolution of Egyptian democracy.

Mubarak's party received 70 percent of the 6.8 million votes and 308 of the 448 elected seats. That is, the ruling party's share of elected seats in the People's Assembly fell to 69 percent, one of the lowest figures in history. The well-financed Muslim Brothers transferred their support from the Wafd to Socialist Labor, and their candidates gained 56 seats. The Wafd, deserted by the Brotherhood in the pre-election bargaining, dropped to 36 seats. Independents won 48 seats. This parliament duly nominated Mubarak for a second term, for which he was endorsed in a referendum.

Weeks after the election, the walls of Cairo and Alexandria were still plastered with the posters and placards of the various parties and slates, but popular participation in the election process had remained very low. Well under half the 14 million eligible voters went to the polls, and turnout was lower in Cairo and Alexandria than in the countryside. The campaign was "quite boring with the results known in advance," said *al-Ahali.*

More interesting than the numbers were the circumstances that surrounded the election. Mubarak gained credit and credibility by his willingness to accede to the authority of the courts and by his deft maneuvering to neutralize the opposition. The amendments to the election law enhanced the legitimacy of the parliament that nominated Mubarak for a second term. The party lists and the independent candidates included a high percentage of new faces, including many who have come to maturity since Nasser died. The overt participation of the Muslim Brothers and some known communists gave de facto legality to political campaigns by organizations that are nominally excluded from the political process.

It may be that Mubarak's flexibility and the decision of the Muslim Brotherhood to participate overtly in mainstream politics, rather than foment trouble clandestinely as in the past, will have the desired effect of channeling the opposition into legal and thus nonthreatening activity. Certainly Mubarak faces no serious threat from the left.

A few weeks after the election I went to see Ismail Sabry Abdallah, a prominent leftist and former minister of planning under Sadat. He observed ruefully that "there isn't any revolutionary environment" in Egypt. "I wish there were," he said. "I want radical solutions." Abdallah said that "the generation under 30, which is two-thirds of all Egyptians, is very frustrated, but they aren't revolutionary. They tend to boil over in three-day episodes that are easily put down."

Whether Mubarak is equally secure on his right flank is much more debatable. Recent history has amply demonstrated that Egypt in the best of times is fertile ground for agitation and violence by clandestine groups of religious extremists. The indifference of the masses to organized and conventional politics, reflected in their abstention from voting in the parliamentary elections, does not necessarily mean acquiescence. The inevitable failure of the leadership to lead the country to prosperity—or at least to an appearance of equity—and the sterility of the thinking among the recognized opposition present an open invitation to a well-financed, mosque-centered underground to take matters into its own hands.

CHAPTER

9

Islam and the State

The face glaring out from the front pages of Cairo's newspapers bore an uncanny resemblance to that of Charles Manson, the California mass murderer. With glaring eyes and sneering mouth and unkempt beard, the man hardly looked Egyptian at all, which is probably why that particular photo was used—the government wanted only to discredit the man it portrayed. He was Shukry Ahmed Mustafa, who for a few weeks in the summer of 1977 was the most talked-about man in Egypt.

Mustafa was a true fanatic, a zealot who was convinced that Egypt had fallen away from the correct path of Islam into corruption and immorality. He was the leader of a cult that called itself *Takfeer w'al-Hijra;* there is no precise translation of this, but it may be rendered into English as Atonement and Migration, or Repentance and Isolation. *Takfeer* was a group of puritanical young men and women who, not content with such external appurtenances of traditional Islamic behavior as beards and ankle-length dresses, believed they should withdraw entirely from what looked to them like a pagan society, as Muhammad had withdrawn from Mecca and migrated to Medina. Mustafa and his followers were known to the police as participants in previous terrorist attacks against government facilities. Mustafa had been imprisoned for religious agitation in 1965; he was known to have been influenced by Sayyid Qutb, a prominent voice of religious reaction who had been executed in 1966. In July 1977, Mustafa's band shocked the country by attempting to organize a mass uprising against the government. The target was not just Sadat but the entire political and social structure of Egypt, which they said had been tainted by hedonism, by materialism and by alien—that is, Western—influences.

Many Egyptians, from armchair Marxists to Muslim theologians, share those views to some extent. But when Mustafa surfaced they did not respond to the group's call, because Mustafa was an isolated figure committed to violence and intimidation, not to reasoned discourse. After all, Mustafa and his group were not appealing to the religious establishment and the pious laymen, they were attacking them as corrupt and un-Islamic. *Takfeer w'al-Hijra* was clearly outside the mainstream. But at the same time the mainstream was changing, largely unperceived by conventional politicians and traditional religious authorities. A decade later, after the peace treaty with Israel, the Iranian revolution and the assassination of Sadat by a group even more extreme than Mustafa's, religion has become Egypt's most volatile domestic issue, and the groups commonly described as fundamentalist cannot be ignored or dismissed as a lunatic fringe.

"The forces which conspired against Sadat," Heikal said, "were just as much a part of the mainstream in Egyptian society as were the forces which overthrew the Shah from the mainstream in Iran." This overstates the case. The conspirators were like other Egyptians in that they appeared to be ordinary citizens, soldiers, doctors and teachers. But their espousal of violence set them apart. In effect, they went to war against their own society. For most Egyptians, the religious question is not one of violence; it is one of cultural alignment, of social priorities, and of the government's role in enforcing the tenets of Islam.

Modern Egypt has lived through many cycles of rising and falling religious agitation, which is never totally absent. The conflict has ebbed and flowed since 1798, when French artillerymen in Napoleon's army shelled al-Azhar mosque to put down resistance to foreign occupation. As recounted in a pamphlet distributed by al-Azhar University to modern-day visitors, the French

> kept shelling the mosque and crowded lanes in its neigh-
> borhood, until the collapse of resistance. Then, brandishing
> their swords, horsemen rushed into the mosque, killed those
> present and carried away carpets, chandeliers, manuscripts and
> even the modest belongings of students. They even trampled on
> copies of the Koran and used the mosque as a latrine and urinal.

This desecration of the center of Muslim learning is still cited by reactionary elements in Egypt as emblematic of the pernicious effects of Western influences.

In the 1940s and 1950s, the Muslim Brotherhood terrorized Egypt with bombings and assassinations, which ended only when Nasser crushed the organization. Sadat, encouraging religious activism as a counterweight to leftist influence on the campuses, allowed the Brotherhood to reappear openly, but the current version is not the threat to stability that it once was. The Brotherhood often dissents from government policies, especially as regards relations with Israel, but for the past decade it has generally contented itself with organizing prayer rallies, encouraging religiously oriented political candidates, campaigning among the students and making money through a network of corporations and financial institutions. It is no longer clandestine—it operates out of a clearly marked office in a shabby Cairo building. Its program emphasizes political pluralism and advocacy of its views through conventional channels, as was reflected in the participation of Brotherhood candidates as members of slates organized by legal political parties in the parliamentary elections of 1984 and 1987. The more serious threat to stability comes from underground groups such as *al-Jihad*, which carried out the assassination of Sadat on October 6, 1981, and *Takfeer w'al-Hijra*.

Mustafa's band was armed and dedicated. Several members, including Mustafa, had been in and out of prison for a decade because of previous incidents of terrorism. They joined members of another extremist group influenced by Sayyid Qutb in an armed attack on the Military Technical College near Cairo in 1974, an incident that was apparently a prelude to an attempt to assassinate Sadat. Some of the men arrested in that episode were still in jail when *Takfeer* struck again two years later. The group kidnapped and executed Sheikh Muhammad al-Dhahabi, a former minister of religious affairs who was a pillar of the traditional religious establishment and a prominent opponent of the extremist groups. Mustafa's followers made clear that they regarded this murder as the signal for an armed uprising against an immoral and corrupt government.

But they lacked the organization, training, political skill and sense of the popular mood that had made the Muslim Brotherhood so powerful under a weak regime 30 years earlier. *Takfeer*'s pronouncements evoked the terror atmosphere of Saigon in the 1960s or of Algiers in the 1950s, but the Egyptians went quietly about their business and the "uprising" never went much beyond the original incident. Mustafa was arrested a few days later, and he and four of his followers were hanged. Lesser members of the group were imprisoned but, according to Heikal, released in time to supply the weapons used by the conspirators of *al-Jihad* in Sadat's assassination.

The public's response to Mustafa showed that the Egyptians, who are amiable and reasonable people, cannot automatically be whipped into revolutionary frenzy by agitators who seize upon Islam as their banner. The same could be said about the popular response to *al-Jihad* when its assassins burst from their truck and gunned down Sadat during a military parade. The Egyptians did not grieve over the loss of Sadat, but neither did they follow *al-Jihad* in its call for a bloody uprising against the established order.

Nevertheless, such incidents seem certain to erupt from time to time, especially as economic progress continues to elude most of the population. They constitute a challenge to the balance of religious and secular power that has evolved in Egypt since the beginning of the nineteenth century. And they illuminate the dark currents that flow beneath Egypt's tranquil surface; religion, and especially the absolutist form of religion espoused by some clandestine groups, cannot be factored out of Egypt's political equation.

As a young revolutionary, Sadat was the "Free Officers'" contact man with the Muslim Brotherhood, and he favored cooperation between the two movements until the Brotherhood opted for terrorism. In *Revolt on the Nile,* Sadat wrote of learning from the experience that

> the Egyptian is a religious man. He has a deep respect for all religions, and for spiritual values. But religion is one thing, its exploitation for political purposes quite another. It must not be given a purpose which it does not inherently possess. If a religion is turned into a political system, then fanaticism is born. The confusion of temporal power with the spiritual has been the downfall of many oriental societies.

The lesson of the *Takfeer* uprising 20 years later, however, and of Sadat's own assassination, was that in Egypt religion and statecraft cannot be so neatly separated. Islam teaches that no area of human endeavor is beyond its purview, including politics and government. This often means that pious or zealous individuals feel obliged to enter into active opposition to a government or political system that they believe has strayed from the true Islamic path. Islam does not teach acceptance.

There is no ordained clergy in Islam. Religious institutions such as al-Azhar train "men of religion," professional scholars and theologians who run the mosques and other religious establishments. But the Koran speaks to the individual: there is no central doctrinal authority, no Muslim Vatican, no cadre of theologians whose religious interpretations must be accepted. This means that any group of pious laymen can study the Koran and the sayings of the Prophet Muhammad and come to its own conclusions, conclusions which the members will espouse even if the established "men of religion" dispute them. The effect of this in Egypt has been to encourage religious agitation from the bottom up, from the man in the street, so to speak, as opposed to the religious revolution in Iran, which was developed from the top down, spreading from the professional religious hierarchy into the streets. The leading members of the Muslim Brotherhood, and of *Takfeer w'al Hijra* and *al-Jihad*, have been laymen, students, military officers and engineers, not religious professionals.

The interplay of religion and public affairs in Egypt is subtle and not immediately apparent to outsiders. Women flying to Cairo on international airliners do not retire to the restrooms to don full-length dresses and cover their faces, as they do upon approaching Saudi Arabia or Qatar. Factories and offices do not come to a halt at prayer time; individuals are free to leave their desks or lathes to pray, but many do not. It is possible to negotiate a contract with the Investment Authority, organize a drilling expedition in the oil fields, discuss international affairs at the foreign ministry, drink beer, send a telex, give a cocktail party, tour the monuments at Luxor, buy bacon, swim in the Suez Canal, read the front page of a newspaper, play tennis, go to a movie, study Arabic, visit the battlefield at el-Alamein, climb the Pyramids or tour a factory without encountering any restrictions based on religion, or even any reference to religion. Nevertheless, Islam constitutes a presence, a force, that has no counterpart in our own society, and a Muslim by definition is part of an international network of spiritual alliance that cannot be severed by secular considerations.

Speeches by Egyptian public officials and private citizens alike begin with the invocation that opens each *surah,* or chapter, of the Koran: "In the name of God, the merciful, the compassionate." That phrase is imprinted at the top of public documents, bills of sale and election campaign flyers. It appears on door knockers and truck bumpers. The traffic department ledger in which the sale of my car was recorded included the designation of my religion. Identity cards specify the bearer's religion. Cab drivers have sun-bleached copies of the Koran affixed to their dashboards.

The policeman who stands guard outside the Central Bank in downtown Cairo keeps a grimy piece of cardboard in his little booth to use as a mat when he drops to his knees for prayer, which he does several times during each tour of duty regardless of whatever else is going on. Millions of farmers, factory hands, soldiers, and students lay aside their worldly occupations for a few minutes of spiritual communion with an uncomplicated God. No one compels them to do it; Egypt is not Pakistan or Saudi Arabia, where the governments police the religion. Some Egyptians pray out of habit, but most do it out of simple conviction.

In the cities, polished business shoes and battered sandals are lined up side by side at the doors of mosques while their owners, lawyers and cobblers, clerks and peddlers, pray together in a setting that bridges the gaps of money and education that divide them at all other times. At any hour, men can be found chatting or snoozing in the mosques, traditionally places of meeting and shelter as well as worship.

In the villages, bright murals painted on the walls depict camels, railroad trains and airplanes, the means by which the inhabitants traveled to Mecca on their pilgrimages. In the marketplaces, tape recordings of sermons by popular imams are big sellers, especially if the preachers deviate from whatever line is being put out by the orthodox, government-controlled religious leaders who have access to television time and space in the newspapers. Political parties can be banned—sermons cannot.

The Koran remains the source not only of religious guidance but of language itself: unlike the Bible, compiled by many men in different languages over centuries, the Koran can be traced to one man and one language, and it is the standard by which all other Arabic expression is measured. Little boys in Egypt spend years in preparation for Koran recitation contests, and the finals are televised.

During the month of pilgrimage each year, a special section of
Cairo Airport is thronged with white-robed men and women of all
social classes waiting for extra flights to Saudi Arabia. Others go by
ship, down the Red Sea from Suez. Some of the pilgrims have new
robes and clean feet and leather-bound Korans; others have old
robes and dirty feet and are illiterate, but Islam is one of the few
forces in Egyptian life that can overpower class distinctions. University students, the most privileged of Egyptian youth, are often as
fervent as the *fellahin* in their devotion. Conservatives and religious
activists have dominated student government organizations since
the mid-1970s.

When those pilgrims arrive in Mecca, they find themselves
surrounded by millions of spiritual comrades of every race and
social class. This is part of Islam's appeal. It is the least racist of
faiths. It is not a white man's religion preached by missionaries who
represented colonial powers.

Islam is Egypt's state religion. Code names for military campaigns are taken from Islamic history: The 1973 attack on the
Israelis was Operation Badr, in honor of a victory by Muhammad's
followers over the pagans in 626. School children receive religious
instruction in class. Newspapers devote columns to theological
arguments, such as whether the Koran actually does prescribe death
for apostasy. The state television carries religious programs, Friday
sermons and highlights of the annual pilgrimage, beamed in by
satellite from Mecca. Egyptian leaders routinely seek *fetwas,* or
decrees issued by the leaders of the religious establishment, to
support them in controversial decisions.

The People's Assembly deals often with religion and maintains
a standing committee on religious affairs, the chairman of which is a
theologian from al-Azhar, the university that has been the center of
Islamic scholarship for a thousand years. (Although al-Azhar has
been a full-scale university since Nasser's time, offering instruction
in science, medicine and commerce, it is dominated by religious
studies. In the 1985–86 academic year, it reported 20,760 students
enrolled in the theology department, 15,533 in religious law, and
about 6,000 in other religion-related programs, out of a total
student body of 114,000.) Early in 1979, when the echoes of the
Iranian revolution were being heard throughout the Muslim world,
the People's Assembly suddenly voted to ban as heretical a murky
800-year-old religious treatise called "Meccan Conquests." Egyp-

tian friends told me that the book, while well known to scholars, is so difficult and complex that there are probably not a hundred living Egyptians who have read it, nor was it even intended for mass consumption. The Assembly vote touched off a new debate about whether that was the proper function of the parliament; critics suggested that there were more urgent issues, such as the housing shortage. But the Assembly is frequently confronted with more substantive religious questions that are legitimately within its purview, such as the reltionship of the civil code to Islamic law, or health and quarantine measures to be taken for the pilgrimage.

Most of the time the influence of religion on state and society appears to be as benign as it is ubiquitous—that is to say, Egypt generally conducts its affairs by standards and policies that seem reasonable and forward-looking to non-Muslims. This is precisely the indictment against the Egyptian system delivered by the religious absolutists. The Egyptians are not given to the vengeful impulses that characterize Shi'a Islam in Iran, nor does Egyptian policy countenance the beheadings and maimings practiced in the name of Islam in some other countries. Egypt is long past the era of debating whether scientific and technical innovation is compatible with Islam. Over the past two centuries, the state has gradually but decisively asserted its control over Islamic organizations and institutions, opening the way for social and technological innovations from coeducation to contraceptives. Movie theaters, still banned in Saudi Arabia, have been in Egypt since the beginning of this century.

There is no religious path to secular power, which is why *Takfeer w'al-Hijra* and *al-Jihad,* like the old Muslim Brotherhood, had to go outside the law. The Napoleonic invasion shocked Egypt by demonstrating the power of technology over tradition. Since then, Western influence and education, the development of the bureaucracy and a technocratic elite and the rise of the army under Nasser have eclipsed religion as the sources of state authority. Egypt has no ayatollahs; under Mubarak and Sadat, as under Nasser, engineering degrees and the command of troops have been the credentials that lead to influence. The conspirators of *al-Jihad* appear to have been genuinely surprised when the nation did not respond to their call to arms after Sadat's assassination. In the city of Asyut, 250 miles up the Nile from Cairo, their followers believed the murder of Sadat signaled the start of a nationwide uprising.

They attacked government buildings in a shootout that killed 82
policemen, but they brought only terror to the streets, not religious
fervor. Had they examined the events that followed similar acts of
violence by earlier groups, they might have anticipated the inevitable outcome. In the words of Michael Youssef, an Egyptian scholar
who interviewed members of *al-Jihad,* "they were crushed by the
power of the state machine which they had intended to destroy."

Because Islam is so deeply rooted in the collective soul of the
people and because it lends itself to absolutist and aggressive interpretations, religion is likely to remain a source of tension and
conflict that will threaten the stability of the state or at least compli-
cate the formation of state policy. When Sadat talked of establishing
the "state of institutions," he was talking in a language his audience,
Egyptian and Western, could understand: self-sustaining institutions in a democratic state would supplant the whim of the ruler.
But if the institutions are not specifically religious in nature, they
will never acquire legitimacy in the eyes of a certain number of
Egypt's citizens. This is the nature of Islam, which holds itself out
as applicable to all fields of endeavor and all institutions of human
society.

As a result, Egypt is destined always to grapple with a built-in
conflict, which exists in two forms: a sputtering, controllable rivalry
between Muslims and the Christian minority, and the struggle between secular and religious control over government policy. The
latter is more complex; it crosses a line between religion and government that the country's leaders have been unable to define as
clearly in practice as in theory—the very line of which the religious
activists deny the existence.

On the crucial issues of foreign policy there is virtually no
religious input. The Muslim Brotherhood and the clandestine
groups vigorously opposed the peace agreement with Israel, but it
remains in place. (One of Sadat's inner circle of friends and advisers,
Hassan Touhaimi, was known as "Sadat's Rasputin" because of his
deep religious convictions and his association with Islamic causes.
But it was Touhaimi who met secretly with Moshe Dayan of Israel
to seek a basis for negotiations before Sadat's Jerusalem breakthrough.)

On domestic matters, however, such as coeducation, state
support for family planning programs, divorce law, curriculum
development and employment of women, it is impossible to sepa-

rate public policy from religious input, and here the state is obliged to give some weight to the sensitivities of the Christians as well as those of the Muslims.

Islam supplanted Christianity as Egypt's dominant religion after the Arab conquest in the seventh century, but the Christian community was not eradicated. The census of 1976 reported that there were 2,315,560 Christians in Egypt, or 6.32 percent of the population. Officials of the Coptic Orthodox Church, the church of most of the Christians, claimed much higher figures—up to six million.

The source of the church numbers was the office of Bishop Samweel, a senior member of the Coptic hierarchy who was, in effect, the church's minister of foreign affairs until he was killed with Sadat in the 1981 uprising by *al-Jihad*. I went to see him when I was looking into the question of whether the armed conflict between Muslim and Christian that was then destroying Lebanon might be repeated in Egypt. The answer Bishop Samweel gave me was the same as that of every Egyptian, Christian or Muslim, to whom I put the question: There was no such possibility.

That is because Egypt's Copts, unlike Lebanon's Maronites, have no political power and do not expect to have any. They are linguistically and ethnically indistinguishable from the Muslims and they have a long record of patriotism, nationalism and honorable military service. It is inconceivable that the Copts today could play the role ascribed to some of them by Lawrence Durrell in the *Alexandria Quartet*—that of a fifth column secretly supporting Israel because they saw security for themselves in the establishment of sectarian enclaves in the Middle East. The Christians of Lebanon have played that part, flagrantly, but they also have territorial and political interests separate from those of their fellow Lebanese. Egypt's Copts have no territory and no armed militia defending it.

Nevertheless, the very existence of a large non-Muslim minority in a Muslim state is bound to be a cause of tension. Islam has for centuries had rules about the treatment of Jews and Christians in Islamic communities: they are protected peoples, subject to a special tax and excluded from military service. But Egypt has not applied these rules to its own subjects. The Christians have been more than second-class citizens. Their levels of income and education are among the country's highest, and Christians were prominent among the *haute bourgeoisie* most affected by sequestration

under Nasser. They naturally oppose attempts to bring Egyptian
law into conformity with *shari'a,* or Muslim religious law. The zeal
of the Muslims and the pride of the Christians almost inevitably
result in violence from time to time, usually over such issues as the
location of a church, or university politics, or differences in courting practices that offend Muslim conservatives.

Sadat preached harmony. He appointed Copts to prominent
positions in the government. Authorized by the constitution to
appoint 10 members of the People's Assembly, he gave many of
those seats to Christians. He installed Fikry Makram Ebeid, a well-
known Christian lawyer, as deputy prime minister and head of his
National Democratic Party. After Camp David, he named Boutros
Boutros-Ghali, a prominent international lawyer who is a Copt
married to a Jew, as minister of state for foreign affairs. Boutros-
Ghali has retained that position under Mubarak, representing
Egypt in international conferences at the highest level. I have had a
dozen or more conversations with Boutros-Ghali over a 10-year
period, about topics ranging from Cuban influence in Africa to
Palestinian autonomy, and I have heard him address audiences in
Egypt and the United States. No one could have guessed from
anything he said that he was a Christian—he spoke as a representative of Egypt. Similarly, Sadat appointed Moussa Sabry chairman
and chief editor of the newspaper *al-Akhbar.* Sabry was the most
sycophantic and extreme of the leading editors in his enthusiasm for
everything Sadat did, but like other Copts who are prominent in
public life he approached the issues as an Egyptian first.

Questions about the patriotism of the Copts can be countered
by examples, going back to Coptic involvement in the nationalist
struggle after World War I. Leading figures in the Wafd were
Christians. As Heikal puts it, "politically, economically and socially
the Copts were becoming integrated in the mainstream of Egyptian
life."

After yet another round of religious disturbance at Asyut in
1980, Interior Minister Nabawy Ismail reported on the incident to
the People's Assembly and urged religious tolerance. "In our battles
and wars the enemy never differentiated between Muslim and
Christian, who both fell and whose blood mixed in the liberation
battles. . . . These few incidents [at Asyut] cannot possibly affect
our course together as Muslims and Christians." The Assembly
responded with a resolution affirming that "national unity among

all Egyptians—Muslims and Christians—is a firm fact. Its roots extend deep in history and it is the secret of Egypt's strength and grandeur."

This is the official line, always reiterated in periods of tension. It is unacceptable to the Muslim extremists, who simply cannot find any support for it in the Koran or in the sayings of the prophet, the only true sources of doctrine in Islam. Michael Youssef quotes one of the members of *al-Jihad* whom he interviewed after Sadat's assassination: "It makes us sick every time we see Boutros-Ghali's picture in the paper. Can't they find a Muslim to be in this important position? How can Egypt be represented in the foreign arena by a Copt? Egypt is an Islamic nation and must at least give this impression to the world."

Emphasizing domestic stability as essential for progress, Sadat and Mubarak have tried to head off the occasional outbreak of sectarian strife. After the 1973 war, when a rumor circulated that the Israeli breakthrough to the west bank of the Suez Canal had been made possible by a Coptic traitor among the Egyptian troops, Sadat responded by appointing Fuad Aziz Ghali, a Coptic general, as commander of the Second Field Army, a critical post. A ceremony was held to honor the soldier said to have been the first to cross the canal, who received a free house as a reward. That soldier was a Copt. At times of national tension, such as when he embarked for Jerusalem, or celebration, such as at the return of el-Arish in the Sinai to Egyptian rule, Sadat had leaders of the Coptic hierarchy as well as leading Muslims at his side. That is how Bishop Samweel came to be gunned down with him at the fateful military parade.

But Sadat could not tolerate the independent-minded and colorful prelate who in 1971 became the leader of the Coptic Church, Pope Shenouda III. Shenouda challenged restrictions on the construction of new churches and he went to the United States to promote the Coptic cause, meeting with President Carter and appearing on television with inflated claims of church membership. He infuriated Sadat by threatening to excommunicate Copts who went as pilgrims to Jerusalem after the peace treaty. Sadat's response was to order Shenouda stripped of his temporal powers and exiled to a monastery in the western desert, where he remained for 40 months until Mubarak cancelled the decree and restored him to his post in 1985.

The Coptic Church became independent of Roman Catholicism after the Council of Chalcedon in 451, refusing to accept the Council's edict in a dispute over the nature of Christ's divinity. (The Copts believe that Christ on Earth had but one nature, the divine, instead of a dual nature, divine and human.) The word Copt is the European form of the Arabic *kibt,* itself derived from the Greek word *Aiguptioi,* meaning Egyptian. Coptic Christianity was the dominant creed in Egypt until the Muslim conquest. Even the few Christians who resisted conversion to Islam yielded to the conquerors' language: Coptic, a relic of the ancient Egyptian language written in Greek script, survives only in religious texts that can be read by few scholars.

The very antiquity of Coptic tradition provokes resentment among some Muslims, because Copts occasionally behave as if they are alone are true Egyptians, rightful heirs of the Pharaohs. Bishop Samweel's office, for example, handed out copies of a tract entitled "Who Are the Copts?" It says that "the genuine Egyptians of today are the Christian Copts who alone trace direct descent from the ancient Egyptian races to whom the civilization and culture of the world are so largely due."

Copts have been unpopular because they developed a prosperous and Western-oriented bourgeoisie and controlled a disproportionate share of the administrative and clerical positions and of land. They also traditionally served the government as tax collectors. In 1975, only a year after the U.S. embassy reopened, the foreign ministry requested that the embassy hire more Muslims and fewer Copts because the percentage of Christians in those desirable jobs was too high; similar restrictions have been enforced on other employers. But the power and wealth of the old bourgeoisie were effectively broken by Nasser, and Muslims now cannot legitimately complain that Coptic citizens have any unfair advantages. On the contrary, the Copts increasingly complain of discrimination against them and harassment by Muslims, especially in Asyut, a city that is home to both the most extreme Muslim activists and a large Christian community.

After a new round of Muslim-Christian violence early in 1987—a mosque burned down, and Muslims accused Christians of torching it—Mubarak called on Egyptians to "stand firm in the face of any attempt aimed at inciting religious sects against each other." He warned that no one should "foment sectarian conflicts and sow the seeds of hatred and hostility between Muslims and Christians."

Sadat said exactly the same things about religious conflict when he was president.

Sometimes the religious antagonism takes harmless forms, as in the "bumper sticker war" of 1985, in which Muslim and Christian activists took to displaying their affiliation on their automobiles. But every so often, despite admonitions from the leadership, Muslim-Christian tension erupts into violence. Rumors touch off neighborhood brawls; insults provoke fights among students. The government always moves swiftly to contain these episodes, but there does not seem to be any way to prevent them.

However much an Egyptian president wishes to live in harmony with the Christian minority, he is a Muslim in a Muslim state and must satisfy his larger constituency. The relationship between Muslim and Muslim is more subtle, complex and explosive than that between Muslim and Christian. There is a perpetual struggle, now almost two centuries old, between those who look to Islam— and, by extension, to the Arab and Muslim world—for their political and cultural guidance and wish to see the principles of Islam dominate public policy, and those who want Egypt to be a secular country, with governmental systems and institutions modeled on those of the West. In a secular community, Islam would be an honored religion but not a rigid doctrine controlling law and society.

There are extremists on both sides, and the country's pattern of response has been cyclical. The so-called secular modernists prevail for a decade or so, then there is a reaction in favor of the traditionalists. The later cycle began in the latter years of Sadat's presidency and has continued through the 1980s, creating one of the most troublesome sources of political discomfort for Mubarak. A balanced policy that would satisfy both tendencies and keep the Copts happy is extremely difficult to achieve.

The Muslims actively involved in religious matters fall generally into three groups. The first and most visible is the established religious hierarchy, the *ulama* or learned elders, which consists of senior officials, such as the minister of religious affairs, the grand sheikh of al-Azhar and the senior scholars from whom the vast network of neighborhood imams and religious societies takes guidance. These men are employees of the state, which means that any of them who becomes a nuisance can be dismissed. The second group consists of the pacified remnants of the Muslim Brotherhood, no longer clandestine, and charismatic individual preachers who develop personal followings, often through the spread of tape-recorded sermons. The third is the violence-prone, extremist clandestine fringe, consisting of groups such as *al-Jihad*.

The Arabic word *jihad* means religious struggle. It is a basic theme of Islam, but Muslims have disagreed for 13 centuries about the nature of this struggle. Does *jihad* mean violence, or does it mean any kind of struggle or effort on behalf of the faith? If it means violence, does it mean violence against unbelievers only, or violence even against Muslims if their commitment to the religion is less than sufficient? According to the manifesto left by members of the group that slew Sadat, *jihad* required the shedding of blood, if necessary the blood of Muslims, to purge the society of infidels, apostates and hypocrites and to achieve the pure Islamic community that they believed God demanded.

All three groupings of religious activists have some objectives in common. They want Islam to shape the political and cultural life of the state and they want the state to enforce Islam's basic precepts, such as the collection of the *zakat,* or religious tax. They want, in differing degrees, to purge the society of the Western influence that in their eyes brings not progress but moral corruption. They do not want Egypt to yield to what the Arab-American scholar Fouad Ajami, who was born in Lebanon, calls "the Mediterranean temptation" or "the dream of turning Cairo into Paris."

The hostility to the West is not based on material and social considerations alone. It has to do with the entire definition of knowledge, with the essence of existence. It is as Michael Youssef described the Egyptian response to the invasion of occupiers from Europe: "The confrontation was one between Europe, which believed in the power of man's will to change the present and determine his future, and Islam, which conceded all knowledge as given and the process of learning as accumulation of the known rather than a process of discovery."

For the first few years of his tenure, Sadat and the groups commonly referred to as fundamentalists were on good terms, especially because he looked so benign by comparison with Nasser, a relentless secularizer. Sadat, personally pious, released Muslim Brothers from prison and allowed them to publish a magazine. His leadership in the 1973 war polished his credentials as a Muslim and Arab leader in the struggle against the infidel. He encouraged

Muslim activism in the universities as a counterweight to leftism, and by the middle of the 1970s religious conservatives dominated student governments.

But the romance faded as it became clear that Sadat was going to make peace with Israel and open the nation to Western economic, and inevitably cultural, influences. There were early signs of trouble: the attack on the Military Technical College, the torching of nightclubs and clip joints on the Pyramids road during the 1977 bread riots, the murder of Dhahabi, the immense popularity of anti-establishment preachers whose tape-recorded messages swept the country.

By the end of the decade, the prevailing atmosphere was one of enthusiastic welcome for the Americans who were flooding into Egypt and of admiration for the United States, tied to the hope that the American-engineered peace treaty would lead to a better standard of living. But there were more and more dissenting voices too, putting out the message that the values of Islam were incompatible with those of the West, that *infitah* would not bring social justice and that the peace treaty was a deal with Jews that served only American and Israeli interests. These dissenters were encouraged by the Iranian revolution, which seemed to represent a triumph of Islam over alien influences.

In his long colloquy with professors at Asyut University in April 1979, Sadat denounced two of the religious dissenters by name: Sheikh Abdel Hamid Kishk and Omar Tilmassani.

Kishk is a blind scholar whose weekly sermons at a Cairo mosque, peppered with criticisms of the government, denunciations of corruption in high places and anti-American broadsides, were drawing enthusiastic crowds from the working classes. Everyone knew who Kishk was; he had first been arrested by Nasser, and tapes of his sermons were distributed all over Egypt. But he was hardly ever mentioned in the official press. Intellectuals tended to dismiss him as a rabble-rouser with a limited audience. But Kishk has the rhetorical flair of the demagogue and a sense of which issues appeal to the underprivileged. He was railing at the "Zionist gangsters" with whom Sadat had made peace, at the government's failure to deal with the housing shortage, at public officials enriching themselves while the masses were suffering.

Kishk's writings generally emphasized personal piety more than public activism, but his sermons certainly had political overtones. His assertion that 60,000 foreigners were living in apartments that might otherwise be available to Egyptians was nonsense, but it had a certain demagogic appeal. Kishk was among the irritating individuals picked up in the mass-arrest dragnet shortly before Sadat's assassination. Mubarak released him the following January, and he resumed his criticisms of anything he deemed un-Islamic.

The other target of Sadat's criticism, Omar Tilmassani, was then editor of al-Dawa, or The Call, the magazine of the Muslim Brotherhood. Tilmassani, who has since died, was then a lawyer in his late seventies. He had been active in the Brotherhood for decades and, like other religious activists, had spent years in prison. He was understood to have a larger role in the Brotherhood than that of editor of its magazine; but when I asked him who was the current leader of the organization he said, "Sheikh el-Banna." Hassan el-Banna, the founder of the Muslim Brotherhood, was murdered in 1949.

Nasser crushed the Brotherhood and drove its adherents underground because it had a long record of terrorism and assassination, including an attempt to kill Nasser in 1954, and represented a rival for power. Nasser said that the Brotherhood

seeks rule by assassination in an era that has outlived such practices . . . reactionary religious groups such as the Muslim Brotherhood are neither genuinely political nor genuinely religious. Their ultimate aim is power and to realize it they adopt methods contrary to the spirit of Islam and the spirit of the age. Islam derives from a comprehensive philosophy which never fails to accommodate various human feelings and aspirations. In this sense it is not only humanitarian but elastic and tolerant. It has ubiquitous principles applicable to time and place and mindful of the rights of men. It condemns intolerance, terrorism, prejudice and organized hatred.

Perhaps Nasser's Islam was not intolerant, but that of Egypt's religious dissenters certainly is—intolerant and xenophobic. Tilmassani, for example, insisted in our conversation that the "Muslim Brothers were never terrorists or fanatics" and that "foreign hands, aimed at destroying the Islamic nation," were behind such accusations. He said that "East and West, the U.S. and the Russians, are alike in that they don't want Egypt to flourish and rise to prosperity," because "for both of them the Middle East is a favorite market. This has been true ever since the Crusades, which were not religious wars but an imperialist search for trade . . . the Brotherhood wants Islam to be powerful so that nobody from either side can control us." Similarly, in the sermons of Sheikh Kishk, we hear that Western ideas are responsible for slavery, two world wars, apartheid in South Africa, the existence of Israel and the corrupt thinking of Freud and Sartre. This is a view of the world essentially incompatible with the outward-looking, progressive policies espoused by Egypt's leadership and, inevitably, a constant source of political tension.

Tilmassani was one of hundreds of Muslim Brothers released from prison in the early 1970s when Sadat freed those jailed by Nasser for crimes that were political rather than violent. The Brotherhood quickly became a visible force in the country, organizing prayer rallies, sponsoring candidates in parliamentary elections (though prohibited from organizing a religious party), and putting out its magazine. The magazine opposed the peace treaty with Israel, attacked the government of the Philippines—a country Mrs. Sadat had recently visited—for its alleged repression of Muslims, and promoted the adoption of an Islamic legal system.

One article reported on a conference of Arab justice ministers at which statistics were distributed showing that for every million residents, 32,000 commit crimes yearly in France, 63,000 in Finland and 75,000 in Canada but only 22 in Saudi Arabia, where thieves still have their hands cut off and rapists are stoned, as prescribed in the Koran. (Saudi Arabia is indeed virtually crime free by comparison with Western countries.)

Another article said that the Grand Sheikh of al-Azhar should be elected by all the imams, not appointed by the president. The power to make that appointment is, of course, one of the Egyptian president's most useful tools in ensuring the cooperation of the orthodox religious hierarchy.

After the 1979 outbreak of religious agitation at Asyut University, Sadat denounced an article in *al-Dawa* claiming that the government of the United States had approached former Prime Minister Mamdouh Salem to warn him that the Muslim organizations were dangerous and tell him they must be broken up.

That article had a threefold appeal: defense of Islam against infidels, discredit to the Sadat government and denunciation of the

Americans, who were becoming more and more influential. In his discussion with the Asyut faculty, Sadat said he was upset not only by what the articles said but by the fact that some students believed it.

"The newspaper *al-Dawa* is the organ of the Muslim Brotherhood," he said.

> I allowed this newspaper to be published although the Muslim Brotherhood was dissolved by order of the Revolutionary Command Council in 1954, a decision that has never been repealed. . . . You all know that I have released every Muslim Brother from the detention camps and prisons and reinstated them in their jobs. I let the newspaper continue publication. Today it came out to confuse our young people about the United States . . . In whose interests are our children being told these days that the United States had warned the Mamdouh Salem government against the religious movements and to eliminate the religious movements? Tilmassani and his deceived sons want to attribute something to the religious movements.

The appeal of the Brotherhood, however, was a symptom, not a cause. By the late 1970s, the Islamic movements were gaining strength, fed by deepening resentment against Sadat and his policies. The president's espousal of "science and faith" as a national motto was increasingly perceived as a sham. Evidence proliferated that Egypt had entered a cycle of religious activism, especially among the young, who embraced a conservative, ascetic Islam that was outside the controlled framework of al-Azhar and the ministry of religious affairs.

Students representing fundamentalist and conservative Islamic groups controlled student governments at the universities, especially in Alexandria and Asyut. Young women in increasing numbers took to wearing monochromatic, ankle-length, long-sleeved dresses with shawls that covered their hair. They spurned makeup, in a show of contrast to their contemporaries in tight jeans who were lining up in the cosmetic shops. A few even resorted to wearing the veil, which Egyptian women had happily cast off half a century before. (The medical faculty at al-Azhar drew the line at veils on female medical students, insisting that face coverings interfered with laboratory work and impeded contact with patients.)

By 1980 the Brotherhood was able to organize large rallies and meetings of young people by openly advertising on buses and in mosques and by working with the student groups. Their targets included jazz concerts on the campuses, Western dress for women, diplomatic relations with Israel, movie videos and "impure" elements in the press, a reference to the Coptic editor Moussa Sabry.

Sadat was losing touch with popular sentiment. Peace had brought materialism but not prosperity; the "Open Door" was an open door to corrupting Western influences but not to Western investment and defiance of the Arabs had brought a disconcerting isolation from Egypt's heritage. What Egyptians were seeing was what Hassan el-Banna had seen 30 years before:

> The social life of the beloved Egyptian nation was oscillating between her dear and precious Islamism, which she had inherited, defended, lived with and became accustomed to and made powerful during thirteen centuries, and this severe Western invasion which is armed and equipped with all the destructive and degenerative influences of money, wealth, prestige, ostentation, material enjoyment, power and means of propaganda.

Sadat's prescription for domestic stability and order was based on endorsement and reinforcement of Egypt's traditional social values, which are deeply conservative even without religious context. He emphasized discipline and tradition: Students should study, young people should defer to their parents, and the police should crack down on vice. But it was difficult to blend that approach with economic and foreign policies that gave the Egyptian more access to Western ideas, films and publications, more opportunity to travel to Europe, more contact with Americans and Europeans, more consumer goods and more money, without at the same time giving them much more opportunity to achieve political or corporate power to satisfy their new ambitions. To many Egyptians, Western influence is by nature corrupting. They want money and cars and television and refrigerators but they do not want extramarital sex or drugs for their children or free choice in vocation or marriage, or pornography on the newsstands. Islam was, and remains, their most natural weapon of defense.

In the absense of a great unifying national cause, Egyptians were unsettled and confused by what semed to be an erosion of their culture. The sentiments that inspired Hassan el-Banna were stirred again by the encroachment of materialism and morally neutral ideas. The smashing of the nightclubs in the 1977 riots was an early manifestation of the potential for reaction. The reaction appeared in a more subtle form when Ismail Hakim died.

The story of Ismail Hakim's short life and unhappy death read like the plot of a Hollywood potboiler. But to Egyptians who knew what killed him, it was more like a morality play that raised disturbing questions about the impact of wealth and Westernization on Egypt and its youth.

Hakim died at the age of 30 in 1978. The newspapers said he died of liver disease, which is common in Egypt, mostly because of bilharzia. The popular singer Abdel Halim Hafez had succumbed to it the year before. But whereas Hafez had died the death of a true son of Egypt, his liver destroyed by a parasite he had picked up in his village as a boy, Hakim apparently died of cirrhosis caused by alcoholism. As one of his relatives told me at the time, "He drank himself to death."

Ismail Hakim's death made the newspapers because he was the only son of a rich and famous father, one of the most revered figures in Egypt, Tawfik el-Hakim, whose sharp features under his ever-present beret had been known to Egyptians long before Nasser was ever heard of. The elder Hakim, who died in 1987, was probably Egypt's most influential writer and playwright of this century. He was a literary pioneer whose works celebrated patriotism, national reawakening and the common man. He is said to have been the first Egyptian author to use colloquial Arabic in his dialogues.

Ismail was born when his father was 50 years old, and he took advantage of his aging, doting father's indulgence to grow up in a most unconventional way. He spurned the traditional careers of the upper classes to throw himself into rock music. He took on the coloration of a hard-rock performer of the 1970s, and in the newspaper photograph that accompanied the story of his death he looked a little like Jimi Hendrix.

He was a cultural aberration, but by all accounts he was an aberration whom growing numbers of young Egyptians admired—not because he drank or was a social renegade but because he had access to, and mastered, the music, dress and style of life that represented the affluence, spontaneity and opportunity of life in Europe and the United States. His widow, Hedy, a singer who helped make his "Black Coats" band the most popular in Egypt, said that "the musical map of Egypt has changed enormously since Ismail first started strumming his electric guitar in 1963," and it was obvious.

A blue-jean and discotheque society was mushrooming in Cairo and Alexandria; pirated rock tapes were advertised for sale on campus bulletin boards. Cairo radio appealed to young listeners with a dedication show in English ("for Sami from Hoda, for Mustafa from Magda"). Tape recordings of American rock music broadcasts, made by Egyptian students in the United States, were played on the state-owned radio, sometimes complete with commercials and station breaks. The gap between university students who wear traditional Islamic dress and go to religious meetings and those who wear jeans and spend their time at expensive watering holes was visible and volatile. Egyptians of every shade of political opinion were at least uncomfortable with the sudden emergence of Cairo as an international playground where gambling was legal, rich Arabs came to buy Egyptian girls, young people asserted their independence and young women of good family danced at discotheques with young men whom their parents had not met. The story of Ismail Hakim was upsetting even to the Westernized bourgeoisie; to the religious activists, it was just more evidence of what they already knew.

When Sadat went to Asyut to talk to the professors, a pharmacy teacher named Nabil Hakim rose to complain about the religious reaction. "The power of the communists" among the students had been overtaken, he said, by "religious bigotry" and "religious fanaticism" that had interrupted study and research and led students to challenge the morality of their fathers' occupations and styles of life.

"Mr. President," he said,

> the students are in revolution. There is no dialogue, contact or channels to the children. How long will we continue like that? If we wait until the start of the next academic year, it will be too late, for catastrophe will have taken place. I beg you and I insist that you guide us, Mr. President. You have emphasized freedom and more freedom, but what I can see is that we are losing our way and that freedom will one day lead us to anarchy.

Sadat responded by denouncing the strongarm tactics of the extremist Muslim groups as "unacceptable in form or substance." He said he would not permit them to take on the role of "caretakers of God's religion on earth" or to form "a state within a state." And he issued a warning: "Whoever wishes to learn, the state is prepared to accommodate him. We will give our children a chance. But whoever clings to and continues to take this path, he should leave. . . . We and all the people are amicably giving a warning, but afterward whoever persists will be dealt with differently."

It was too late for such admonitions. To the religious activists, Sadat had squandered the moral capital that would have lent weight to his warnings. The storm that would blow him away was already rising, not on the campuses or in the Brotherhood but in the clandestine organization known as *al-Jihad*.

The extremists could not accept Sadat's professions of piety because to them his actions were not those of a true Muslim. The bill of particulars was extensive, and included matters both great and trivial. He made peace with the Zionist occupiers of Jerusalem, and prayed at al-Aqsa mosque while it was under the control of infidels. He riased a glass of wine in a toast at a dinner with President Carter and permitted state-owned distilleries to continue producing alcoholic beverages. He allowed his wife to go around Egypt and around the world preaching the doctrine of family planning and population control. He supported the Shah of Iran against that country's religious revolution and gave the Shah refuge in Egypt after he had been deposed. He kissed Rosalynn Carter in public. He insisted on separating affairs of state from affairs of the pulpit: "No religion in politics, no politics in religion," Sadat often said, a formula that is the antithesis of Muslim teaching. He lived in luxury while his people lived in poverty. He supported moderniza-tion of the status of women: Divorce was restricted and the role of women in public life was expanded. He tolerated the production and sale of pork. He allowed Egypt to be drummed out of the worldwide fraternity of Muslim nations. He encouraged the spread of Western economic and cultural influence, which meant sexually alluring advertisements on television.

Nasser had engaged in frontal assaults on religious tradition and the religious establishment in ways that Sadat never did. It was Nasser who forced al-Azhar, the religious university, to establish nonreligious departments with secular curricula. It was Nasser who nationalized the religious endowments, including their vast land-holdings, and who abolished the religious courts. Nasser sup-pressed the Muslim Brotherhood, while Sadat permitted its re-suscitation. But Nasser was not guilty of peace with Israel, friendship with the Shah, personal ostentation or the embrace of Western lifestyles. The high-priced Frank Sinatra concerts and celebrity parties that seemed more and more to be Sadat's natural milieu were not for Nasser.

Nor for Mubarak, who is much more circumspect in personal style than was Sadat. Mubarak began almost immediately to pull back from some of the extreme positions that provoked Sadat's opponents. But Mubarak will never be at peace with the religious absolutists and cultural isolationists. He preaches that technology is the key to progress, that knowledge remains to be developed, that enlightenment comes from many sources. "Our education policy," he said near the end of his first six-year term,

> must be directed toward building an Egyptian character capable of facing the future while stressing our Arab and Islamic cultural identity without fanatacism, which would isolate us from the world. Fanaticism would blind us to the progress made in the way of thinking in the world. Thinking is the highest form of man's activities and must therefore become part of the heritage of all peoples.

These ideas are incompatible with the view of those who believe that all knowledge derives from the Koran.

So the agitation continues. Mubarak has been unable to escape questions about the stability of his regime and the threat from the religious right. Hermann F. Eilts, who was the U.S. ambassador to Egypt during most of the Sadat years, found during his 1986 visit that "not all Egyptians share the official view that the Islamic fundamentalists are under control. The gnawing fear exists that sooner or later one or another such group may spawn new violence. The belief exists, too, that covert Islamic fundamentalist groups receive Iranian, Libyan and even Saudi Arabian financial aid."

Sure enough, within weeks after Eilts's report was published in the *Washington Quarterly,* there was a new round of shootings and assassination attempts that the authorities attributed to clandestine Muslim extremists who were branches of the same ideological tree as *Takfeer w'a-Hijra* and *al-Jihad.* The suspects were said to be associated with yet another previously unknown group called "Those Spared From Hell" or "Those Saved From the Flames," and to have been influenced by the same manifesto of absolutism and violence that guided *al-Jihad.*

I happened to be in Cairo when one of the assassination attempts occurred. As usual, the incident had no effect whatsoever

on the daily routine of the country. The police rounded up the
usual suspects, as they say, and everyone went about his business.
But the political effect was also predictable: a new round of doubt,
questions and fear. Could Egypt go the way of Iran? What would
become of Egypt if the agitation were to evolve into a successful
movement to impose rigid Muslim doctrine on the country?

Uncertainty about the strength of the militant movement con-
tributes to the anxiety. Estimates of the numerical strength of the
activist groups are almost meaningless, partly because their clandestine nature makes it difficult to count the membership, and
partly because their pattern of organization is designed to foil
penetration and betrayal. The groups are said to be organized as an
anqud, or bunch of grapes, in which each cell is independent of the
others.

Eilts, who would have access to the best available intelligence
information, said that "no one seems sure how many Islamic fundamentalists there are. Estimates vary between 3,000 and 12,000
activists. There are, of course, hundreds of thousands of passive
supporters, either out of conviction or fear, who would lend aid
and comfort" to the extremists if called upon. Hinnebusch notes
that circulation of *al-Dawa,* the Brotherhood's magazine, peaked at
150,000, and that the campus groups such as the Youth of Muhammad had about 100,000 members.

In a population of more than 50 million, these seem like small
numbers, but the impact of the whole movement has been greater
than the sum of its parts. It is hard to argue with Hinnebusch's
conclusion that

> the emergence of an Islamic movement in Egypt increasingly at
> odds with the regime was perhaps the most important ingre-
> dient in the pluralization of the political arena: it added a depth
> to the opposition of which neither the left nor the liberal right
> was capable. . . . The mobilizational capacity of the Islamic
> movement, while perhaps still falling short of its peak in the
> thirties, had, by the late seventies, produced one of the most
> formidable political forces in Egypt.

Even members of the educated elite who are not sympathetic
to the religious movement understand its appeal. European-style
liberal politics, as practiced between the world wars, failed to bring
prosperity and failed to get rid of the British. State socialism, as

practiced under Nasser, failed to bring prosperity and failed to defend the country. Sadat's internationalism failed to bring prosperity and severed Egypt from its spiritual roots. Pan-Arabism was a chimera. What then remains but Islam, an indigenous and independent ideology from which the masses are not excluded?

Morroe Berger, in his landmark study *Islam in Egypt Today,* found Egypt dotted with charitable and educational foundations known collectively as Associations for the Preservation of the Koran. At the time of Berger's research, in the last years of Nasser, there were 291 of them, more than half in the villages, and they did much more than propagate study of the Koran. Berger found that most of their outlay went for "general education, cash assistance, vocational training, recreation, and medical and health care." These are not malevolent activities. But today there are more than 2,000 such associations, by government figures, and religious activists find these organizations useful because they provide legal coloration for the inculcation of an activist doctrine that might be suppressed if presented in an overtly political form. Supplemented by private schools, they make up a network through which the message of the religious absolutists is spread to Egyptians from an early age. That message is not one of tolerance or polyculturalism.

From the point of view of the United States, which has such a big political and economic investment in Egypt, the most troubling question is whether Egypt could become another Iran. Eilts, in a farewell interview with me before his retirement as ambassador in 1979, was one of the first high-ranking American officials to articulate this fear publicly. "We all remember Iran," he said, expressing his discomfort over the fast-growing American mission in Egypt, its increasing visibility and its potential as a target for agitation. Sadat too was aware of the potential parallels. He made sure that television cameras were present when he pressed his forehead to the dirt floor of a village mosque, the message being that he, unlike the Shah whom he befriended, was a pious man of the people.

But Egypt and Iran are more different than alike. The conditions that led to the triumph of the mullahs in Iran do not exist in Egypt.

Iran is home to the Shiite form of Islam, which emphasizes the role of the imam, or heir to the prophet, in leading the community. No living person is recognized as the imam, but the ayatollahs at the top of the hierarchy fill that role. In Sunni Islam as practiced in

Egypt, no religious authority commands the allegiance of the
faithful as the ayatollahs do. In Egypt, the orthodox religious
leaders are employees of the state. They do not have the political or
financial independence of the Shiite ayatollahs. The corollary of this
is that the grass-roots groups in Egypt, while sincere and dedicated,
are also fragmented. They do not agree among themselves on such
essential questions as the nature of an Islamic state, the definition of
jihad, the place in society of religious minorities or the com-
patibility of Islam and technological innovation. Supporters of the
Muslim Brotherhood, for example, were active participants in the
1987 parliamentary elections and won 37 seats; but groups such as
Takfeer reject the entire existing governmental structure as un-
Islamic and refuse to participate in it. In the nearly 40 years since
the death of Hassan el-Banna, no one individual has surfaced as a
consensus leader of Egypt's Islamic movement.

Egypt also came into the 1980s with a modern political and
economic experience vastly different from that of Iran. Egypt has a
long tradition of secular liberal politics and of nonreligious nationalism. Its leadership, which arose from the ranks of the armed
forces and rid the country of foreign domination, was not installed
by the "Great Satan" against the wishes of the people. Its diverse
economy was not disrupted by overnight wealth conspicuously
diverted to the enrichment of a few well-connected families.

Some Westernized intellectuals, perhaps whistling through the
graveyard, minimize the clout of the religious movement. The
Mubarak government, though, is hardly complacent and has en-
deavored to confront it, not just through police vigilance but
directly. It sponsors televised debates between establishment religious figures and the militants, publishes detailed scholarly re-
sponses to the fundamentalists' doctrinal pronouncements, and
sends conventional religious teachers into the prisons to "correct"
the thinking of jailed extremists.

Egypt is unlikely to be swept by a united mass movement that
would propel a fundamentalist regime to power, as happened in
Iran. More likely than a mass rising, and harder to defend against,
would be a coup d'etat, probably from within the armed forces. But
the events that followed Sadat's assassination were instructive on
this point. The assassins of *al-Jihad* penetrated the armed forces,
infiltrated a ceremonial parade, killed the president and other high
officials, and prepared themselves to take over the country—but

nothing happened except their arrest. No one followed them. In the words of Fahmy Howaidi, religious affairs writer for *al-Ahram,* "The silent majority is ready to vote for the Islamicists but not to fight their fight."

And the army has held: Twice in a decade, during the food riots of 1977 and the police revolt of 1986, the army was called into the streets to restore order and defend the civilian leadership, and twice the troops did their duty. Opponents of the regime, who asserted with confidence that Egypt's Muslim soliders would not take up arms against their coreligionists, were shown not to know what they were talking about. A military seizure of power is always possible in a country where the armed forces are the ultimate repository of power, but a military coup based on religious motivation could succeed only if the military as a group supported the conspirators, which did not happen when Sadat was killed. As P. J. Vatikiotis put it, "The growth of the armed forces into a vast military institution (c. 500,000 men) may have minimized the chances of conspiracies similar to the one in 1952. On the other hand, the growth of a large conscript army facilitated such infiltration by militant Islamic groups."

Eilts, in his report, said that "Egyptian authorities at the highest level are aware of the Islamic fundamentalist threat." But whom does it threaten? Assuming that some unlikely convergence of events would bring to power in Cairo a regime dedicated to religious activism and the establishment of an Islamic state, what would that state be like?

It is often said that the religious opposition has no program, no platform. It is true that there is no single document, not even "The Neglected Duty," the manifesto of *al-Jihad,* in which all the religious groups have laid down a unified program of action. There is no known document approved by all the groups, the overt and the clandestine, the violent and the nonviolent, that says, If we come to power, we will do the following. The Muslim Brotherhood itself, for example, moved over the course of a generation from an emphasis on state involvement in the economy and nationalization of certain industries to an insistence on private enterprise, free from government interference. Leaders of the Brotherhood have said they favor a multiparty system, in which they would be one of the parties, but *al-Jihad* rejected the formation of a party because its members believed the entire structure of the state to be corrupt and non-Islamic. Still, from the writings of Hassan al-Banna, from "The Neglected Duty," from public statements and sermons of religious activists and from legislation proposed by Muslim Brothers in the People's Assembly, it is possible to envision the political, social and economic structure of an Egypt dominated by the religious activists.

The legal system embodied in the *shari'a* would apply to all functions of the state, economic, social, educational and political. This is a goal that Muslims have espoused since the foundation of the faith and have rarely if ever achieved. To accept *shari'a* requires agreement on its scope, on its applicability to modern life; where is it written that religious law requires the banning of Western classical music, as in Iran, or forbids women to drive, as in Saudi Arabia? Is the law immutable, or does it evolve? These are debatable matters; what is not debatable is that in the religious state, religion and only religion will provide the framework in which the debate will be conducted. Whereas under Nasser "all significant religious institutions were made subject to the control of the state," as Abdel Monem Said Aly and Manfred W. Wenner wrote in a study of the contemporary Muslim Brotherhood, under a religious regime it would be the other way around.

Religious considerations would be imposed on state functions: work schedules would be set to encourage participation in prayer. Religious officials would be stationed in the workplace.

Economic transactions would be conducted according to Koranic principles: the charging of interest, for example, would be restricted as a violation of Islam's prohibition of usury. (This is a good example of an issue on which Islamic law and the requirements of a twentieth-century nation cannot be reconciled.)

Questions of family law and personal status, such as inheritance and divorce, would be resolved according to religious law. In practice, this would mean the exclusion of women from active public life.

National policy would stress the solidarity of the worldwide Muslim community, the ummah. What this would mean for relations with Israel can be deduced from the comments of Hamid Abu al-Nasr, a leading official of the Brotherhood, in a 1987 interview with the magazine *October:*

> The Muslim Brotherhood believes that the only solution is through holy *jihad* for the sake of Palestine. As for treaties,

negotiations, and agreements, the Zionist entity will be the only beneficiary. The Zionist entity exploited the Camp David accords and continues its bullying after attacking the Iraqi nuclear reactor, dismembering Lebanon and dispersing the people of Palestine. This shows that *jihad* is the only way to confront it.

Of course, Muslims are deeply divided over the meaning of *jihad:* does it imply violence, as the group called *al-Jihad* insisted, or can it take the form of nonviolent confrontation and effort?

Education and mass media of communications, such as television, would stress religious precepts as applicable to all aspects of life. Egypt is a conservative society in any case; nudity in the movies and passionate kissing on television are already taboo. But the religious activists would go beyond prohibition into active promotion: using the state's channels of communication to emphasize religious precepts to the exclusion of others. Again, this would raise difficult questions. Islam teaches that souls and bodies will be reunited at the last judgment. Should medical students then be allowed to work on cadavers? Should autopsies be permitted? Whatever the answers, they would be couched in religious terms and handed down by religious authorities.

Alcohol and pork would be banned; men would be prohibited from working in hairdressing salons for women; Western-style bathing suits for women, and sexually integrated swimming, would be banned, regardless of the impact of such measures on the tourist industry. Basic requirements of the Muslim religion, such as the daylight fast in the month of Ramadan, would be enforced by the state.

Non-Muslim minorities, which in Egypt means the Copts, would be excluded from authority even more than they are now, and their role in all aspects of national life would be circumscribed. Muslim law would forbid outright persecution, but it is unlikely that Copts would be accepted as officers in the army or diplomats in the foreign service. The construction of churches would be further restricted. Apostasy from Islam would be a crime, probably punishable by death.

For most Egyptians, life in a country ruled by these precepts would not be greatly different. The *fellahin* and the urban factory hands don't drink alcohol; they have deeply conservative views on women and family life, observe the Ramadan fast, have no objection to religion in education and have little sympathy for Israel. But

the educated elite and the Westernized bourgeoisie would be quite
uncomfortable, just as they are in Iran, and Egypt's relations with
the rest of the world would be drastically different. What is unclear
is the extent to which such precepts would be translated into action,
and how quickly. The Islamic state has always defied definition; it is
still argued whether Muhammad intended to found a state at all or
merely a community of believers within a state. The violence-prone
absolutists personified by the *al-Jihad* group would insist on overnight transformation, according to religious interpretations handed
down by them. Such a course is unlikely, especially because the
Muslim Brothers, now ensconced within the existing system, would
not support it. Hamid Abu al-Nasr gave the Brotherhood's view in
his *October* magazine interview:

> I believe that Islamic law must be applied gradually. We must
> first put an Islamic stamp on the state. Initially, we must imple-
> ment what the people feel they need. We will wait for matters
> that need time before being carried out, as Islamic law was
> established in phases. Alcoholic drinks were banned in three
> stages. Slavery was also banned in stages. Gradual implementa-
> tion is one of the hallmarks of Islamic law.

An Egypt pursuing a gradual course toward an Islamic state
would not necessarily be at odds with the United States, except on
the question of Israel. If the United States can have a cooperative
relationship with the theocratic regime in Saudi Arabia, it can stay
on good terms with a religious regime in Egypt, unless Egypt were
to revert to active hostility against the Jewish state. A "cold peace"
between Egypt and Israel, such as existed after the 1982 Israeli
invasion of Lebanon, would not necessarily terminate American
relations with Egypt.

More troubling is the question of what life would become for
the urbane, sophisticated and cosmopolitan Egyptians who have
earned a place in the larger world through cultural adaptability.
They draw their guidance from Europe; their backs are turned
toward Mecca. As Fouad Ajami says of these Egyptians in his
analysis of the country's cultural dualism,

> The coveted membership in that glamorous world is partly real,
> for the bourgeois age did leave many things behind on Egyptian

soil, and partly an attempt to conceal and legitimate dependency. In that we see the fundamental dilemma of any liberalism removed from the core of the world system. Weak societies at the periphery of the world desperately flaunt the outward trappings of modernity, because the cosmopolitan layers intuitively feel their own isolation.

That this attitude prevailed among Egypt's "elite circles," in Hinnebusch's perceptive words,

> was apparent from Sadat's plea that Egypt be accepted in the West as a civilized outpost in the barbarous Middle East, from Tawfik al-Hakim's denigration of the Arabs and embracing of "civilized" Israel. There was an economic dimension to this, too. The view that everything Western was superior, everything *baladi* [was] inferior returned—an attitude captured by the cartoonist Salah Jaheen who depicts two Egyptians marveling over the Great Pyramid: "Fantastic, it must be imported."

If Egypt is a "weak society at the periphery of the world," that helps to explain the resiliency of the religious activists: to them, the path from weakness to strength lies across the familiar and indigenous terrain of Islam. And if, as seems certain, Egypt will be unable to bridge the gulf of wealth, opportunity and exposure to imported influences that divides its privileged classes from the masses, which group will prevail? This is Egypt's fundamental identity crisis, and it is not new; it has been going on for more than century, from the time when the Khedive Ismail, though bankrupt and at the mercy of the European powers, insisted on playing in their arena, on their terms.

The culture of the Arab village meant nothing to the Khedive Ismail, or to the liberal thinkers such as Taha Hussein who set the agenda of Egyptian intellectuals in this century. Contemporary Egyptians did not respond to Sadat's efforts to turn his native village into a cultural fountainhead. They knew what life in an Arab village was like and they wanted to put it behind them.

But Arabism also is ineradicable from Egyptian culture, inseparable from Islam yet not the same as Islam. It was often said of Sadat that in abandoning Egypt's role as leader of "the Arab nation" he was leading Egypt back into pharaonic self-consciousness, into a pre-Arab identity. He apparently miscalculated the extent to which

Egyptians, however envious and contemptuous of their Arab brethren, cherish their Arab heritage.

Arabism as a political doctrine, linking Egypt's fate to that of lesser states, did not arise naturally in Egypt. Only in the early years of this century was it grafted on by such events as the Balfour Declaration and revelation of the Sykes-Picot Agreement, and it was dominant only under Nasser. After the collapse of the union with Syria and the disastrous military intervention in Yemen, Arabism was widely understood to be only a slogan, not a serious policy.

Except for a few leftover Nasserites, Egyptians recognize that pan-Arabism was an ephemeral doctrine. The collective euphoria of the Arabs over their performance in the 1973 war and the subsequent oil embargo had dissolved in recrimination and suspicion long before Camp David. Egypt fought a brief border war with Libya in 1977 and broke relations with the so-called "steadfastness states" after Sadat went to Jerusalem. Resentment of the Palestinians, on whose behalf Egypt had fought and suffered, was expressed openly when the Palestine Liberation Organization adhered to the "Steadfastness Front" of Sadat's opponents, and it crystallized when a prominent Egyptian writer and editor, Yusef Sebai, was assassinated in Cyprus by Palestinian gunmen.

Thus when the Arabs gathered at Baghdad after the peace initiative and imposed political and economic sanctions on Egypt—and moved the headquarters of the Arab League from Cairo to Tunis—it was not as if the Egyptians had suddenly been thrown out of a happy family. Relations between Egypt and other Arab countries have been poisonous as often as they have been cordial, and in their enthusiasm for peace the Egyptians were willing to accept a divorce from the Iraqis and the Saudis and the Algerians. At that time, many Egyptians were angry at their fellow Arabs for other reasons.

Fouad Ajami had noted that there was "widespread discontent over the fact that Cairo had become the Bangkok of the Arab world, that outside Arab capital was violating Egypt's honor and integrity and its women. . . . Arab wealth challenged Egypt's sense of self; possessed by arriviste bedouins, it underlined the cruelty of a world that had gone awry."

Egyptians felt it unfair that the "shoeless goatherds" of the

Arabian peninsula and Libya should be so rich while they, historic defenders of Arab civilization, were so poor. They resented the parsimony of the Libyan and Kuwaiti governments toward Egypt, and they resented the showy vulgarity of the Saudis and Qataris who came to Egypt to flaunt their money, gamble and buy Egyptian women.

But political quarrels with particular Arab governments, and disgruntlement over the vulgarity of certain individuals, did not mean that the Egyptians were cut loose from their Arab consciousness. Despite what the Egyptians regard as the cultural shallowness and political immaturity of other Arabs, they share with them what Boutros Boutros-Ghali calls a "common market of the mind," a web of personal and cultural ties based on religion, language, the experience of war and centuries of migration and pilgrimage. They became increasingly uncomfortable and restive as Sadat engaged in a long-running rhetorical flogging of all Arabs who did not agree with him.

Sadat never let up. Much of what he said about the other Arabs was true, but the intemperance of his language began to cause deep pain among his people. Even the most Europeanized Egyptians were proud of Cairo's place at the historic center of Arab civilization and Muslim thought. Sadat's rhetoric played into the hands of the religious activists.

An excerpt from one of his speeches conveys the tone of his rhetoric. Referring to Arab complaints that Nasser had failed to consult them before nationalizing the Suez Canal in 1956, he said,

> They met in 1978 in Bagdhad, 22 years after 1956, with the same mentality, the same hatred and bitterness. Well, if Abdel Nasser had advised Nuri as-Said [of Iraq] and Camille Shamoun [of Lebanon] and Abdullah [of Jordan] that he intended to nationalize the canal—bearing in mind that they were stooges—would he have been able to carry the nationalization through? It is as if 22 years did not help those people transcend this rotten mentality, when they met in Beirut and then they met in Baghdad and poured out their curses. They came out with attacks and took decisions full of invective against Egypt, which represented a deviation from all true values. Their main decision was to starve the Egyptian people, those dwarfs who have been fed, protected and educated by Egypt and are still being educated by Egypt. You heard me say that Egypt was not only sending professors and teachers to one of these dwarfs'

emirates but also schoolbooks, pencils and chalk. The steadfastness of the new Baghdad pact, its plan to liberate Palestine
and solve the Arab issue, its struggle and all the slogans we have
heard, all of this manifests itself in attacks against Egypt and
attempts to starve the Egyptian people so as to keep them in the
same position as prior to the October war: a defeated and
wounded people, and this at a time when their own coffers are
bulging with gold and dinars amassed at the expense of our
people's sacrifices of blood and resources.

The reference to a "new Baghdad pact" was a nasty thrust. If
there is one thing on which all Arabs agree, it is that the original
Baghdad pact of 1955 was an imperialist plot to draw the Arabs
into the cold war and that the regime in Iraq, the only Arab state to
sign the pact, had to be overthrown for doing so.
"Without Egypt, the Arabs are zero," Sadat said.

Egypt is the heart and mind of the Arab world and for the next
generations to come they will never catch up with Egypt and it
is not oil that builds Egypt, no. The fortune of Egypt is not like
Saudi Arabia and the others, it is here a complete economy of
agriculture, industry, assets, all this. And the biggest asset in
Egypt is the human being, the Egyptian man, who is a doctor,
engineer, laborer, teacher, with 13 universities here and with
the pride and heritage of seven thousand years.

Sadat called Qaddafi a "lunatic" and a "mad boy." He called
Hafez al-Assad of Syria, his erstwhile ally, "the Alawite," a below-
the-belt slur on Assad's membership in the minority sect that dominates Syria. King Hussein of Jordan was, to Sadat, a descendant of
King Abdullah, "the number one traitor to the Arab cause," and
was himself responsible for the "Black September" massacre of the
Palestinians in whose name he was now denouncing Egypt. As for
the Saudis, Sadat smeared them by praising the strength and no-
bility of Faisal, the king who died in 1975. He scorned the princes
of the House of Saud as bunglers and poseurs, unreliable men who
backed out of their solemn commitments to finance Egypt's arms
purchases, who surrendered to pressure from other Arabs, who
were unable to protect the great mosque at Mecca from being
defiled by extremists who took it over in 1979. Collectively, he
scorned all his Arab critics as "the leaders of polytheism and
ignorance"—polytheism, of course, being the blackest libel on any
Muslim.

Mubarak held his peace during the years of these tirades, but he recognized their futility and he put a stop to them immediately upon taking office. One of his first acts was to order the state-owned press to call off the mudslinging, and he began a patient effort to restore Egypt's political ties to the Arabs, which finally paid off in 1987 with their decision to permit restoration of full diplomatic relations. But the achievement of a political truce is not the same as a resolution of Egypt's cultural ambivalence.

For nearly a century, the greatest symbol of that ambivalence, of the attempt to graft European culture onto Egypt, was the Cairo Opera House. It was built by the profligate Khedive Ismail, who commissioned Verdi to write "Aida" to mark the opening of the Suez Canal. The opera house burned down in 1971; but a replacement, a Lincoln Center of Cairo, is scheduled to open in 1988, thanks to $30 million in aid from the government of Japan. The spectacle of Japan helping Egypt construct a lavish center for an art form alien to both cultures is beyond irony.

When officials of Sadat's government began to talk seriously about building a new opera house, I went to talk to Louis Awad about the idea. Awad, one of the country's senior writers and cultural critics, is an unshaven, ramshackle man who looks like an unmade bed; but his knowledge of Egypt's cultural experience is vast, as is his willingness to share it.

I expected him to oppose reconstruction of the opera house as a frivolous use of scarce capital in a country where people are desperate for shelter and transportation, but he said he was strongly in favor of it. "Opera is a symbol to us," he said, "because it points to the direction in which we are going. Are we in Egypt going to be multicultural, to be part of the large body of humanity, or are we going to live in the isolated inferno called the East?"

That is the real challenge presented by the Islamic movement. Egypt is weaker than, and dependent on, the societies its political and educational leaders have tried to emulate. What then, Egyptians ask, is the merit of that emulation? Isolation, xenophobia and a retreat into the sheltering, indigenous surroundings of Islam and Arabism offer a natural defense against the assault of a culture most Egyptians can never master.

Nor is the isolationist impulse confined to the religious right. When Egypt established diplomatic relations with Israel, Khaled Mohieddin's leftist party warned of the cultural consequences:

The loss of the distinct identity of our national culture and consequently of our personality, which rests on nationalist, ideological, liberationist concepts hostile to foreign colonialism and economic subjugation; [and] the isolation of Egyptian culture from the broad Arab base in which the Egyptian intellectual finds inspiration for his thinking and to which he directs his technical experience and his literary, artistic and scientific creativity.

Sentiments such as these provide a natural line of defense for a proud people searching for excuses for their own backwardness. They cannot be eradicated. We ignore them at our peril. It cannot be assumed that Muslims, exposed to Western ideas and American influence, will respond favorably to them. In Egypt, prosperity may not be achievable; democracy may be a superficial concept of the political elite. The one force that is universal and eternal, the one to which rich and poor have equal access, the one untainted by cultural self-doubt, is Islam.

FURTHER READING

The literature on contemporary Egypt is extensive. The following list consists of books and articles that are quoted in the text or may be helpful to readers seeking more detailed information.

Abu-Lughod, Janet. *Cairo: 1001 Years of the City Victorious*. (Princeton, Princeton University Press, 1971).

Adams, Richard H., Jr. *Development and Social Change in Rural Egypt*. (Syracuse, Syracuse University Press, 1986).

Ajami, Fouad. *The Arab Predicament*. (Cambridge, England: Cambridge University Press, 1981).

————. "The End of Pan-Arabism." *Foreign Affairs*, Winter 1978–79.

Aldridge, James. *Cairo: Biography of a City*. (London, Macmillan, 1969).

Aliboni, Roberto (Ed.). *Egypt's Economic Potential*. (London, Croom Helm, 1984).

Aly, Abdel Moneim Said. "Democratization in Egypt." *American-Arab Affairs*, No. 22, Fall 1987.

————, and Wenner, Manfred. "Modern Islamic Reform Movements: The Muslim Brotherhood in Contemporary Egypt." *Middle East Journal*, Vol. 36, No. 3, Summer 1982.

Aronson, Shlomo. *Conflict and Bargaining in the Middle East*. (Baltimore, Johns Hopkins University Press, 1978).

Atherton, Alfred L., Jr. *Egypt and U.S. Interests*. (Washington: Foreign Policy Institute, Johns Hopkins University, 1988).

Aulas, Marie-Christine, et al. *L'Egypte d'Aujourd'hui*: Permanence et Changements 1805–1976. (Paris, Editions du Centre National de la Recherche Scientifique, 1977).

Baker, Raymond William. *Egypt's Uncertain Revolution Under Nasser and Sadat*. (Cambridge, MA: Harvard University Press, 1978).

Berger, Morroe: *Islam in Egypt Today*. (Cambridge, England: Cambridge University Press, 1970).

————: *Bureaucracy and Society in Modern Egypt*. (Princeton, Princeton University Press, 1957).

Copeland, Miles. *The Game of Nations*. (London, Weidenfeld and Nicolson, 1969).

Critchfield, Richard. *Shahhat, An Egyptian.* (Syracuse, Syracuse University Press, 1978).

Dean, Charles; el-Bindary, Salah, et al. *Housing and Community Upgrading for Low-Income Egyptians.* (Issued by the Ministry of Housing and Reconstruction and the Ministry of Planning, Arab Republic of Egypt, and the U.S. Agency for International Development, 1977).

Dekmejian, R. Hrair. *Islam in Revolution.* (Syracuse, Syracuse University Press, 1985).

Dessouki, A. E. H. (Ed.). "Democracy in Egypt." *Cairo Papers in Social Science,* Vol. 1, Monograph 2, American University in Cairo Press, 1979.

————. *Islamic Resurgence in the Arab World.* (New York, Praeger, 1982).

Dodge, Bayard. *Al-Azhar: A Millennium of Muslim Learning.* (Washington, The Middle East Institute, 1961).

Egypt, Arab Republic of. *White Paper on the Peace Initiative Undertaken by President Anwar el-Sadat, 1971–1977.* (Cairo, Ministry of Foreign Affairs, 1978).

Eilts, Hermann F. "Egypt in 1986: Political Disappointments and Economic Dilemmas." *The Washington Quarterly,* Spring 1987.

Fahmy, Ismail. *Negotiating for Peace in the Middle East.* (Baltimore, Johns Hopkins University Press, 1983).

Heikal, Mohamed. *The Road to Ramadan.* (London, Collins, 1975).

————. *Autumn of Fury.* (London, Andre Deutsch,1983).

Herzog, Chaim. *The War of Atonement.* (Jerusalem, Steimatzky, 1975).

Hinnebusch, Raymond A., Jr. *Egyptian Politics Under Sadat.* (Cambridge, England: Cambridge University Press, 1985).

Hirst, David, and Beeson, Irene. *Sadat.* (London, Faber and Faber, 1981).

Hopwood, Derek. *Egypt: Politics and Society 1945–84.* (London, Allen & Unwin, 1985).

Ikram, Khalid, et al. *Egypt: Economic Management in a Period of Transition.* [A World Bank Country Economic Report]. (Baltimore, Johns Hopkins University Press, 1980).

Jansen, Johannes J. G. *The Neglected Duty: The Creed of Sadat's Assassins and Islamic Resurgence in the Middle East.* (New York, Macmillan, 1986).

Kays, Doreen. *Frogs and Scorpions: Egypt, Sadat and the Media.* (London, Frederick Muller, 1984).

Kishtainy, Khalid. *Arab Political Humor.* (London, Quartet, 1985).

Kissinger, Henry A. *White House Years.* (Boston, Little Brown & Co., 1979).

Laipson, Ellen B. *Egypt and the United States.* (Washington, Congressional Research Service, 1981).

Lane, Edward. *Manners and Customs of the Modern Egyptians.* First published in 1836; facsimile of the 1895 edition issued in 1978 by East-West Publications, the Hague and London, and by Livres de France, Cairo.

Lippman, Thomas W. *Understanding Islam.* (New York, New American Library, 1982).

Mahfouz, Naguib. *Midaq Alley*. (Translated by Trevor Le Gassick) (London, Heinemann, 1975).

Mansfield, Peter. *The Arabs*. (Second Edition) (New York, Penguin, 1985).

Mitchell, Richard P. *The Society of the Muslim Brothers*. (New York, Oxford University Press, 1969).

Mohie el-Din, Amr. *Income Distribution and Basic Needs in Urban Egypt*. (Cairo, The American University in Cairo Press, 1982).

Moorehead, Alan. *The Blue Nile*. (London, Hamish Hamilton, 1962).

Nelson, Cynthia, and Koch, Klaus-Friedrich, editors. *Law and Social Change in Contemporary Egypt*. (Second Edition) (Cairo, The American University in Cairo Press, 1983).

Nyrop, Richard (Ed.). *Egypt, A Country Study*. (Washington, The American University, Foreign Area Studies Series, 1983).

Omran, Abdel R. (Ed.). *Egypt: Population Problems and Prospects*. (Chapel Hill, Carolina Population Center, University of North Carolina, 1973).

Peretz, Don. "Reform and Revolution in Egypt." *New Outlook*, Volume III, Number 1, 1959.

Pipes, Daniel. *In the Path of God: Islam and Political Power*. (New York, Basic Books, 1983).

Quandt, William B. *Camp David: Peacemaking and Politics*. (Washington, The Brookings Institution, 1986).

Rubenstein, Alvin. *Red Star on the Nile*. (Princeton, Princeton University Press, 1977).

Sadat, Anwar. *Revolt on the Nile*. (New York, John Day, 1957).

———. *In Search of Identity*. (New York, Harper and Row, 1977).

Sadat, Jehan. *A Woman of Egypt*. (New York, Simon & Schuster, 1987.)

Sheehan, Edward R. F.: "The Real Sadat and the Demythologized Nasser." *The New York Times Magazine*, July 18, 1971.

Stephens, Robert. *Nasser: A Political Biography*. (London, Penguin, 1971).

Tuma, Elias H. "Neglected Aspects in Rural Development Aid Policy: Illustrations From Egypt." *Journal of Arab Affairs*, Volume 6, No. 1, Spring 1987.

Vatikiotis, P. J. *The History of Egypt*. (Baltimore, Johns Hopkins University Press, (Third Edition), 1985).

———. *Nasser and His Generation*. (London, Croom Helm, 1978).

Waterbury, John. *The Egypt of Nasser and Sadat*. (Princeton, Princeton University Press, 1983).

———. *Egypt: Burdens of the Past. Options for the Future*. (Bloomington, Indiana University Press, 1978).

———. *Hydropolitics of the Nile Valley*. (Syracuse, Syracuse University Press, 1979).

Weinbaum, Marvin G. *Egypt and the Politics of U.S. Economic Aid*. (Boulder, CO, Westview Press, 1986).

Weizman, Ezer. *The Battle for Peace*. (New York, Bantam Books, 1981).

Youssef, Michael. *Revolt Against Modernity*. (Leiden, The Netherlands, E. J. Brill, 1985).

INDEX

R0159281695   SSC   962
       22.95   L766

LIPPMAN, THOMAS W
       EGYPT AFTER NASSER
SADAT PEACE AND THE
MIRAGE OF PROSPERI   TY

R0159281695   SSC   962
                        L766

HOUSTON PUBLIC LIBRARY

CENTRAL LIBRARY
500 MCKINNEY

© THE BAKER & TAYLOR CO.